VIRTUAL KNOWLEDGE

VIRTUAL KNOWLEDGE

EXPERIMENTING IN THE HUMANITIES AND THE SOCIAL SCIENCES

EDITED BY PAUL WOUTERS, ANNE BEAULIEU, ANDREA SCHARNHORST, AND SALLY WYATT

THE MIT PRESS

CAMBRIDGE, MASSACHUSETTS

LONDON, ENGLAND

MIT Press books may be purchased at special quantity discounts for business or sales promotional use. For information, please email special_sales@mitpress.mit.edu or write to Special Sales Department, The MIT Press, 55 Hayward Street, Cambridge, MA 02142.

Set in Engravers Gothic and Bembo by the MIT Press. Printed and bound in the United States of America.

Library of Congress Cataloging-in-Publication Data

Virtual knowledge : experimenting in the humanites and the social sciences / edited by Paul Wouters, Anne Beaulieu, Andrea Scharnhorst, and Sally Wyatt.
    pages cm
Includes bibliographical references and index.
ISBN 978-0-262-01839-5 (hardcover)—ISBN 978-0-262-51791-1 (paperback)
1. Communication in learning and scholarship—Technological innovations. 2. Humanities--Information technology. 3. Social sciences—Information technology. 4. Humanities--Research. 5. Social sciences—Research. 6. Internet research. 7. Information visualization. 8. Knowledge, Theory of. I. Wouters, Paul, 1951– II. Beaulieu, Anne, 1970- III. Scharnhorst, Andrea. IV. Wyatt, Sally, 1959–
AZ195.V57 2013
001.2—dc23
2012013564

10 9 8 7 6 5 4 3 2 1

for all of those who contributed to the Virtual Knowledge Studio in the years 2006–2010

CONTENTS

ACKNOWLEDGMENTS

Many people have been involved in the production of this book. We would particularly like to thank Paul Edwards, Melissa Gregg, Willem Halffman, Sonia Liff, Eric Meyer, Janice Reiff, and Patrik Svensson for providing comments on early drafts. Neil Milne provided editorial help at an early stage of the project. We would also like to thank the anonymous referees as well as Marguerite Avery, Katie Persons, and Paul Bethge of the MIT Press for helping us to improve the manuscript in various ways. Janet Armstrong provided assistance in preparing the figures in chapter 3. The following provided permission to reproduce material: Arthur Petersen for table 3.1; Mundaneum in Mons, Belgium for use of the photograph reproduced as figure 3.2; and Pegasus Communications for figures 3.3 and 3.4. We are very grateful to Jeannette Haagsma, Anja de Haas, and Marja Koster for their help in preparing the manuscript and their invaluable support during the years of the Virtual Knowledge Studio.

INTRODUCTION TO VIRTUAL KNOWLEDGE

SALLY WYATT, ANDREA SCHARNHORST, ANNE BEAULIEU, AND PAUL WOUTERS

This book is about newly emerging forms of knowledge. Since the late 1990s, many scientists, scholars, and funding agencies have paid attention to the application of advanced information and communication technologies in academic research. Initially, this was framed as a revolution to be triggered by computational technologies (NRC 1999). This wave of enthusiasm enabled the mobilization of large-scale resources for the further development of new paradigms in computer science, ultimately leading to the creation of a cyberinfrastructure for research in the United States (Atkins et al. 2003) and the e-science program in the United Kingdom (Hey and Trefethen 2002), among other initiatives. However powerful in attracting resources, this vision tended to reduce the debate to the creation and subsequent uptake of computational tools and network technologies. Not surprisingly, social scientists and humanities scholars, especially those versed in science and technology studies, criticized these approaches from the very beginning as shallow and biased (Dutton 1996; Hine 2006b; Woolgar 2002; Wouters and Beaulieu 2006). After all, knowledge is not a purely cognitive operation of analytical tools on data, but a complex and highly structured set of practices of interpretation (Hackett et al. 2007). The styles of working and reasoning in different fields are quite different, and the differences have been analyzed both historically (Crombie 1994) and sociologically (Whitley 2000; Collins 1998; Knorr Cetina 1999). It therefore seems plausible that the implications of new digital networked research tools and research environments should be different for different fields. Research on the interaction between practices and digital network technologies has confirmed this variation (Virtual Knowledge Studio 2008; Borgman 2007). It is now almost common sense that enabling new forms of knowledge creation via digital technologies is not simply a matter of handing over the technical tools or a matter of adopting the tools and techniques used in some highly reputed field. Of course, this does not in any way diminish the seductiveness of the promise of the "World Brain" in new guises. Claims of revolution will continue to be made, and they may also play a productive role in generating more resources for research, as promises and expectations tend to do (Brown and Michael 2003). But they should not be taken at face value.

So how should one think about these developments and about the exciting challenges of the information revolution and the data deluges that seem to come with it? To begin, it is necessary to look closely at the practices that are developed and sustained by both "expert" and "non-expert" knowledge creators in a variety of fields. This empirical analysis of how science is actually conducted is, however, not a direct reflection of reality, but a result of interaction between the imagination and expertise of analysts and their objects of research (Woolgar 1988; Ashmore 1989). Every empirical analysis of the purported transformation in research is based on a theoretical framing of what counts as knowledge and as knowledge practices. It is, moreover, based on some theory of (infra-)structure and practice—and of the ways they interact (e.g., Latour 1987; Giddens 1979; Foucault 1966; Rheinberger 1997). In this book—one of the fruits of a five-year (2005–2010) research endeavor at the Virtual Knowledge Studio—we build on this theoretical work to refine the main concepts further. We focus on the quest for new forms of expertise which we call *virtual knowledge*.

Three notions of knowledge have shaped this work. First, knowledge is always inscribed in and by technology and instruments, either social (Derksen and Beaulieu 2011) or material (Bowker 2005; van Dijck 2007). Second, knowledge is deeply social. For knowledge to be more than simply the record of what an individual knows, it has to be embedded in, and performed by, infrastructures (Star and Ruhleder 1996). Paul Edwards puts it this way: "Get rid of the infrastructure and you are left with claims you can't back up, facts you can't verify, comprehension you can't share, and data you can't trust." (2010, 19) Third, the creation of knowledge enters into a cyclical feedback loop in which there is interaction between knowledge and infrastructures, through the practices of knowledge producers and users. In these interactions, new practices co-evolve with new infrastructures. For example, the crucial invention of the European seventeenth-century "scientific revolution" was the creation of science as a new social institution enthralled by the creation of novelties, stuff that did not exist before (Collins 1998). Today we are witnessing a new wave of changes in the ways scientific and scholarly knowledge are created, codified, and communicated. These transformations are related to the use of digital technologies and to the virtualization of knowledge production. Although we are reluctant to call it a revolution, we do think that these changes are quite profound because they affect the social fabric of science and scholarship.

Scholars, industrialists, politicians, and policy makers are all engaged in discussing, analyzing, and even promoting knowledge-based economies. This book focuses on the question of whether there is anything new when knowledge is produced in the digital age. Does knowledge itself change when the tools with which knowledge is acquired, represented, and distributed become digital? Do new actors become involved, and/or do traditional actors become less prominent in knowledge production? Are there shifts in power relations around knowledge? Are traditional definitions of knowledge affected? What new opportunities might emerge, and how should they be taken up? These questions are addressed in this book in relation to the academic system and to scholarly and professional practices. Change is not always for the better; thus, it is also necessary to raise questions, from the perspective of researchers and from the perspective of society more generally, about what kinds of changes and innovations are desirable and worthy of being promoted. We use the term *virtual knowledge* throughout this book to evoke these questions. Before we explain this term more fully, we will present five vignettes that illustrate the kinds of changes in knowledge production with which we are concerned.

• In 2004, scholars of Dutch language and literature in the Netherlands, in Belgium, and in South Africa were involved in an emotionally charged controversy about the digitization of a major research resource: the Bibliography of the Dutch Language and Literature. Printed versions of it were still being published, though much of the work of cataloguing the material was already being done digitally and there was an email newsletter. Thus, what was at issue was not the use of digital technologies but, rather, how a literary scholar should work in the twenty-first century, and with what sorts of professional support. Long-standing disagreements between literary studies and linguistics resurfaced. Dutch literary study is conducted largely by researchers who interpret texts on their own. Linguists tend to work in teams, using quantitative methods and supported by an international computational infrastructure. The controversy involved scholarly identities, both individual and collective. The crucial question was not whether the field should go digital, but rather what kind of digitization should be pursued for what purposes and at what costs (Kaltenbrunner and Wouters 2009).

• Historians of global economic history, who used to exchange data in spreadsheet files attached to email messages, are building what they hope will become a sustainable "data hub" with related topic-oriented collaboratories (laboratories without walls spanning institutional and national borders). This is not a simple matter. Those involved are confronted with the need to negotiate how to classify and present data as well as with the social configuration of data sharing. Questions of who can publish what, using what data, and questions about the most effective ways of working in a shared Web-based work space are at the core of what it means to work and be recognized as a historian. Perhaps, in the longer term, this collaboratory-building will change the dominant mode of scholarship from individual authors regularly co-authoring with colleagues of their own choice to large, distributed research teams requiring different forms of management and accountability. Or perhaps the collaboratory will turn out to be a temporary, project-bound experiment without any long-term effect on the structure of the field (Dormans and Kok 2010).

• Individual scholars, using tools now considered mundane, can already collaborate and communicate in creative ways, as the experiences of a prominent women's studies research group in Europe exemplify. The group's members did not identify themselves as being in any way related to "e-research," yet they made innovative use of email lists in research and teaching. Through the use of lists and of supporting websites, these scholars were creating and sustaining national, European, and international networks. The use of these Web-based resources contributed to increasing the visibility and the consolidation of women's studies. Furthermore, the use of email—widely available to those outside formal academic institutions—made it much easier for feminist activists and others interested in gender equality to participate in Internet-based discussions, thus facilitating wider dissemination and production of knowledge. Changes in knowledge production can therefore occur gradually, without much conscious investment in explicitly technological promises, and even without being recognized as "e-science" or "digitization of the field" (Wouters and Beaulieu 2006).

• New forms of visualization and simulation, some developed by the computer games and entertainment industries and some for military purposes, are increasingly finding application in the social sciences and the humanities. Digital technologies can be used to enhance the presentation and circulation of maps by, for example, visualizing the technical reliability of information. The historical evidence associated with original maps can also be made visible by means of annotations that enable users to establish the suitability of a map for their own research purposes, whether professional or amateur historical or archeological research, or for purposes of restoration. But the reliability of maps cannot be separated from their original functions and contexts of use. By combining (parts of) maps made for different purposes and (re-)used in different historical contexts, "messages" are mixed, making it difficult for users to know how historical information is represented in digital town plans and virtual reconstructions of cities. Using such maps for research and other purposes demands critical skills of users in order to assess the reliability and veracity of historical representations (van den Heuvel 2006).

• With the use of digital technologies almost ubiquitous in advanced industrialized countries, large amounts of data are generated as individuals, households, and organizations go about their everyday activities. These data are routinely collected and processed, not only by academic social scientists but also by market and social researchers in policy settings and in private-sector institutions. In an example of social science research, Peters, Kloppenburg, and Wyatt (2010) combined qualitative and quantitative data in novel ways when researching how people incorporate transport and communication technologies into their busy lives. Both in-depth interviews and numeric data from mobile phone records were used. The availability of such data offers the promise of solving what some researchers see as problems inherent to interviews, such as imperfect memory and socially desirable answers, but it may also exacerbate ethical and methodological problems arising from a lack of contextual information about what everyday activities mean to those engaged in them. Furthermore, even though there are many digital tools that facilitate analysis of large-scale data, the divide between social scientists trained in qualitative methods and those trained in quantitative methods may widen.

These vignettes illustrate phenomena and themes that will recur in this volume. They make visible the diversity of applications, tools, techniques, software, and hardware that have been described as *e-research* or *e-science*. They also illustrate the variety of changes in knowledge production. In analyzing newness, we concentrate on the makers and the processes rather than on the new products themselves. We are not primarily interested in the new instruments, tools, and technologies *per se*, but rather in the contradictions and tensions scholars face when alternating between the roles of producing knowledge and using knowledge. We pose the overarching question of what is actually new in e-research at three analytically distinct levels (which may overlap in practice): the form and content of research, the practice of research, and the organizational context in which research and knowledge production are conducted. The tensions always present in discussions of the development and use of new technologies—those between transformation and tradition, between change and continuity, between hope and fear, and between control and autonomy—are often expressions of normative struggles. These tensions are important not only for those participating in knowledge production across a variety of settings, but also for those who are the objects of research, and for society as a whole (which invests substantially in research and is the main stakeholder in the production of knowledge).

In the next section, we discuss how the research context in which digital technologies have been developed and used has changed in many advanced industrialized countries. We then turn to the emergence of e-research, focusing on its relationship to related concepts such as e-science or virtual knowledge, and further elaborate on why we use the term *virtual knowledge*. Finally, we outline the contents of the book, not only providing an overview of the chapters but also identifying cross-cutting themes.

THE CHANGING RESEARCH CONTEXT

Long-established hierarchies and practices of scholarly knowledge production are undergoing change, challenged from within and by broader social developments. At a systemic level we can distinguish four developments, which we label *growth*, *accountability*, *network effects*, and *technology*. The first two, associated primarily with the decline of autonomous science in practice and as an ideal, point to the myriad ways in which a wider group of social actors are involved not only in setting the agenda for science but also in knowledge creation itself. The third and the fourth relate to the socio-material relations and to conditions of knowledge production.

First, the growth of the university system after World War II in advanced industrialized countries was part of the overall growth of research and development and was accompanied by a concomitant increase in the diversity of students, staff, and subjects. In the second half of the twentieth century, universities became accessible to a wider range of people. Many new disciplines and interdisciplinary fields emerged, such as media studies, cultural studies, women's studies, and gender studies. Sometimes, as in the case of women's studies, these new disciplines could be attributed to the greater diversity of people entering universities. In other cases, the emergence of a new field is related to the widespread availability of a new object or medium, such as television in the case of media studies. Promoting interdisciplinarity is not new, and it can be used to disrupt power relationships in a field by uprooting extant research practices and norms of quality and relevance. The push to become interdisciplinary, sometimes by importing instruments and ways of working and thinking from other fields, can be instigated by funding agencies, organizations of researchers and individual scholars. If it is successful, those involved become pioneers. If not, the experiments and those promoting them tend to be erased from the disciplinary collective memory, perhaps to become objects of research for future historians of science (Joerges and Shinn 2002). Over the same period, the institutional frames for knowledge production have changed and new forms of governance and organization have emerged (Stichweh 1996).

Second, and related to new institutional forms and modes of governance mentioned above, researchers are increasingly called to account for the quality and quantity of their output and its relevance for non-academic social actors. National and international science and other policy makers have played an increasingly important role in steering and evaluating academic output in both teaching and research. A wider range of social actors, including for-profit corporations as well as civil society organizations, are no longer simply the passive recipients of knowledge produced elsewhere but are increasingly active in its production. Though many positive outcomes can be observed arising from new forms of governance and participation, modes of accountability nevertheless have a range of effects on the work of scholars and on institutions (Strathern 2000).

Third, the apparent success of "big science" in the physical and biological sciences in the postwar period means that large teams working across institutional and disciplinary boundaries have become the ideal for research managers and policy makers. Makers of science policy have been promoting particular forms of work organization by investing in research infrastructures and by encouraging large–scale, interdisciplinary and/or international collaboration (Bell, Hey, and Szalay 2009; Hine 2008; Edwards 2010). Not only has networked research emerged as a new ideal organizational form; network science, as a new research field that systematically analyzes network effects in nature and society, has grown. Moreover, the diversity of research networks has increased, partly as the result of increased collaboration between publicly funded research institutions and for-profit companies.

Fourth, as the vignettes above illustrate, digital technologies have been taken up in all stages of knowledge production (Hine 2005; Jankowski 2009; Virtual Knowledge Studio 2008). Furthermore, digital technologies have a role to play in the processes mentioned above. Digital technologies shape collaboration, monitoring, and evaluation and the communication of results, both within the scientific community and to wider audiences. This fourth development is the main focus of this book.

The implications of growth, globalization, commercialization, and digitization for the natural sciences and for engineering have already received a great deal of attention in the literature. They have been given various labels, including *Mode 2* (Nowotny, Scott, and Gibbons 2001), *post-normal science* (Funtowicz and Ravetz 1993), *technoscience* (Latour 1987; Haraway 1985), and *the triple helix* (Leydesdorff and Etzkowitz 1998). Their counterparts in the social sciences and the humanities have not been studied as systematically. This volume aims to help remedy that.

We start from the observation that the social sciences and the humanities (SSH) are also undergoing profound changes that bring to the fore the very notion of knowledge. Growth, accountability, network effects, and technology, the four developments outlined above, also affect SSH. But, given that society and the products of human creativity and interaction are the main objects of study in SSH, the implications of changing the modes of governance and organization are likely to be different for SSH than for natural sciences and engineering. Changes in society not only reconfigure the conditions under which new knowledge is produced; they are, at the same time, objects of study. The tools and methodologies used to gain knowledge change, but these changes also affect the object under study (Giddens 1984). These changes take place concurrently and interactively, though not always in the same direction or at the same rate. These changes cannot simply be reduced to developments in research technologies (although some policy actors certainly think they can). However, analyzing the use of technology provides a valuable analytical focus, giving indications about changing circumstances of use and of how traditional hierarchies, locations, and processes of knowledge production in SSH are being disrupted.

There are a number of analytical advantages to taking technology as a starting point when striving to understand changes in SSH. As was mentioned above, it is not the technical tools *per se* that are most interesting but the ways in which new technologies stimulate reflection about objects, methods, and practices of research. First, most efforts to use digital technologies in research involve the formalization of research practices and of research objects (van Zundert et al. 2012). Such processes require actors to consider their practices and negotiations about standards for communication or for data formats. These processes make explicit aspects of research and values of research communities, which themselves provide an interesting starting point for analysis. Such negotiations may enhance the reflexivity of practitioners and the likelihood of being able to enter into discussion with them about their work. Second, in part because the infrastructures were first adopted in physics and computer science, digital infrastructures tend to be built at scales that are "large" by SSH standards. Coalitions across institutions and disciplines are thus needed to reach the scale at which infrastructural projects are pitched by funding agencies, resulting in encounters between epistemic cultures. Such processes are again moments when differences within SSH become visible to the analyst. Third, e-research and e-science projects provoke hopes, resistance, and controversies. Controversies have a long tradition in STS and in history of science as moments that are analytically rich (Martin and Richards 1995). They have also been identified as "early warning indicators" for the development of new ideas, emerging paradigms, and methodological innovations. When scholars become involved in ongoing controversies, they can play a role in articulating what is at stake for actors, thereby opening up the possibility of analytically informed interventions.

As was mentioned above, there are already a number of concepts in circulation, including Mode 2, post-normal science, and technoscience, that aim to convey how knowledge production has been changing in recent decades. There are also a number of more specific concepts, including cyberscience, e-science, and e-research, that aim to capture how digital technologies have affected the research process. In the next section, we discuss these more fully and explain why the concept of virtual knowledge best captures the interplay between the various changes that can be observed in the social sciences and in the humanities.

THE EMERGENCE OF VIRTUAL KNOWLEDGE

In the course of the research presented in this volume, a wide variety of terms have been encountered in different settings, whether used by actors in the field (*e-science, cyberinfrastructure, grid, semantic web*), used by colleagues in academic discussions (*digital humanities, computational humanities, collaboratories, virtual research environments*), or generated by us in the course of our work (*e-research, virtual knowledge*). At times these settings have overlapped considerably. Each of these terms (and their use in paired opposition) has a particular connotation, and none of them arrive free of history and context. Some of these histories have been recounted recently—for example, by Jankowski (2009) for e-science and e-research, by Borgman (2007) for cyberinfrastructure and digital scholarship, and by Hine (2008) for cyberscience. (See also Nentwich 2003.) These histories are especially interesting and important because these terms have been used to articulate the promises of change in relation to technology (Brown and Michael 2003; Hine 2006a). Though we will not recount all the histories here, the contributors to this volume signal and contextualize the uses of terms that have played such promissory roles, and make explicit their decision to take on these vocabularies. Instead of trying to set definitions in stone, it is more important to interrogate the use of these terms, especially their use to evoke positive or threatening futures for those who encounter them.

In this section, we focus on two of these labels. We choose to do so because they play an especially important role in analyzing the developments under discussion and in positioning the contributions of this book as a whole. The first is *e-research* (Jankowski 2009; Wouters 2004; Wouters and Beaulieu 2006; Virtual Knowledge Studio 2008). The use of this term brings the practice of research to the fore rather than hardware or infrastructure, and acknowledges forms of research that are not reliant on high-performance computing, thereby including the use of new media and digital networks. We have used *e-research* to indicate an object of research and intervention that would be more inclusive of a variety of research modes (Wouters 2004). Sensitivity to disciplinary practices (Fry 2006; Kling and

McKim 2000) is therefore a central assumption in the use of this term. Because of the analytic terrain this term opened up, it seems to have become far more widespread recently. Most significantly for the point to be made here, we use *e-research* specifically in contrast to *e-science*, which emphasizes data-oriented, computational, or quantitative analysis. Not only does this oppositional redefinition enable us to evoke an interesting object of study; it was also important in establishing the mission and research program that led to much of the work presented in this book (Wouters 2004).

The second term we wish to discuss is *virtual knowledge*. We use this term to characterize the contents and object of this book. Both words, 'virtual' and 'knowledge', denote important analytic and theoretical decisions, as well as a sensitivity to the context of our work. *Knowledge* may be a better term for the practices that interest us, because it is both broader than *research* and closer to the perception that the humanities are engaged in scholarship rather than research. Furthermore, whereas research can be seen as a rather specialized activity pursued largely in academic institutions or in corporate labs, knowledge enables us to incorporate a wider range of social actors and practices.

To speak of *the virtual* is also to use an evocative term, and to signal one's analytic distance from the technological. Although in the 1990s the term *the virtual* was associated mainly with digital environments and with simulated spaces such as "virtual reality," it is broader in meaning than *the digital*, or *simulation*, or *the artificial*. An important line of thought on virtuality emphasizes that the virtual is a mode of reality implicated in the emergence of new potentials (Massumi 1998). In this sense, virtual knowledge is not simply the use of a digital tool; it is also the potential for change that it carries. We approach e-research empirically, combining our commitment to study practice and use with attention to the power and transformative potential of the virtual. To address the virtuality of knowledge empirically means that we consider the very actual, material, institutional implications of such potential. These are, in each particular case, limitations on virtuality, since the actual situations we analyze constitute an instantiation of virtuality. Virtuality is generative of all kinds of changes in practice. Contributors to this volume constantly pose the question "What is really new?" To ask this question is to engage with the potential for change while seeking to witness it.

The term *virtual knowledge* therefore invokes creativity, potential, and dynamism in combination with actual practices and understandings. It also emphasizes the ongoing dynamics of change, both in the form and content of knowledge and in the craft of generating new knowledge. When we speak of our work as simultaneously *being* virtual knowledge and being *about* virtual knowledge, we emphasize that it is both an ontological and an epistemological concept. We therefore emphasize that our concerns encompass the changing core of how others, as well as ourselves, pursue science, research, and scholarship, while being aware of the situatedness of any such changes. Virtual knowledge is not "just" about data, tool, or method; it is also about the epistemological and ontological consequences of the changing conditions of knowledge production. Virtual knowledge signals a new attention to the becoming of such potentials, and to the consequences of virtual knowing.

Virtual knowledge is strongly related to the notion that knowledge is embedded in and performed by infrastructures. In his recent book on the history of climate science, *A Vast Machine*, Paul Edwards points to the centrality of infrastructures in knowledge and in society: "To be modern is to live within and by means of infrastructures: basic systems and services that are reliable, standardized, and wisely accessible, at least within a community." (2010, 8) Infrastructures are noticed only when they fail, but they are usually transparent and taken for granted (Star and Ruhleder 1996). It is mainly in the form of newly emerging infrastructures that virtual knowledge becomes real. Many e-science programs claim to build the scientific infrastructure of the future. As Edwards has shown, this is a misnomer. Infrastructures cannot be built; they can only evolve. We would go even further: In the best case, they co-evolve with the research practices they aim to support. Rather than decouple infrastructures from research practices, it is better to state that what most e-science programs have built are systems and tools—potential components of new infrastructures that may or may not be included in the evolving knowledge infrastructures. The infrastructures that are now taking shape are not developed to support well-defined research projects as to the generation of streams of yet undefined research. Most of the data infrastructures that have been built so far have promised the discovery of new patterns and the formation of new data-driven fields of research. Networks of young researchers hope to generate new combinations of very different disciplines. New funding schemes specifically target unusual combinations of people, machines, and institutions. Increasingly, infrastructures and their component network technologies try to support possibility rather than actuality—though, as these chapters show, certain possibilities are better supported by the kinds of infrastructures being developed. This is underlined by the term *virtual knowledge*. How to further develop and sustain this type of knowledge is as much an empirical question as a theoretical one.

OUTLINE OF THE BOOK AND COMMON THEMES

In this book, the emergence of virtual knowledge is examined from a variety of perspectives, using many different empirical examples. Insofar as virtual knowledge is itself characterized by diversity, it makes sense to examine its emergence from different disciplinary, methodological, and empirical perspectives. Two main themes frame the contributions. The first is how novelty and promises of novelty are themselves deployed in the discourses and practices accompanying the introduction, the diffusion, and the use of the wide range of applications, tools, and techniques that can be collectively described as virtual knowledge. The second theme is the normative implications of these changes, what they mean for winners and losers in the changing landscape of knowledge production, and whether the reconfiguration of academic autonomy in favor of more involvement from nonacademic actors results not only in purported democratization but also in better knowledge. Thus, the contributions are explicit about the emergence and implications of the changes they describe. Each chapter draws on one or more examples about the form and content of research, about the practice of research, or about the organizational context in which research and knowledge production are conducted.

In line with the contemporary orthodoxy in science and technology studies (STS), the chapters are based on empirical research. STS has been very successful in developing theoretical and methodological tools for analyzing epistemic cultures and practices, drawing attention to local contingencies and specificities. Also in line with STS, contributions include insights from other disciplines—especially history, information science, and cultural studies. The volume adds to STS through its focus on the social sciences and the humanities, hitherto neglected in comparison to the huge number of studies in STS about natural, engineering, and medical sciences. This book is also a contribution to a more recent development in STS that distances itself from the single case study (Wyatt and Balmer 2007) and puts more emphasis on using comparative analysis to draw out common themes. The book shares this trait with recent books on e-research that have aimed to give a critical overview of a large number of recent developments and interesting case studies (Dutton and Jeffreys 2010; Hine 2006a; Jankowski 2009). For example, Dutton and Jeffreys ask how "technical change in research is enabling the reconfiguration of access to information, expertise, and experience across the disciplines." Jankowski (2009) draws attention to the ways in which change is dependent on disciplinary and other contextual factors, and suggests that change in scholarly practice is gradual. Access is a central theme in all of these books. Interestingly, Jankowski performs this theme by freely providing an "enriched publication" on the Web (http://scholarly-transformations.virtualknowledgestudio.nl/). We also share the critical perspective, developed by Hine (2006b, 2008), in which practices and promises are confronted with each other. Our book adds to the current discourse by shedding light on practices that have not yet received much attention in the debates on contemporary changes in knowledge making—changes that may or may not lead to more fundamental epistemic transformations.

Each chapter in this book integrates several case studies and theoretical approaches revolving around a particular theoretically relevant theme. The book is not formally divided into parts or sections; however, there is a logic guiding the order of the chapters. Chapter 1 questions the novelty of recent developments and the book ends with a chapter focused on the future. In the first chapter, Anne Beaulieu, Sarah de Rijcke, and Bas van Heur argue that the "realization of promise" and emerging forms of epistemic authority are shaped by pre-existent institutional and infrastructural elements. The chapter is based on three case studies of new networked sites of knowledge production: the collection database of an ethnographic museum, the use of the photo-sharing site Flickr by researchers and professionals concerned with the phenomenon of street art, and the development of a municipal website to support local cultural heritage. The analysis of these cases explicitly challenges the popular claim that new technologies will radically reconfigure existing sociotechnical relations and dramatically alter the basis for scientific and scholarly authority. The chapter shows the importance of the constitutive tension between reproduction and innovation in thinking about new sites of knowledge production and the forms of authority and expertise they sustain.

In chapter 2, Smiljana Antonijević, Stefan Dormans, and Sally Wyatt focus on the everyday work practices of scholars in the social sciences and the humanities. The topic of that chapter—affective work in professional relationships—is rarely addressed in scholarly studies of e-research and information technologies. Antonijević et al. draw on debates about immaterial and affective labor in order to present a set of conceptual tools for understanding the range of tasks involved in scholarly collaboration and how they are affected by the use of digital technologies. Their analysis is based on their research on large-scale international collaborations among social and economic historians and on their own smaller-scale cooperation in writing their chapter. They distinguish among care work, articulation work, and persuasion work, all of which are being affected by the introduction of digital technologies, with consequences for the ways in which some work and some workers are visible and valued. Their analysis also contains some thought-provoking messages for system builders and e-researchers alike. And by asking if invisible work should perhaps not better remain invisible, they also question the current trends in research evaluation and assessments in which visibility is *de rigueur*.

In chapter 3, Matthijs Kouw, Charles van den Heuvel, and Andrea Scharnhorst address, at an epistemological level, the issue of what counts as valid and valuable. They explore how uncertainty can be a source of knowledge rather than simply a sign of lack of knowledge. They also argue that the natural sciences and the computational sciences have a lot to learn from the humanities, thereby inverting the usual hierarchy in the sciences. After reviewing recent debates about the role of uncertainty in knowledge practices in the natural and social sciences, Kouw et al. present three examples from the history of information sciences, the history of architecture, and the history of complexity research. The examples concern the role of data and classification, the design of interactions, and the inclusion of dynamics in formal approaches to complex systems. Using these examples, they reflect on how people involved with e-research in the humanities and social sciences and people working in multi-disciplinary environments can engage uncertainty and appreciate its productive and disruptive effects, especially in the areas of interfaces, interactions, and models.

Yet another dimension of what it means to make something visible is explored by Rebecca Moody, Matthijs Kouw, and Victor Bekkers in chapter 4, the topic of which is the policy dimensions of visual knowledge. Moody et al. address how the introduction of a new technology (in their case, geographic information systems) challenges ways of producing and using knowledge in policy-making settings. They discuss a theoretically and methodologically novel approach to public administration and management made possible by the availability of geographic information systems; they also discuss the increased challenge of mastering complex interwoven natural, economic, social, and political networks by governmental organizations. In doing so, they combine insights from governance studies with science and technology studies. Using examples from water management, concentrations of particulate matter, and contagious livestock diseases, Moody et al. illustrate the barriers and potentials of new technologies in policy settings. They argue in favor of implementing new technologies in a theoretically well-guided way that roots new possibilities for conveying knowledge in existing and emerging social systems.

In chapter 5, Clement Levallois, Stephanie Steinmetz, and Paul Wouters examine the challenges facing social sciences as a result of "data floods," the massive increase in the quantity of data available to researchers arising from the use of new technologies. Focusing on the use of Web-based surveys in sociology and the use of brain imaging data in economics, they address the implications of emerging forms of data-intensive research for the role of social theory in e-social science. They argue, in line with the overall argument of this volume, that what is taking place is not so much a shift from one paradigm to another as a complicated set of changes at the interfaces between disciplines. They deal with virtual knowledge in two ways. They discuss the implications of virtual technologies and of data about social transactions embedded in these virtual technologies for sociology and economics. They also posit that the claim that the data deluge disempowers theoretical discourse in academic sociology and economics hasn't yet been realized and may never be realized, though it still affects the researchers' self-esteem in these fields.

In chapter 6, Clifford Tatum and Nicholas Jankowski take as their starting point the ongoing crisis in scholarly communication associated with increasing costs of periodicals, the growth of scientific literature, and the transitions to digital environments. They then elaborate the concept of openness, and use it to analyze emerging forms of formal scholarly communication, such as publication of journals and monographs that are solely Web-based, and to analyze rapidly proliferating new forms of informal exchange, such as blogs, social networks, and discussion lists. They consider whether new digital technologies may give rise to new forms of scholarly communication, blurring the traditional distinction between formal and informal modes of scholarly exchange and between scholarly communication and research practices. Their focus is on openness, perhaps one of the concepts most frequently invoked in the scholarly debate on e-research. Tatum and Jankowski contribute to the debate by analyzing openness both as an infrastructure and as an interface.

In chapter 7, Jan Kok and Paul Wouters return to the role of visions and expectations in shaping the ways in which research is conducted. In doing this, they examine how promissory documents that have shaped e-science, cyberinfrastructure, and e-research as a whole (discussed at the beginning of this introduction) affect a specific field. They analyze the role of technology in shaping research agendas in the history of the family, a field at the interface between the humanities and the social sciences. The authors examine the visions and "dreams" of researchers and policy makers as a way of understanding how research agendas and research technologies are intertwined. They excavate these visions by combining the sociology of expectations with elements of narrative analysis and of studies of science, technology, and innovation. This most explicitly future-oriented chapter goes well beyond family history and examines the constructive role of visions in the development for new research ideas, which is often accompanied by a struggle for new research technologies. The generative potential of the virtual in the form of research dreams and proposals for new infrastructures is real, irrespective of its later success. Even if a particular expectation isn't met, it has real consequences for the field.

The book has two overarching themes: the novelty and promises of novelty associated with e-research and the normative implications of their realization. These themes are addressed at three levels: that of form or representation, that of the content of research or disciplinary commitments, and that of the organization and the practice of research. By focusing the practice of research, contributors are able to analyze transformative changes and continuities in the creation of scholarly knowledge. This allows the contributors to draw upon a range of approaches, including technologically oriented ones, without falling into the trap of technological determinism (Wyatt 2008); it also allows them to draw on cognitive approaches, which start from theoretical or methodological concerns particular to individual disciplines.

The first theme regarding the promise of novelty appears in all chapters. Individually and together, the chapters call for a historical perspective

comparing the novelty of virtual knowledge with earlier revolutions, paradigm changes, and visions. Chapters 3 and 7 show the value of considering
how new research practices are embedded in past ones, allowing for comparison and points of reference. Though the explicit claims and the most
prominent promises of e-science tend to be easiest to deconstruct, a focus
on practice can help identify novelty in relation to new technologies. By
considering the low-level and mundane aspects of research practices, we
highlight the really novel, which often takes unexpected forms (chapters
1 and 2). Furthermore, the "new" in e-research ranges from new theoretical frameworks (chapter 4), the epistemic challenges (and even dan-
gers) resulting from new data (chapter 5) to imagined and practiced forms
of navigating through information and knowledge (chapter 3), and new
modes of publishing and presentation (chapter 6). The quest for the new
in e-research practices is simultaneously the quest for the sustainability of
virtual knowledge.

Our diachronic perspective on the practice of e-research and the emergence of virtual knowledge draws attention to the importance of temporality. Temporality can be a cause of friction in the adoption of new research
practices as discussed by Beaulieu et al. in chapter 1. In that chapter, the tension between the relative temporal stability of institutions and infrastructures
and the more fluid dynamics of interaction around Web and digital projects are analyzed. Temporality (more specifically its control in mathematical
models) is also a driving force for new forms of knowledge visualization. To
contrast change against stability, and to choose the appropriate elements for
both, is a major challenge for information sciences (chapter 3).

Modes of research become visible when one is discussing the role of data,
the "beyond data" questions, and the data-driven paradigm of e-research
(chapter 5). In chapter 7, Kok and Wouters explain how new forms of data
may trigger epistemic changes in a field. In most accounts of e-science, especially those originating from life sciences and physics, data are presented as
the driving force behind new divisions of labor (chapter 2) and professional
practices. But new research practices also create new forms of data, such as
research notes in the form of blogs (chapter 6). Data can take different forms,
including numbers, text, and images (chapter 3). By following the shape and
the role of data in knowledge production, the variety of e-research practices
becomes more prominent. The possibility of switching between different
forms of data representation itself has consequences. As Moody et al. argue

in chapter 4, visualizing data can have a major effect on the actual selection of data and thereby on the empirical ground and the theoretical framework of a field. The availability of new data or new methods highlights their role as communication devices within and across disciplines.

Although data may be visual and visualizations may drive data selection, the epistemic role of visualizations is also addressed in several chapters. Visualizations are not simply representations; they carry their own epistemic potential, and they have a much longer history than text. Visualizations that are legitimate in one research tradition may lead to controversies when imported into another field, and may also open up knowledge production to new audiences (de Rijcke and Beaulieu 2007). Kouw et al. provide examples of the epistemic role of representations in their account of the production and consumption of uncertainties and the ideal of "complete knowledge." Beaulieu et al. bring another aspect to the fore in their discussion of the apparently easy availability of visual material in digital settings, which creates challenges for cross-institutional and cross-disciplinary work in networked environments. Moreover, as Moody et al. demonstrate, skill and craft are needed by individuals and teams to produce visualizations that subsequently shape the way scholarship is understood and agreed upon. Technically mediated collaboration challenges existing divisions of labor and reconfigures the nature and distribution of affective labor (chapter 2), and not only in relation to visual material.

Analyzing the role of creative labor in the cycle of value creation in society draws attention to the limits of the economization, valorization, and accountability of research (chapter 2). The tension between self-exploitation, academic freedom, collectively produced knowledge, institutional boundaries, and societal recognition influences what is accepted as knowledge and the demarcation of research and scholarship. Digital settings do not mean that the social dynamics surrounding disputes about what counts as authoritative knowledge disappear, nor do they render knowledge and its production in completely transparent ways (chapter 1). Who counts as a researcher? What is academia? What roles can and do academic institutions play in the production of knowledge and innovation? How does virtual knowledge affect the relationship among social sciences, humanities, and other forms of knowledge production? This book traces the emergence of virtual knowledge in the humanities and the social sciences and shows what is at stake in pursuing and studying it. Ultimately, in the chapters that follow, the normative dimensions of what these changes mean for the future of the social sciences and the humanities come to the fore.

REFERENCES

Ashmore, Malcolm. 1989. *The Reflexive Thesis: Wrighting Sociology of Scientific Knowledge*. University of Chicago Press.

Atkins, Daniel, Kelvin Droegemeier, Stuart Feldman, Hector Garcia-Molina, Michael Klein, David Messerschmidt, Paul Messina, Jeremiah Ostriker, and Margaret Wright. 2003. *Revolutionizing Science and Engineering Through Cyberinfrastructure*. National Science Foundation.

Bell, Gordon, Tony Hey, and Alex Szalay. 2009. Computer science: Beyond the data deluge. *Science* 323 (5919): 1297–1298.

Borgman, Christine L. 2007. *Scholarship in the Digital Age: Information, Infrastructure and the Internet*. MIT Press.

Bowker, Geoffrey C. 2005. *Memory Practices in the Sciences*. MIT Press.

Brown, Nik, and Mike Michael. 2003. A Sociology of expectations: Retrospecting prospects and prospecting retrospects. *Technology Analysis and Strategic Management* 15 (1): 3–18.

Collins, Randall. 1998. *The Sociology of Philosophies: A Global Theory of Intellectual Change*. Belknap.

Crombie, Alistair Cameron. 1994. *Styles of Scientific Thinking in the European Tradition*. Duckworth.

de Rijcke, Sarah, and Anne Beaulieu. 2007. Taking a good look at why scientific images don't speak for themselves. *Theory & Psychology* 7 (5): 733–742.

Derksen, Maarten, and Anne Beaulieu. 2011. Social technology. In *The Handbook of Philosophy of Social Science*, ed. I. Jarvie and J. Zamora-Bonilla. Sage.

Dormans, Stefan, and Jan Kok. 2010. An alternative approach to large historical databases. Exploring best practices with collaboratories. *Historical Methods* 43 (3): 97–107.

Dutton, William H. 1996. *Information and Communication Technologies: Visions and Realities*. Oxford University Press.

Dutton, William H., and Paul W. Jeffreys, eds. 2010. *World Wide Research: Reshaping the Sciences and Humanities*. MIT Press.

Edwards, Paul N. 2010. *A Vast Machine: Computer Models, Climate Data, and the Politics of Global Warming*. MIT Press.

Foucault, Michel. 1966. *Les Mots et les Choses, Archéologie des Sciences Humaines.* Gallimard.

Fry, Jenny. 2006. Studying the scholarly web: How disciplinary culture shapes online representations. *Cybermetrics: International Journal of Scientometrics, Informetrics and Bibliometrics* 10 (1) (available at http://cybermetrics.cindoc.csic.es).

Funtowicz, Silvio, and Jerome Ravetz. 1993. Science for the post-normal age. *Futures* 25: 739–755.

Giddens, Anthony. 1979. *Central Problems in Social Theory.* University of California Press.

Giddens, Anthony. 1984. *The Constitution of Society.* Polity.

Hackett, Edward J., Olga Amsterdamska, Michael Lynch, and Judy Wajcman, eds. 2007. *The Handbook of Science and Technology Studies,* third edition. MIT Press.

Haraway, Donna. 1985. Manifesto for cyborgs: Science, technology and socialist feminism in the 1980s. *Socialist Review* 80: 65–108.

Hey, Tony, and Anne E. Trefethen. 2002. The UK e-science core programme and the grid. *Future Generation Computer Systems* 18 (8): 1017–1031.

Hine, Christine, ed. 2005. *Virtual Methods: Issues in Social Research on the Internet.* Berg.

Hine, Christine. 2006a. *New Infrastructures for Knowledge Production: Understanding E-Science.* Idea Group.

Hine, Christine. 2006b. Computerization movements and scientific disciplines: The reflexive potential of new technologies. In *New Infrastructures for Knowledge Production: Understanding E-Science,* ed. C. Hine. Idea Group.

Hine, Christine. 2008. *Systematics as Cyberscience: Computers, Change and Continuity in Science.* MIT Press.

Jankowski, Nicholas W., ed. 2009. *E-Research: Transformation in Scholarly Practice.* Routledge.

Joerges, Bernard, and Terry Shinn, eds. 2002. *Instrumentation: Between Science, State and Industry.* Kluwer.

Kaltenbrunner, Wolfgang, and Paul Wouters. 2009. Controversial digitization: e-Humanities between cost-reduction and methodological innovation. In Proceedings of the Fifth International Conference on e-Social Science, Cologne.

Kling, Rob, and Geoffrey McKim. 2000. Not just a matter of time: Field differences and the shaping of electronic media in supporting scientific communication. *Journal of the American Society for Information Science* 51 (14): 1306–1320.

Knorr Cetina, Karin. 1999. *Epistemic Cultures: How the Sciences Make Knowledge.* Harvard University Press.

Latour, Bruno. 1987. *Science in Action.* Open University Press.

Leydesdorff, Loet, and Henry Etzkowitz. 1998. The triple helix as a model for innovation studies. *Science & Public Policy* 25 (3): 195–203.

Martin, Brian, and Evelleen Richards. 1995. Scientific knowledge, controversy, and public decision making. In *Handbook of Science and Technology Studies*, ed. S. Jasanoff, G. Markle, J. Petersen, and T. Pinch. Sage.

Massumi, Brian. 1998. Sensing the virtual, building the insensible. In *Hypersurface Architecture,* ed. S. Perrella. *Architectural Design* 68 (5/6): 16–24.

Nentwich, Michael. 2003. *Cyberscience: Research in the Age of the Internet.* Austrian Academy of Sciences Press.

Nowotny, Helga, Peter Scott, and Michael Gibbons. 2001. *Re-thinking Science: Knowledge and the Public in an Age of Uncertainty.* Polity.

NRC (National Research Council). 1999. *Funding a Revolution: Government Support for Computing Research.* National Academy Press.

Peters, Peter, Sanneke Kloppenburg, and Sally Wyatt. 2010. Co-ordinating passages: Understanding the resources needed for everyday mobility. *Mobilities* 5 (3): 349–368.

Rheinberger, Hans-Jorg. 1997. *Toward a History of Epistemic Things: Synthesizing Proteins in the Test Tube.* Stanford University Press.

Star, Susan Leigh, and Karen Ruhleder. 1996. Steps toward an ecology of infrastructure: Design and access for large information spaces. *Information Systems Research* 7 (1): 111–134.

Stichweh, Rudolf. 1996. Science in the system of world society. *Social Sciences Information* 35 (2): 327–340.

Strathern, Marilyn. 2000. *Audit Cultures: Anthropological Studies in Accountability, Ethics and the Academy.* Routledge.

van den Heuvel, Charles. 2006. Modeling historical evidence in digital maps: A preliminary sketch. *e-Perimetron* 1 (2): 113–126.

van Dijck, José. 2007. *Mediated Memories in the Digital Age.* Stanford University Press.

Virtual Knowledge Studio. 2008. Messy shapes of knowledge—STS explores informatization, new media, and academic work. In *Handbook of Science and Technology Studies*, ed. E. Hackett, O. Amsterdamska, M. Lynch, and J. Wajcman. MIT Press.

Whitley, Richard. 2000. *The Intellectual and Social Organization of the Sciences.* Oxford University Press.

Woolgar, Steve. 1988. *Science: The Very Idea.* Tavistock.

Woolgar, Steve, ed. 2002. *Virtual Society? Technology, Cyberbole, Reality.* Oxford University Press.

Wouters, Paul. 2004. The Virtual Knowledge Studio for the Humanities and Social Sciences @ The Royal Netherlands Academy of Arts and Sciences. Research program, KNAW (available at http://citeseerx.ist.psu.edu).

Wouters, Paul, and Anne Beaulieu. 2006. Imagining e-science beyond computation. In *New Infrastructures for Knowledge Production: Understanding E-Science,* ed. C. Hine. Idea Group.

Wyatt, Sally, and Brian Balmer. 2007. Home on the range: What and where is the middle in science and technology studies? *Science, Technology & Human Values* 32 (6): 619–626.

Wyatt, Sally. 2008. Technological determinism is dead. Long live technological determinism. In *Handbook of Science and Technology Studies,* ed. E. Hackett, O. Amsterdamska, M. Lynch, and J. Wajcman. MIT Press.

van Zundert, Joris, Smiljana Antonijević, Anne Beaulieu, Karina van Dalen-Oskam, Douwe Zeldenrust, and Tara Andrews. 2012. Cultures of formalization: Towards an encounter between humanities and computing. In *Understanding Digital Humanities: The Computational Turn and New Technology,* ed. D. Berry. Palgrave Macmillan.

I AUTHORITY AND EXPERTISE IN NEW SITES OF KNOWLEDGE PRODUCTION

ANNE BEAULIEU, SARAH DE RIJCKE, AND BAS VAN HEUR

Much has been written recently about user-generated content entering and reshaping circulatory matrices of media and power, and about how new media practices redefine the role of cultural producers (Jenkins 2006; Bruns 2008). For example, platforms like Flickr have been hailed as sites of new literacies and creativities (Burgess 2009), and blogs are implicated in debates about how new dynamics in information and news production are reshaping the public sphere. Changes also seem to be taking place in other areas of knowledge production, as evidenced by phenomena such as crowd sourcing and social information filtering, implemented and arising from sites such as Wikipedia and Delicious. These and other participatory new media phenomena, although diverse, are often characterized as taking place via or in infrastructures as new sites of knowledge production, such as networked databases or websites designed for interaction and participation. Claiming the presence of a new territory in relation to digital networked media is a well-known trope and one frequently evoked in relation to the "virtual-think" of virtual worlds or virtual cities. Martin Hand's (2008) analysis of this trope as a discursive and conceptual instrument reveals its consequences. To write of a new site of knowledge production is to posit a new geography of power—one that is often considered to be outside institutions, and enabled by new infrastructure. In other words, a particular technological platform is assumed to realize the potential of the virtual. While we are aware of the promissory potential of the metaphor of a new site of knowledge, we also welcome the connotation of possibilities for action and interaction that it invokes. We agree with Hand that the sense of newness felt and expressed by participants is empirically important. At the same time, we explicitly seek to include institutional (and not solely technological) elements in discussions of these sites at the level of practice and theory.

While much attention has been paid to the influence of these new sites on fields such as journalism, the creative industries, and politics, the ways in which they are mediated through and inflected by the often highly institutionalized contexts of scholarly and professional research are only beginning to be addressed (RIN 2010). The central question posed in this chapter is, therefore, the following: Given the traditional importance of institutions in the production of knowledge, what are the relations between these wider mediated networks as new sites of knowledge production and traditional, institutionalized modes of research?

We consider this question in relation to three sites we have studied: the use of Flickr by lay experts and accredited researchers for the study of street art, the practices of collection database of the Tropenmuseum in Amsterdam, and the development of the heritage website of the Municipality of Maastricht. All three sites operate at the intersection of the humanities, cultural heritage, and art. In all three sites, the work of knowledge production is pursued in settings that reach out beyond established organizations (in the cases discussed here, universities, museums, and local governments) and through new mediated research activities (Hayles 2002, 2006; Hine 2008). In focusing on new sites of knowledge production, we emphasize that the phenomena we analyze are in development as forms of virtual knowledge. The phrase "new sites of knowledge production" also highlights the tension between existing practices and the need for innovation: a new site draws on existing resources while also calling forth expectations that something new will come out of their deployment—something beyond current, routine, business-as-usual practices. Finally, the phrase orients our analysis to the composition of these practices, which draws on both infrastructural and institutional elements. In the sites at hand, the relation between institutions and infrastructure takes on different configurations. These reveal three important aspects of knowledge production: how new actors come to be involved in knowledge production, how empirical material is legitimized in these settings, and how knowledge claims are validated in relation to existing and emergent forms of order. We will argue that both infrastructural and institutional elements play important roles in shaping promises and various aspects of authoritative knowledge production at these sites.

We write here, in short, of the promise of new sites of knowledge production, and we use that phrase to evoke the importance of positive expectations for both infrastructural and institutional dimensions of knowledge production—and indeed for the conditions that enable our own research. (See the introduction to this volume.) Expectations generate enthusiasm, mobilize resources at multiple scales in order to make the virtual actual, and bring together highly diverse groups of actors in the pursuit of a new project (Brown and Michael 2003; Borup et al. 2006; chapter 7 below). This is the truly emergent moment of expectations, since they are most clearly visible in the early phases of "infrastructural imagination" (Sparke 2000; Jackson et al. 2007) and infrastructure development. In our sites, the early phases of infrastructure development can be characterized by high expectations of cross-institutional and cross-disciplinary work. That these developments may also challenge institutionalized academic and professional systems of accreditation can be an unexpected corollary. On the other hand, expectations are also usefully understood as shaped by institutional elements in that they manage and order change along relatively fixed and pre-established lines and according to existing epistemic resources.

EXPERTISE AND AUTHORITY

For each of the three sites discussed in more depth below, we address how configurations of expertise and authority, two important aspects of knowledge production, are re-shaped in a dynamic interaction with existing and emergent institutional and infrastructural elements. As our discussion of these sites shows, there is no reorganization of knowledge production into a single mode. In view of discussions of new forms of cultural production that tend to posit these developments as largely uniform or as convergent (Jenkins 2006; Bruns 2008), we feel it is crucial to show the plurality and diversity of these configurations. Instead of either uncritically welcoming these developments as breaking the barriers of traditional power relations in a knowledge-stratified society or (the reverse argument) criticizing them as incapable of being truly democratic or as leading to mediocre science, we offer a more contextual argument that highlights the constitutive tension between socio-technical reproduction and innovation.

The role of expertise and the importance of experts in shaping this constitutive tension have been widely noted by STS scholars. A result of the differentiation of modern society and its complex divisions of labor is that experts of all kinds (in relation to scientific, technical, legal, aesthetic, and other knowledges) have become increasingly important in shaping the dynamics of knowledge production. STS research has played a major role in analyzing these different forms of expertise and in deconstructing the epistemological claim that expertise offers a neutral representation of a particular independent reality. By doing so, it has questioned this cognitive bias and has shown expertise to be historically and socially constructed and shot through with a wide variety of cultural, political, and economic considerations (Shapin 1995; Collins and Evans 2002; de Rijcke 2008a, 2010; Lynch 2007).

In this chapter, we want to emphasize more strongly the relation between expertise and authority that is implicit in most of the STS literature. Complementing the processual and constructivist line of argumentation in STS, a focus on authority allows us to analyze in more depth the ways in which the sedimentation of expertise creates particular forms of socio-technical order that, in turn, shape the emergent role of expertise in new sites of knowledge production. According to Max Weber's well-known formulation, authority is the "probability that a command with a given specific content will be obeyed by a given group of persons" (1968, 53). Weber might be too focused on rationalism for today's sensibilities, and his interest in legitimate authority (by distinguishing among rational-bureaucratic, traditional, and charismatic authority) may be too limited for our purposes, but his concern with identifying the shaping force of established forms of order remains relevant. Indeed, many studies on expertise address this authoritative dimension in one way or another. Critical accounts in development studies (for example, those focusing on the rhetoric of participatory development and the role of experts) have shown that in development projects certain authoritative principles are in place in which the expert is assigned the role of identifying and categorizing problems and the power to intervene and fix them (Kothari 2005). Similarly, in research on governmentality, authors have suggested that we need to understand experts as mediating between specific forms of authority and subjectivity (Rose 1993). Expertise, in this Foucauldian version, associates itself with particular authoritative rules (such as neo-liberalism or advanced liberalism) and links these rules to individual and collective conduct. At the same time, expertise depoliticizes these linkages by transforming fundamentally political questions into technical ones. STS has zoomed in on the politics behind the construction of these and other dichotomies—technical vs. political, fact vs. value, objective vs.

subjective, scientific vs. commonsense (see Lynch 2007, 20)—in supposedly meritocratic societies. Attention has been paid to the roles of trust, reputation, credentials, and moral standards within epistemic communities (Shapin 1995; van House 2002a), roles shaped as much by contingent interactions in particular sites as by path-dependent learning (Rip 2003). Sheila Jasanoff has made a particularly strong argument for investigating the institutional dimensions of these processes, describing institutions as "stable repositories of knowledge and power" that "offer ready-made instruments for putting things in their places at times of uncertainty and disorder" (2004, 39–40). On many occasions, Jasanoff has singled out the continuous reproduction of institutionalized epistemic traditions. This work is concerned with the effect of cultural, political, and indeed institutional settings on markers of credibility and authority (Jasanoff 1990). When the co-construction of expertise and institutional imperatives is taken into account, questions as to where, when, and under what conditions knowledge is validated, and for which audiences, then become pertinent (Beaulieu 2002; Callon and Rip 1992; Rip 2003).

INSTITUTIONAL-INFRASTRUCTURAL REPRODUCTION AND INNOVATION

In thinking through the relations between expertise and authoritative institutions, we find it useful to connect the STS literature to debates in institutional sociology, following Jasanoff's proposal to explore points of contact between the predominant concerns in STS and those of "traditional social sciences" (2004, 2; cf. Wouters and van Heur 2009). While STS has developed a range of approaches to describe the complexity of emergent knowledge production in investigating the ways in which these new sites are ordered by institutionalized ways of knowing and doing things, it seems to us that STS can benefit from such an interdisciplinary discussion. At the same time, institutional sociology can learn from STS by paying more attention to the roles of materiality and technological objects in shaping and transforming relations of authority and expertise (Pinch 2008).

We use 'institution' as distinct from 'organization', which denotes an actual social arrangement that adopts particular procedures and methods of coordination to pursue a specific goal. The notion of institution, on the other hand, refers to those reproductive elements that contribute to social order and stable behaviors. Scott (2008) distinguishes among three kinds of elements that constitute social order: regulative, normative, and cultural-cognitive elements. Regulative elements refer to rules, monitoring, and sanctioning; normative elements highlight the moral obligations in social interaction; cultural-cognitive elements emphasize the assumptions and classifications underlying institutional logics. We want to emphasize the need to pay attention to the *process* of institutionalization in order to counter the perceived static and functionalist tendencies of early institutional theory. Furthermore, this processual perspective on institutional analysis can be complementary for approaches used in science and technology studies. We emphasize the heterogeneity of institutional logics (Friedland and Alford 1991) and seek to remain sensitive to the extent to which institutional logics can actually shape particular organizational cultures, since logics are always counteracted by other logics (Krasner 1988).

In drawing on institutional sociology, our analysis overlaps with recent debates on information infrastructures (Virtual Knowledge Studio 2008; Bowker et al. 2010). As the discussion of the three sites will also show, the development of new infrastructures is often seen as central to successful innovation, but recent infrastructure studies have increasingly questioned this technology-centered expectation by putting more emphasis on the organizational and institutional context of digital infrastructures. Following Edwards et al. (2009, 366), we emphasize the fact that "any new infrastructure must somehow integrate with an installed base that includes not only artifacts but human habits, norms, and roles that may prove it most intractable elements." This unavoidably leads to a "recurring issue of adjustment" (369) in which infrastructure projects adapt to and reshape their environment, and to failure when these mutual adjustments do not generate substantive embeddedness of infrastructures in everyday working practices. Infrastructural innovation, in other words, is constantly confronted with the persistence of institutional reproduction.

THREE DIMENSIONS OF KNOWLEDGE PRODUCTION

Using the theoretical framing discussed above, our analysis shows that a constitutive tension between reproduction and innovation is played out on a number of levels in new sites of knowledge production.

First, as has already been noted, we pay particular attention to how knowledge claims are validated in relation to existing and emergent forms of order.

A second, related issue was also briefly alluded to above. A number of STS studies take the investiture of new sites of knowledge production as informative of the relation between knowledge and power. Important interfaces between experts and others are constantly being modulated through protocols, hierarchical relations, and boundaries (Gieryn 1983, 1999; Derksen 1997; Waterton and Ellis 2004). The aggregation and acceleration of data flows in new media forms, such as networked databases, may indeed contribute to the blurring of boundaries between knowledge produced by governments, universities, research institutes, private companies, cultural institutions, and "the public" (see also Castells 1996), but this is by no means certain. Correspondingly, a second aspect we incorporate in our analysis is that of struggles over which actors are entitled to produce, have access to, and distribute knowledge, and how these roles, in turn, affects existing power relations (Wynne 1992; Epstein 1996).

Third, if the Internet has been found to "make more, and more varied information available from a growing range of formal and informal sources" (van House 2002a, 101) and to play a role in the circulation of scientific information (van House 2002b), it becomes crucial to consider how such information is constituted and evaluated as legitimate empirical material. In the discussion of our three new sites, we therefore also focus on how empirical material becomes authorized, and under which conditions it can best be taken up in research. This part of our work rejoins issues raised by Levallois, Steinmetz, and Wouters (in chapter 5 of this volume) in relation to methodological and epistemological debates in social science, but offers a complementary view by considering them at the level of research practices. We analyze whether there are shifts in the way access to materials is organized and in the way epistemic privileges are established (Sekula 1985).

AUTHORIZING ACTORS AND THE TROPENMUSEUM'S NETWORKED IMAGE DATABASE

The question of who has the authority to make, handle, and disseminate knowledge is pertinent to the particular infrastructural and institutional practices of the Tropenmuseum's networked image database (in a software package called The Museum System, available at http://www.gallerysystems.com), and of other digital visual resources related to the collection. At the Tropenmuseum (an ethnographic museum in Amsterdam), the main institutional investments in producing knowledge about the collection have been made in the development of this networked image database. The word 'networked' has a threefold meaning here. It refers, first, to the local network of computers that allows museum employees to simultaneously use the image database. Second, the database is networked, or "relational," in the sense that each element in the database (i.e., a photograph of an ancient book formerly used by Batak priests in Sumatra) can be linked to multiple other elements, and vice versa (i.e., to exhibitions on influential cultures in Southeast Asia, or to other objects from the collection originating from Sumatra). Third, the word 'networked' refers to the embeddedness of the database in the networked infrastructure of the Web, and to the accessibility of the Tropenmuseum collection database by means of a Web-based interface.

The Tropenmuseum, founded in 1871 in Haarlem as the Koloniaal Museum, has a collection that encompasses the whole of the tropics. The collection consists of roughly 175,000 objects, 155,000 photographs, albums, slides, and negatives, and 10,000 paintings, drawings, and other documents. The collection is housed in various depots and is mainly documented using The Museum System (TMS). But these visual documentation practices are increasingly blending with new forms of visual knowledge production and dissemination via other networked image infrastructures (de Rijcke and Beaulieu 2011). We investigated these existing and emergent ways of visual knowing at and around the Tropenmuseum by means of ethnographic fieldwork, which comprised systematic participant observation, qualitative interviews with museum employees and visitors, a detailed scrutiny of new Web-based initiatives around the museum collection, and an analysis of official policy documents, relevant archival material, and funding applications relating to digitization and information management. Below we will concentrate on shifts in the ways in which different actors are mandated to make, access, and disseminate knowledge about the museum collection in relation to existing power structures.

DISTRIBUTION OF POWER

Depending on the time and money invested, TMS can be a relatively unpretentious database with rudimentary categorizations of museum objects or a highly complex tool for capturing, managing, and accessing collection information. The latter is the case at the Tropenmuseum. Expectations regarding TMS at the Tropenmuseum were rather high when the museum first started working with the database around the year 2000. Although the actual integration and institutionalization of TMS was messier, TMS is now deployed with the goal of changing interactions with the collection, and not only for employees. It is hoped that TMS will reduce the number of times the collection is physically handled by replacing the practice of handling physical objects by that of consulting a database and by standardizing and making transparent complete work processes around collection conservation, management, presentation, and research. TMS also changes who is interacting with the collections, and it makes these interactions visible. It is hoped that TMS will help make the complete collection accessible to a wider audience, and that it will increase the numbers of visitors to the website and to the museum.

The entwinement of the TMS infrastructure with the Tropenmuseum shapes many of the practices and roles within the museum. One result of the large-scale digitization of the work processes at the museum is a distribution of power to the computer application manager, one of the few employees to be highly competent in the new digital infrastructure at a technical level. He is also an important player in other digitization initiatives. The organizational hierarchy and its accompanying division of labor are therefore inscribed in the way TMS is implemented. Roles of workers at the museum are also shaped by the way TMS is produced and used. For example, "data entry" is done by registrars, while validation of this material is done by documentalists and curators. The amount and type of data employees can enter into TMS depends on the number of fields they have access to, which is directly related to their job description. This is not simply an issue of quality control. It also shapes whether the data can travel or not, since the data are progressively "released" for circulation in the system, depending on whether they have been reviewed, and by whom. Once material is embedded in TMS, its circulation is also restricted to certain actors, so that work must be coordinated around the involvement of others in the museum. This coordination work is also partly necessary for another reason. Namely, the Tropenmuseum owns 15 TMS licenses, and this number determines how many employees can be logged onto the system simultaneously. On busy days, it regularly happens that people do not have access to the database and either have to wait until one of their colleagues logs off, have to work around the database, and/or have to attend to other responsibilities. The cost of licenses sometimes

means that staff cannot interact with TMS, a situation which the organization has to accommodate.

INVOLVING NEW ACTORS

As we have described, TMS is a focus of major investments at the Tropenmuseum. It is also an object that has carried a number of promises—
of modernizing the museum, of improving management, and of enabling
the museum to become a better caretaker of its collections. While TMS is
extremely important to the museum and its collections, other projects are
also changing the role of actors with regard to the collections. Following
international trends in the museum world, the museum is currently investing in other new, distributed infrastructures for visual knowing, along with
the collection database. Several of these focus on involving new actors. In
July of 2009 the museum began to present the "object of the month." A
photograph of a relatively unfamiliar object is put on the website, and visitors to the website are asked to provide information on the object. Every
month, this new object is introduced by means of Twitter, digital news-
letters, and blogs. Interestingly, the objects are selected by a curator, who
searches through TMS for objects that could not be documented by museum experts. In this case, new actors are sought and authorized only when
in-house expertise has failed. Thus, although new participatory media are
being used in this situation, this example shows that the Tropenmuseum is
also reproducing traditional frameworks of power and authority and building on existing infrastructural and institutional arrangements and how roles
are inscribed in them.

RE-NEGOTIATING AUTHORITY

A third way in which the Tropenmuseum explores new sites of knowledge
production is through cooperation with the Wikimedia Foundation (the organization behind Wikipedia and Wikimedia Commons) on a project called
"Wiki loves art/NL" (hereafter abbreviated WLANL). The initiative sought
to stimulate amateur photography in museums, with the goal of getting
more photographs of cultural heritage on Wikipedia pages under a Creative
Commons license. In June of 2009, a group of 46 museums opened their
doors to the public for special sessions and allowed participants to make photographs of designated objects from their collection. Participants uploaded

their images on Flickr, which thus served as a conduit for the photographic material. A jury, consisting of the organizers and a number of museum employees, decided which photos would subsequently be used on the Wikipedia pages.

The WLANL project is interesting for our purposes because it reveals the continuous negotiation of epistemic authority by the actors involved. In a blog post on WikiLovesArt/NL, the US-based museum exhibit designer Nina Simon recently wondered if the slight changes made to the rules of the game when WikiLovesArt traveled to the Netherlands should really be considered improvements (Simon 2010). The Dutch initiative was a follow-up to the first WikiLovesArt, a co-production of US and UK museums. In the Netherlands, Simon argued, museums had tighter control over the event than they had had in the US or in the UK. As a result, she believed, there was less room for creativity for participating photographers in the Dutch project. Indeed, it seems that museums had a tight hold on the process not only because in many case, museums decided which objects were eligible for the photography contest in the first place but also because museums were represented in the jury responsible for deciding which photos ended up on Wikipedia. On the other hand, as one of the Dutch participants pointed out in reaction to Simon's post, although the formal rules were indeed a bit strict, creativity was certainly stimulated in practice. The type of knowledge produced, and the ways in which different parties were authorized to do so, clearly depended on the parties' different vested interests. Simon mentioned that, although museums may have been mainly interested in making their content digitally accessible without breaking any copyright laws regarding the objects on the photographs, and although the Wikimedia foundation was especially keen on obtaining useful data, a participant in the Dutch project who reacted to Simon's post felt that many photographers were more concerned with "freely making pictures for their own use (or their portfolio)." As it turned out, the commenter argued, "quite a few came to do their own thing and they had ample opportunity to do so."

The WLANL case can also serve as an example of how new sites of knowledge production can help in mediating tensions between different roles *within* an organization. The Tropenmuseum has three photographers on its staff, whose job it is to photograph the ethnographic objects for the collection database, to digitize the many photo albums and negatives the museum possesses (also for the database), and to make photographs on demand (for instance, for public relations purposes, such as to accompany books written by curators, or to be put on exhibition posters or on the museum's website). Some of the photographs taken in the Tropenmuseum during WLANL were considered particularly beautiful by the museum's public relations department, and will most likely be used by that department in the near future. The department is also considering putting participants' photos on display on the museum's multimedia screens. This made one of the in-house photographers quite anxious, as she considered this fusion of her own photos with that of visitors to be a threat to her photographic expertise and professional identity. The WLANL case lays bare the need for a constant re-negotiation of certain boundaries and identities between (new) users and producers in new sites of knowledge production. The particular circumstances that shape how expertise and authority are achieved in this case not only transform existing epistemic configurations but also affect the relations with other electronic settings and networks in which knowledge about the Tropenmuseum collection might circulate. On the other hand, the WLANL example makes visible how certain practices are changing, even gaining institutional anchoring, thereby embedding new sites of knowledge production in the contemporary social and cultural fabric. With Friedland and Alford (1991), we do however want to emphasize that multiple institutional logics are at play here. There is a clear tension between institutional interests in this case, resulting in strategic moves of the PR department, possibly at the expense of the in-house photographers. When it comes to interactions with other networked infrastructures such as Wikipedia or Flickr, the contestation of disciplinary and professional boundaries is most obviously felt by the Tropenmuseum employees responsible for knowledge production in and around the networked database (registrars, photographers, documentalists, curators). Not surprisingly, they remain quite keen to claim jurisdiction over the infrastructure that best "captures" the collections (TMS), as it is their professional identity and symbolic capital that becomes inscribed in this database.

REINFORCING EXISTING CONFIGURATIONS OF EXPERTISE

One final example will serve to illustrate that the infrastructural and institutional dynamics described in this section, in addition to the large investments in The Museum System, probably will continue to shape future Web-based, networked initiatives at the Tropenmuseum. At the time of writing, the recently hired head of museum digitization, after only a few months in his new job, is already facing the challenge of (on the one hand) recognizing the internal social order of the museum and (on the other hand) connecting to broader societal trends to include new actors, new expertise, and new knowledges. As the responsible member of the staff in digitization initiatives, he played a leading role in the last stages of development of a digital search engine that was launched in January of 2010. Months before the launch, he formed an "expert group" consisting of curators and other museum experts. They were asked to critically assess the search engine by performing random and premeditated searches. Because of a strict deadline (agreed upon with the funding agency), the search engine was made public with known bugs still present. At the launch, the challenge of managing conflicting notions of expertise became very apparent when a second group of users was announced by the head of museum digitization, whose role would be to monitor the ongoing development of the search engine. From the perspective of the museum, the co-existence of the two groups, with the first group still carrying the label of experts, reveals that the professional position of museum employees continues to be seen as the most appropriate criterion for the authorization of knowledge, with potential effects on the intended users of the search engine.

AUTHORIZING EMPIRICAL ENCOUNTERS IN FLICKR

Our second site is Flickr and its use by researchers who study graffiti and street art. We focus on the constitution of Flickr as a resource and a means of interaction between researchers and empirical material. We therefore consider not only the photographic material but also the communicative, archival, and interactive aspects that are interwoven in Flickr. In every field, there is an accepted way of constituting one's object of research, and this aspect of research is a crucial aspect of epistemic cultures (Knorr Cetina 1999; Wouters and Beaulieu 2006). Researchers engage with the possibilities of this technology, configuring their presence on the site, interacting with the infrastructure, and/or making contributions to the database (whether via photos, comments, or links), so that 'Flickr' is an important resource for their work.

Best known as a photo-sharing platform, Flickr can also be used to build a personal archive of photos, to browse material uploaded by others, or to engage in a wide variety of activities using photos, including research. Flickr has several features of "ongoing sociability" (Fuller 2003) typically associated with social networking sites. It enables users to represent themselves and to articulate links to other users and the content they upload. Furthermore, Flickr, like other social networking platforms, makes use of traces generated by use of the system and its content. These traces are generated by tagging, by marking as "favorite," by patterns of sharing, by indicating other users as contacts, by frequency of use, and so on. These uses of profiles, of relations to content, and of other self-referential traces are defining features of so-called Web 2.0 applications, and "content" can itself be a source of sociability (Lange 2007). Therefore, although this case does not pretend to generalizability, it is representative of how researchers using qualitative methods might negotiate the use of Web 2.0 applications, with a "bottom-up" motivation of following their object using digital data (in this case, graffiti and street art) rather than a top-down "digitization" motivation.

The researchers studied are mostly (visual) sociologists or anthropologists who focus on urban and/or material culture. Among the huge variety of photos on Flickr, urban photography and the documentation of urban life is a prevalent theme (Petersen 2009). All of the researchers use photography in their research practices, which they define as "fieldwork." The researchers were identified using a snowball approach, through sites such as Art Crimes (graffiti.org). Through interviews, email exchanges, analysis of articles and other output, and the researchers' use (or, in one case, vehement non-use) of Flickr, we were able to characterize how Flickr is used in relation to empirical material in the work of these researchers. The focus here is on practices relating to "empirical material" on Flickr, within the greater range of ways in which Flickr and research intersect. The material discussed here focuses on Flickr as a source or context for material, rather than on the communicative or symbolic aspects of Flickr in researchers' work. Although the practices described here focus on the Flickr platform, Flickr is a highly networked setting, with links to websites or other social networking platforms appearing on Flickr pages and vice versa: Flickr can be a source for newspapers or Web-based forums. In the subsections that follow, we address three aspects of the relation between power and knowledge of interest in this chapter: shifts in archival practices of researchers, the way Flickr becomes an authorized setting for empirical material, and Flickr as a tool for connecting and enriching observations.

NEW ARCHIVING PRACTICES

Archiving practices endorse particular kinds of material as worthwhile sources. As such, archives are infrastructures of power that inscribe categories and imbue archived material with "intrinsic" value. Shifts in modes of archiving therefore involve a re-examination of the values instantiated by archives (Hand 2008; Waterton 2010). Flickr may be leading to new archiving practices for researchers, with consequences for what it means to use or rely on empirical material, and may be reshaping preservation and collection practices. For one thing, the use of Flickr signals a shift to a reliance on companies for backup and archiving of photos (Rubinstein and Sluis 2008). This contrasts with a personal or professional location of this responsibility, where researchers organize their own archives of photographic material, often relying on personal means or personal affiliations to institutions, storing materials in a university or home office or on an institutionally provided server. While many universities and other institutions provide repositories for publications or working papers, these services are text-oriented and are not suitable for archiving of visual material, especially when they are meant to function as sources for research rather than as research output. An increased reliance on company-based archiving of visual material is a result of multiple changes in the work of researchers and of the rise of practices located at the intersection of digital technologies and electronic networks. The use of digital cameras is specifically mentioned by researchers as a challenging new practice.

Increasingly mobile researchers who work with increasingly large numbers of photographs expect to have access to their material to an extent that may not be supported by their home institutions. The desire to share photographs with audiences (whether readers of articles or potential informants) also comes into play, since printed journals (and even some Web-based ones) offer very limited means of showing visual material. Flickr's Web-based interface seems to answer those needs, and researchers entrust their material to the site. Flickr also widens the possibilities for sharing of photos, and researchers mention the growth of a sharing circle through Flickr and other digital technologies, beyond the collegial interactions or student-teacher relations in which sharing has traditionally taken place. In this context, the value of the archive then seems to be leaning toward circulation and presentation of photographic material, rather than preservation. If the highly local and highly personal "shoebox in a drawer" presented an issue for long-term preservation and archiving of printed photographic material, the shift toward privately owned servers as repositories means that preservation (in the form of continuity of access) may remain difficult. Even if researchers are diligent and have the resources needed to back up their material, other problems remain. For example, as Petersen (2009) notes, all the tags, categories, and annotations on photos (which could be termed 'meta-data') form relevant content that is not easily separable from the photos. This increasingly poses problems as users invest time and attention to this kind of content in these platforms: all data generated by and through the platform remain property of the company. As we will see, photos on Flickr are deeply embedded in the networked setting offered by Flickr. The context in which the photos appear lends them authority, validity, quality, or authenticity. Removing them from the setting therefore means a (partial) loss of the meanings that come to be overlaid on the photographs. Because researchers are not in control of that infrastructural aspect of their collections of photos on Flickr, empirical material comes to inhabit a private-public hybrid space in which traditional (academic) institutional values do not prevail when it comes to archiving. What counts as proper preservation and access and what counts as an "object" are reconfigured in this infrastructural setting.

AUTHORIZING CONTENT

A second element relating to the authorization of empirical encounters in this new site of knowledge production is the way researchers evaluate Flickr as a location for finding and presenting empirical material. As was discussed earlier, infrastructural promise is often directed at opening up an empirical field. Infrastructures for research have a long tradition and have been central to empirical work in many disciplines (field stations, observatories, experimental setups) and to communication and validation practices in research (publishing, granting, peer review). But the use of such infrastructure is often accompanied by restriction to specific sets of users with institutional credentials. With Flickr, access to the platform is not a restrictive mechanism, relatively speaking. The promise here is twofold: not only will the set of users who will be granted access expand, but the diversity and richness of empirical material will also greatly increase.

To what extent can we expect such an infrastructure to enable encounters with empirical material in such a way that this material will be considered valid or useful for knowledge production? STS has shown that if infrastructures are to enable new encounters with empirical materials, these materials will be taken up in knowledge production only if the dynamics of validation that authorize these encounters can be reconfigured (Bowker 2000; Beaulieu 2001; de Rijcke 2008b, 2010; Wouters and Schroeder 2003; Arzberger et al. 2004). In using Flickr, the (visual) sociologists and anthropologists studied value above all the identity performance enabled by the platform, as a mechanism to authorize empirical material. This extends in important ways what was already known about the role of content in using Flickr: that "content" also becomes a resource for sociality in these settings (Lange 2007). By uploading particular kinds of photos, users provide implicit but important information about their skills, their access to "the field," and their interests—in addition to the more explicitly stated elements in their user profile pages. Furthermore, content is increasingly redefined to include not only files but also the social meta-data in which content is embedded (Skågeby 2008). The use of photos for identity creation has been analyzed by other scholars (van House et al. 2004; van Dijck 2008). Van Dijck in particular contrasts identity work done with personal photos to memory practices, noting that although identity and communication are increasingly important the role of photos as archive material—as evidence of events—still endures. In analyzing the practices of researchers of street art and graffiti, the link between identity-performance practices and documentation practices comes to the fore even more. On Flickr, content and identity are tightly linked by the infrastructural design of the platform and by users' emerging expectations. One's identity, strongly shaped by one's content, is an important element in the reception, the attention perception, and perhaps even the acceptability of photographic material. This performance of identity affects the authoritativeness of researchers' work by serving as evidence of authentic access to the field. One researcher explains why it is important to be very focused on Flickr in order to maintain credibility and standing:

That's my big problem, because when I post a picture of a rainbow, my followers are either not going to comment, or else they will un-follow me. They're going to say: "What?!!! This guy who photographs graffiti also takes pictures of rainbows! He's too sensitive, he's not a real graffer. Cause a graffer can't like rainbows—he's gotta be a MAN!" And because of that ambiguity, followers are going to be disgusted. And then you're not using the platform as it should be. Not that there IS a way it should be used, but that's how people use it. That's how it's become configured through use. (interview, December 2, 2009)

Having followers (people to whom Flickr will systematically show one's newly uploaded photos), and the followers' active presence through comments, are important dynamics of validation. In this case they are best sustained, the researcher explains, by not being ambiguous about one's interests and commitments. By diversifying the subjects of photos posted, the researcher risks introducing what he calls ambiguity, diluting his claim to specialized interest, which situates him as a legitimate participant and ensures the enduring attention of his followers.

Specialization is therefore explained as an important element in performing a proper identity on Flickr. Specialization is, furthermore, an answer to the huge amount of material on Flickr: sticking to appropriate material is a way of maintaining the interest of followers. In other words, choosing to follow a "person" on Flickr is a way to filter content. But this creates expectations about who this person can be and about what kinds of photos this person will upload. It also highlights the tight coupling between identity and empirical material. This is one way of using Flickr in relation to field material and field relations. This analysis should be understood in terms of a specific dimension of the use of Flickr by researchers committed to fieldwork. There are, of course, other approaches to configuring Flickr as empirical data. Some quantitatively oriented social scientists and computer scientists use photo files on Flickr as data, seeking to strip away most aspects of "identity" (that is, the specifics of individuals) in order to map out networks or to deploy computational approaches to understanding content (Derksen and Beaulieu 2011). In the setting discussed here, it seems that witnessing (Shapin and Schaffer 1985) relies on values of commitment and specialization and on the coherence of identity performance.

CONNECTING EMPIRICAL MATERIAL

Researchers also use Flickr to deepen their analysis of material they have gathered in their fieldwork by connecting different bits of empirical material. This use resembles searching, browsing, and "Googling" on the Web, but more specifically in relation to visual material and to street culture, for which Flickr is an especially good source. Visual material is also notoriously underserved by search engines, which are oriented to textual (and, even more narrowly, ascii) material. For scholars studying the materiality of the city, or graffiti as traces, Flickr can be useful to make connections between graffiti they have observed and photographed and sources, authors, or other instances of similar graffiti. Flickr can also be used to track informants as they move around different cities or as certain styles and images become "viral" and spread to other geographical locations. For example, there is a project, called Constructing Coexistence, to gather photos of paint-based interventions using stencils of Gandhi in cities around the world. This use of Flickr depends on the presence of material from huge numbers of contributors, and, significantly, on the use of recognizable tags or labels. Though often done without much conscious effort, these seemingly banal gestures are important practices that subtend the constitution of Flickr material as authorized sources. Consider that most of these researchers condemn the use of captions on their photos as a parasitic textual practice that undermines the narrative power of the visual material. One researcher recounted in vivid terms her struggle to have images appear without captions in a journal publication. After finding out at the stage of reviewing proofs that captions had again been inserted, she emphatically explained her resistance to this practice: "the caption is detrimental to the argument." Yet all these researchers assign titles and tags to their photos on Flickr. These are usually summary, but nevertheless label the photo with a transcription of the tag text—that is, the "name" of the writer or artist. (Locations are also often used as tags.) This labor enables Flickr to function as a searchable source. This emergent practice brings us back to the issue of archiving and to the constitution of categories and modes of organization of material. Such labeling and tagging, sometimes called "folksonomies," are not purely bottom-up processes, and proper tagging or linking to thematic groups is subject to the same social and reflective dynamics as proper posting.

Interestingly, however, researchers rarely explicate this use of Flickr in their publications. The use of Flickr fulfills an academic need for documentation, whether as a place to display material or to look up material. But the use of Flickr seems to belong to the nitty-gritty of sharing or "finding out stuff" in the course of research. It does not seem to be perceived by researchers as a noble enough practice to be deserving of citation (unlike institutionalized archives of photographic prints), and it is often only indirectly evoked in methodological accounts, and subsumed to "consulting the Web." We argued earlier that the intersections of institution and infrastructure were especially important to consider in order to understand how authoritative knowledge can be constituted at these new sites. If Flickr hardly appears worthy of mention in publications (whether as a reference, as source, or as a "tool"), this points to the use of Flickr as being neither institutionally recognized nor recognizable. When Flickr does appear prominently in academic publications, Flickr usually is taken to be an object of study. Furthermore, some researchers express the desire to publish their photos in a printed magazine, book, journal, or exhibition catalog, and then to post them to Flickr after the photos have a "trail." This would seem to indicate that researchers consider established forms of academic publication to be more effective attribution mechanisms than using Flickr. Yet Flickr is not expected to be a free-for-all, and researchers expect that conventions of ownership as established in academic and artistic institutions will be respected. If they find that their work is being misused, they will protest, or they will alter settings on their material (changing file size or permissions) in order to modulate access to their work.

Institutional dynamics can also be seen in the way researchers' methodological commitments shape how they approach the use of Flickr. Taking one's followers seriously and carefully considering the reactions of informants as part of a developing relationship are evidence of an important ethnographic sensibility. We can see in this case how the relationship to informants gets worked out in terms of the infrastructural possibilities and conventions on Flickr, thereby shaping fieldwork material. Finally, these researchers who have delved into "Web 2.0" platforms sometimes express a desire to have such possibilities offered by their organizations, or a desire to have university infrastructures be at least somewhat open to such platforms (for example, by allowing the researchers to incorporate more diverse and dynamic material in their university homepages). With regard to authorizing empirical encounters, we see the constitution of new kinds of repositories, and their effect on defining the boundaries of what counts as empirical in this intersection of institutional and infrastructural elements. We have also seen the importance of creating proper identities in relation to the material in order to count as a proper witness, to articulate the resource to enhance (others') use of material (through labeling and tagging), and the persistence of expectations about academic forms of ownership and citation.

VALIDATION OF KNOWLEDGE CLAIMS AND EXPERTISE IN THE CULTURAL BIOGRAPHY OF MAASTRICHT

Our third case study also involves knowledge production in a setting that reaches out beyond established organizations. This time, however, the actors are not associated with museums or universities, but with a local govern-ment aiming to rethink its cultural heritage policy. In mid 2002, following a cultural policy for the years 2002–2010 in which a more active engagement with local cultural heritage was advocated, the Dutch city of Maastricht commissioned an Amsterdam-based consulting agency to develop a guid-ing vision and concrete ideas for the management of its cultural heritage. Drawing on the work of Gerard Rooijakkers (1999), a professor of Dutch ethnology at the University of Amsterdam, the notion of cultural biogra-phy was adopted to conceptualize the city of Maastricht as a city of shifting identities over time. At this early stage, the development of a digital heri-tage infrastructure was occasionally mentioned, but always as one element within a much wider-ranging attempt to rethink the presentation and use of cultural heritage in Maastricht. Over the next couple of years, however, it was precisely the development of the digital infrastructure that became the main concern for those involved in the project organization dedicated to the Cultural Biography of Maastricht.

The empirical material for the analysis presented here has been derived from extensive analysis of minutes of steering group meetings, e-mail ex-changes, letters of interest groups, official policy documents, internal reviews, funding applications, and newspaper articles. On the basis of this material and the theoretical discussion above, it becomes possible to identify two main is-sues: (1) a path dependency leading to a narrowing focus on digitization and (2) little or no room for involvement in knowledge production by unauthor-ized experts. As a result, established forms of expertise were reproduced.

NARROWING FOCUS ON DIGITIZATION

With the decision in place to develop the Cultural Biography of Maas-tricht as formulated by the consultancy group, the first phase concentrated largely on making the notion of cultural biography more concrete to fit the particularities of Maastricht and on developing a collaboration model that could be used to actualize the virtual knowledge concerning the imagined infrastructure of a cultural biography. This infrastructure was seen less in digital terms than in narrative and organizational terms. The consultancy re-port emphasized the need to understand the city as a layered, differentiated, and complex phenomenon in which the "life and social meaning of urban artifacts (streets, buildings) and events are inextricably connected with the biographies and genealogies of city users and inhabitants" (LAgroup 2003,

20). Digital technologies were only mentioned briefly as "multimedial support tools" (33) that could aid visitors in selecting historical narratives.

Following the recommendations in the consultancy report, one of the first tasks of the civil servant responsible for the coordination of the Cultural Biography was to find candidates for a steering group that could guide the development of the project. Even before executing this task, however, he commissioned a local website design firm to develop a plan of action concerning the online dimensions of the project, a demo website to show the added value of multimedia, and a project-website to be used for streamlining communication between project participants. In December of 2003, the website designer produced a "step-by-step plan online Cultural Biography of Maastricht" as well as a report on "multimedia and the Cultural Biography of Maastricht" in which the content and form of the envisioned website was described. Leaving behind the original commission of producing a demo website, this step-by-step plan is much more ambitious: a full-blown web-based cultural biography that effectively replaces the less technology-centered vision of the consultancy agency is to be developed. From this moment on, and only six months after the consultancy report advocated a concept-driven and organization-driven project, the Cultural Biography of Maastricht came to revolve primarily around the development of a digital infrastructure and the digitization of heritage information. In line with the literature on path dependence (David 1985; Rip 2003) that highlights the importance of early decisions in ordering subsequent developments, this rather contingent decision to commission the design of a demo website proved to be crucial for the development of the Cultural Biography of Maastricht.

The digital biography was further stabilized by the expectation that it would be essential to the development of the Cultural Biography as a whole, since it was argued that this digital infrastructure would connect producers of heritage information (cultural organizations in Maastricht) with consumers (tourists, local citizens, schools). This is stated quite directly in an early draft:

When the decision is made, as is to be expected, to adopt a phased approach, then the development of a digital cultural biography should be first priority. This digital system ... will play a pivotal role in connecting those who should deliver the contents of the biography (the institutions) with the consumer. The producers of the content can deliver their product digitally in the digital system. Museums and other cultural heritage institutions, the tourist information office, educational institutions, tourists, local citizens, etc. can consult this content directly via the Internet and possibly give comments or add their own stories. (Habets 2004)

In short: by positing the digital biography of Maastricht as a solution to heritage management, substantial financial and time investment in the building of the digital infrastructure was justified.

Although these developments were largely the results of local interactions, this narrowing focus on digitization in the Cultural Biography of Maastricht organization was further institutionalized by linking up with broader trends, in particular debates on the national scale on the value of digitizing the cultural heritage of the Netherlands. (See, for example, Digital Heritage of the Netherlands,www.den.nl.) Following the plans as presented by the website designer, the civil servant responsible for the Cultural Biography submitted a funding application to the Mondriaan Foundation, one of the main foundations that funds projects in the arts, design, and cultural heritage in the Netherlands. Despite criticisms by the Mondriaan Foundation that the project was too top-down and did not involve enough possibilities for user interaction, the application—once revised and resubmitted—was accepted, and funding was granted. This had a rather paradoxical effect on the further development of the Cultural Biography of Maastricht. On the one hand, the criticism by the Mondriaan Foundation led to awareness among the groups involved that the technical choices proposed by the website designer were not necessarily the best choices. On the other hand, the very fact that the Mondriaan Foundation offered substantial funding for the digital biography produced a strong interest in its further development and, as a result, reproduced and even further secured the focus on digitization at the expense of more organizational dimensions of cultural heritage innovation.

ORDERING EXPERTISE

The increasingly narrow focus on digitization was paralleled by an organizational dynamic that prioritized established forms of expertise of academic researchers (and, to an extent, cultural organizations) over alternative forms of knowledge production. Even though a new site of knowledge production was explicitly put in place to manage the development of the Cultural Biography of Maastricht, the already institutionalized environment in which this new site had to operate affected how it functioned. A genealogy of this project, therefore, can be written as a constant struggle between institutionalized, authorized forms of knowledge and alternative, emergent knowledges.

Park Doing has coined the notion of "epistemic politics" to capture these "negotiations and antagonisms/contests over who has what kind of access to different epistemic realms" and the extent to which these contests "are also justifications for who should be in charge of whom and what" (2004, 315). He continues: "Importantly, this dynamic is recursive, as accepted justifications of authority are in turn used to cordon off and fortify epistemic realms that become the wellsprings of "technical' knowledge." (315)

This selective inclusion and exclusion of actors and their expertise became visible throughout different stages of the project. In the early stage of the consultancy report, as described above, and in the setting up of the steering group, four defining historical periods were identified, namely Maastricht as a Roman establishment, as a medieval religious center, as an early modern garrison town, and as an industrial city. The Cultural Biography of Maastricht was in turn seen to consist of three layers: the "collective memory" of the city, including the "source material" of buildings, works of art, literary texts, maps, rituals, archives, stories, and scientific interpretations; the "permanent story," including the four historical periods; and the "temporary stories" not in need of "structural attention or that present the permanent stories from a different (non-direct) perspective" (LAgroup 2003).

Academic researchers contributed to the definition of these four historical identities of Maastricht. They were described in the consultancy report in a chapter co-authored by Ed Taverne, emeritus professor of history of architecture and urban planning at the University of Groningen. Although these four historical periods were not addressed in the think tank and expert discussions preceding and informing the consultancy report, the very idea of distinguishing three layers was present from the beginning. At the same time, one of the reasons for asking an academic historian from Groningen to formulate the four historical periods was that many cultural organizations in Maastricht did not believe the municipality was seriously interested in realizing and financially supporting the Cultural Biography. As a result, the cultural organizations—which included an art museum (the Bonnefantenmuseum), libraries, an exhibition space (the Centre Céramique), a church (the Basilica of Saint Servatius), a tourism organization (VVV Maastricht), and a historical documentation center (the Sociaal Historisch Centrum voor Limburg)—were very reluctant to cooperate in the formulation of the four historical periods. Two years later, in early 2005, these were again presented at a conference in which representatives from the cultural organizations participated. Each identity was discussed in a working group. Although this still led to some discussion, the basic logic of adopting four historical periods to describe the history of Maastricht was accepted.

This problematic relation between the main actors involved in the Cultural Biography project and the cultural organizations in Maastricht can be said to have contributed to a hierarchization of expertise. The Cultural Biography of Maastricht positioned the steering group as central to knowledge control. Six people were selected as members of this group: two civil servants (including the one formally responsible for the Cultural Biography project), two historians, one director of a cultural organization, and the website designer. Parallel to the submission of the revised application for the Mondriaan Foundation grant, the website designer was replaced by a member with extensive experience in researching and organizing digital media projects. The role of the digital infrastructure, which was strong even before the formation of the steering group, was further reinforced by the fact that the steering group's members and the daily manager of the project—were the only actors who could decide on infrastructural changes. The second level of expertise was occupied by the cultural organizations in Maastricht. Although in the original consultancy report they had a prominent role as producers of the information that could be fed into the digital biography, this interactive dimension never really developed, owing to the reluctance of the cultural organizations to contribute. And citizens and tourists were placed on the third level of expertise. Even in the early consultancy report, however, their role was understood rather ambivalently. On the one hand, citizens and tourists were granted a passive role as "recipients" of the Cultural Biography, consuming the information available via the Web. On the other hand, inhabitants were also positioned as potential contributors to the development of the temporary stories (though not the permanent stories) (LAgroup 2003, 32). In exploiting this participatory niche for citizens, a number of oral history interviews have been conducted. But all in all, this kind of contribution has remained a rather marginal aspect of the Cultural Biography of Maastricht.

With the benefit of hindsight, this period, in which a narrowing focus on digitization and established forms of expertise led to a particular institutionalization of the Cultural Biography of Maastricht project, can be understood as a period in which the time-consuming development of the website effectively overshadowed all other concerns. It was only after the completion (in 2007) of the main infrastructure underlying the website that alternative expectations concerning the future development of the cultural biography project could emerge, ranging from the organizing of heritage exhibitions to educational projects with schools and more extensive cooperation with citizens in disadvantaged neighborhoods. Organizationally, this more heterogeneous approach has been further pursued through the integration of the Cultural Biography of Maastricht project into the broader project known as BV Limburg. (Limburg is the Dutch province of which Maastricht is the capital city.) Instead of only focusing on digital heritage presentations, BV Limburg develops innovative heritage formats of various kinds, including websites, theater shows, television programs, exhibitions, books, magazines, and school projects.

CONCLUSIONS

In the projects discussed above, configurations of expertise and authority were (re-)shaped in a dynamic interaction with existing and emergent institutional and infrastructural elements. We see these practices as achievements, resulting from the ongoing process of ordering infrastructural and institutional elements. Rather than insist on the rise of new paradigms in knowledge production, we focused on showing how neither institutional nor infrastructural elements are homogeneous and determinant resources. The way these two elements interact can have far-reaching effects on the very values that denote scientific or scholarly knowledge, and can lead to new articulations of expertise and authority. By combining these dimensions in our analysis, we were able to account for important features of the knowledge produced in the projects.

To see expert knowledge as necessarily located in traditional institutional sites, and folksonomies as new sites of knowledge production standing outside expertise (and leading to knowledge that is multiple, open to alternatives, and deliberative) is to set up a false dichotomy (compare Bruns 2008). As we saw in the case of Flickr, new sites also make demands of and impose constraints on experts; in order to build or maintain their authoritative status, they have to learn to navigate the infrastructure. In contrast, the Tropenmuseum and Biography cases showed how hierarchies can be reproduced in digital and networked settings, where the roles occupied in institutions get reinscribed in work flows in and around digital settings and in the very architectures of infrastructures. Furthermore, we saw in the cases of the Tropenmuseum and Flickr that the performance of identity, through the specific interfaces and possibilities of a database, lends authority to one's material or one's professional position. In considering how important the infrastructural dynamics of identity and sociality can be for the meaning of specific photos, and the value of particular collections, we are reminded of the importance of asking, again and again after Latour, why authority might be ascribed to one particular actor rather than distributed throughout networks of people and devices (Shove et al. 2007, cited in Hand 2008).

In the case of the Cultural Biography of Maastricht, various boundaries between the kinds of knowledge that could be integrated in the project shifted. These shifts can be understood in terms of changing membership of steering groups, and in terms of the decision to move toward a digital biography as the main objective and means of the project. In this case, the shifting configurations of organizational involvement and the resulting decisions to invest in digital infrastructure as the main goal of the project led to a situation where (1) only what is in the system counted as part of the biography and (2) what could be included was further limited by the emphasis on having certain partners deliver certain kinds of material for inclusion in the digital biography. This is also an example of how existing forms of power legitimize expertise and validate particular kinds of knowledge claims by institutionalizing certain practices at the expense of others. In the case of the Tropenmuseum, we saw that different parts of the organization were more open or less open than others. For example, the public relations department was eager to use photos made by visitors, and saw clear benefits in greater interactions and in the visual material produced in new sites such as WLANL. In the case of Flickr, we saw that some of the more innovative practices of researchers went unmentioned in publications and were hardly visible as part of formal knowledge practices, since they were seldom mentioned in methodological sections or included in citations. Fieldwork uncovered a tension between the fact that these practices around Flickr are essential parts of the empirical work of these researchers and the fact that are not (yet) part of institutional routines. Recall also that the formal channels of academia were also considered the preferred ways of reinforcing claims to knowledge production and authorship, with books, articles, or exhibitions in traditional settings counting as sites of publication or attribution of intellectual and artistic ownership. On the other hand, we saw that researchers' expectations about the infrastructural services that their organization should provide (better Web platforms, more support for visual material) were shaped by their experiences in the context of user-driven and commercial platforms.

Our concern with specifying an analytical vocabulary and with examining both infrastructural and institutional aspects of new sites of knowledge production stems from the often-heard promise that new infrastructures (alone) will radically reconfigure how knowledge is produced and valued. Such claims about the potential of new sites to break open monopolies on expertise or cultural production posit that good things will come from new infrastructures, and that institutions (especially in the ways in which they are dysfunctional) will be challenged in the process. The crux of the argument is that roles of actors will change: consumers will become "produsers" (Bruns 2008), and the small minority who in the past have been involved (for instance, as lay experts or as early adopters) will be joined by the masses as they take an active role in producing technological, cultural, and scientific knowledge. As this chapter has shown, changes in knowledge production are more diverse than this scenario claims, even along the specific dimension of authority and expertise. If virtual knowledge arising from new sites of knowledge production has the potential to be radically democratic, heterogeneous, and distributed, it is through such new configurations of interfaces with institutions and infrastructures that actual changes in knowledge production can be understood.

REFERENCES

Arzberger, Peter, Peter Schroeder, Anne Beaulieu, Geoffrey Bowker, Kathleen Casey, Leif Laaksonen, David Moorman, Paul Uhlir, and Paul Wouters. 2004. Science and government: An international framework to promote access to data. *Science* 303 (5665): 1777–1778.

Beaulieu, Anne. 2001. Voxels in the brain: Neuroscience, informatics and changing notions of objectivity. *Social Studies of Science* 31 (5): 635–680.

Beaulieu, Anne. 2002. Images are not the (only) truth: Brain mapping, visual knowledge, and iconoclasm. *Science, Technology & Human Values* 27 (1): 53–86.

Borup, Mads, Nik Brown, Kornelia Konrad, and Harro van Lente. 2006. The sociology of expectations in science and technology. *Technology Analysis and Strategic Management* 18 (3/4): 285–298.

Bowker, Geoffrey C. 2000. Biodiversity datadiversity. *Social Studies of Science* 30 (5): 643–683.

Bowker, Geoffrey C., Karen Baker, Florence Millerand, and David Ribes. 2010. Towards information infrastructure studies: Ways of knowing in a networked environment. In *International Handbook of Internet Research*, ed. J. Hunsinger, L. Klastrup, and M. Allen. Springer.

Brown, Nik, and Mike Michael. 2003. A sociology of expectations: Retrospecting prospects and prospecting retrospects. *Technology Analysis and Strategic Management* 15 (1): 3–18.

Bruns, Axel. 2008. *Blogs, Wikipedia, Second Life, and Beyond: From Production to Produsage*. Peter Lang.

Burgess, Jean. 2009. Remediating vernacular creativity: Photography and cultural citizenship in the Flickr photosharing network. In *Spaces of Vernacular Creativity: Rethinking the Cultural Economy*, ed. T. Edensor, D. Leslie, S. Millington, and N. Rantisi. Routledge.

Callon, Michel, and Arie Rip. 1992. Humains, non-humains: Morale d'une coexistence. In *La Terre outragée: Les Experts sont formels!* ed. J. Theys and B. Kalaora. Autrement.

Castells, Manuel. 1996. *The Rise of the Network Society*. Blackwell.

Collins, Harry M., and Robert Evans. 2002. The third wave of science studies: Studies of expertise and experience. *Social Studies of Science* 32: 235–296.

David, Paul A. 1985. Clio and the economics of QWERTY. *American Economic Review* 75 (2): 332–337.

de Rijcke, Sarah. 2008a. Light tries the expert eye: The introduction of photography in nineteenth century macroscopic neuroanatomy. *Journal of the History of the Neurosciences* 17: 349–366.

de Rijcke, Sarah. 2008b. Drawing into abstraction: Practices of observation and visualization in the work of Santiago Ramón y Cajal. *Interdisciplinary Science Reviews* 33 (4): 287–311.

de Rijcke, Sarah. 2010. Regarding the Brain: Practices of Objectivity in Cerebral Imaging, Seventeenth Century—Present. PhD thesis, University of Groningen.

de Rijcke, Sarah, and Anne Beaulieu. 2011. Image as interface: Consequences for users of museum knowledge. *Library Trends* 59 (4): 663–685.

Derksen, Maarten. 1997. Are we not experimenting then? The rhetorical demarcation of psychology and common sense. *Theory & Psychology* 7 (4): 435–456.

Derksen, Maarten, and Anne Beaulieu. 2011. Social technology. In *The Handbook of Philosophy of Social Science*, ed. I. Jarvie and J. Zamora-Bonilla. Sage.

Doing, Park. 2004. "Lab hands" and the "Scarlet O": Epistemic politics and (scientific) labor. *Social Studies of Science* 34 (3): 299–323.

Epstein, Steven. 1996. *Impure Science: Aids, Activism, and the Politics of Knowledge*. University of California Press.

Edwards, Paul. N., Geoffrey Bowker, Steven J. Jackson, and Robin Williams. 2009. Introduction: An agenda for infrastructure studies. *Journal of the Association for Information Systems* 10 (5): article 6.

Friedland, Roger, and Robert R. Alford. 1991. Bringing society back in: Symbols, practices, and institutional contradictions. In *The New Institutionalism in Organizational Analysis*, ed. W. Powell and P. DiMaggio. University of Chicago Press.

Fuller, Matthew. 2003. *Behind the Blip: Essays on the Culture of Software*. Autonomedia.

Gieryn, Thomas. 1983. Boundary-work and the demarcation of science from nonscience: Strains and interests in professional ideologies of scientists. *American Sociological Review* 48 (6): 781–795.

Gieryn, Thomas. 1999. *Cultural Boundaries of Science: Credibility on the Line*. University of Chicago Press.

Habets, Jan. 2004. Concept Plan van Aanpak Invoering Culturele Biografie. Unpublished archival document.

Hand, Martin. 2008. *Making Digital Cultures: Access, Interactivity and Authenticity*. Ashgate.

Hayles, N. Katherine. 2002. Material metaphors, technotexts, and media-specific analysis. In Writing Machines: Mediaworks Pamphlets, ed. N. Hayles and A. Burdick. MIT Press.

Hine, Christine. 2006. Databases as scientific instruments and their role in the ordering of scientific work. *Social Studies of Science* 36 (2): 269–298.

Hine, Christine. 2008. *Systematics as Cyberscience: Computers, Change, and Continuity in Science*. MIT Press.

Jackson, Steven J., Paul N. Edwards, Geoffrey C. Bowker, and Cory P. Knobel. 2007. Understanding infrastructure: History, heuristics, and cyberinfrastructure policy. *First Monday* 12 (6).

Jasanoff, Sheila. 1990. *The Fifth Branch: Science Advisers as Policymakers*. Harvard University Press.

Jasanoff, Sheila. 2004. Ordering knowledge, ordering society. In *States of Knowledge: The Co-Production of Science and the Social Order*, ed. S. Jasanoff. Routledge.

Jenkins, Henry. 2006. *Convergence Culture: Where Old and New Media Collide*. New York University Press.

Kothari, Uma. 2005. Authority and expertise: The professionalisation of international development and the ordering of dissent. *Antipode* 37 (3): 425–446.

Knorr Cetina, Karin. 1999. *Epistemic Cultures: How the Sciences Make Knowledge.* Harvard University Press.

Krasner, Stephen D. 1988. Sovereignty: An institutional perspective. *Comparative Political Studies* 21 (1): 66–94.

LAgroup. 2003. *Eindrapport: De Culturele Biografie van Maastricht.* LA Group.

Lange, Patricia G. 2007. Publicly private and privately public: Social networking on YouTube. *Journal of Computer-Mediated Communication* 13 (1): 18 (available at http://jcmc.indiana.edu).

Lynch, Michael. 2007. Expertise, skepticism and cynicism. *Spontaneous Generations* 1 (1): 17–23.

Petersen, Søren Møren. 2009. Common Banality: the Affective Character of Photo Sharing, Everyday Life and Produsage Cultures. PhD thesis, IT University of Copenhagen.

Pinch, Trevor. 2008. Technology and institutions: Living in a material world. *Theory and Society* 37 (5): 461–483.

RIN (Research Information Network). 2010. *If You Build It, Will They Come? How Researchers Perceive and Use Web 2.0* (available at http://www.rin.ac.uk).

Rip, Arie. 2003. Constructing expertise: In a third wave of science studies? *Social Studies of Science* 33 (3): 419–434.

Rooijakkers, Gerard. 1999. Het leven van alledag benoemen: Cultureel erfgoed tussen ondernemerschap en nieuwe technologie. *Boekmancahier* 41 (Erfgoed en nieuwe media): 275–289.

Rose, Nikolas. 1993. Government, authority and expertise in advanced liberalism. *Economy and Society* 22 (3): 283–299.

Rubinstein, Daniel, and Katrina Sluis. 2008. A life more photographic: Mapping the networked image. *Photographies* 1 (1): 9–28.

Scott, Richard W. 2008. Approaching adulthood: The maturing of institutional theory. *Theory and Society* 37 (5): 427–442.

Sekula, Allan. 1985. The body and the archive. *October* 39: 2–64.

Shapin, Steven. 1995. *A Social History of Truth: Civility and Science in Seventeenth-Century England.* University of Chicago Press.

Shapin, Steven, and Simon Schaffer. 1985. *Leviathan and the Air Pump: Hobbes, Boyle and the Experimental Life.* Princeton University Press.

Shove, Elizabeth, Martin Hand, Jack Ingram, and Matthew Watson. 2007. *The Design of Everyday Life.* Berg.

Simon, Nina. 2010. Blogpost, http://museumtwo.blogspot.com/2010/01/is-wiki-pedia-loves-art-getting-better.html; accessed 27–01–2010, 16:30 h.

Skågeby, Jörgen. 2008. Semi-public end-user content contributions: A case-study of concerns and intentions in online photo-sharing. *International Journal of Human-Computer Interaction* 66 (4): 287–300.

Sparke, Matthew. 2000. "Chunnel visions": Unpacking the anticipatory geographies of an Anglo-European borderland. *Journal of Borderlands Studies* 15 (1): 187–219.

van Dijck, José. 2008. Digital photography: Communication, identify, memory. *Visual Communication* 7 (1): 57–76.

van House. Nancy. 2002a. Trust in knowledge work: CaliFlora and biodiversity data sharing. In Proceedings of the Second ACM/IEEE-CS Joint Conference on Digital Libraries.

van House, Nancy. 2002b. Digital libraries and the practice of trust: Networked environmental information. *Social Epistemology* 16 (1): 99–114.

van House, Nancy, et al. 2004. From "what?" to "why?": The social uses of personal photos. Presented at ACM Conference on Computer Supported Cooperative Work, Chicago.

Virtual Knowledge Studio. 2008. Messy shapes of knowledge: STS explores infor-matization, new media and academic work. In *The Handbook of Science and Technology Studies*, third edition, ed. E. Hackett, O. Amsterdamska, M. Lynch, and J. Wajcman. MIT Press.

Waterton, Claire. 2010. Experimenting with the archive: STS-ers as analysts and co-constructors of databases and other archival forms. *Science, Technology & Human Values* 35 (5): 645–676.

Waterton, Claire, and Rebecca Ellis. 2004. Environmental citizenship in the making: The participation of volunteer naturalists in UK biological recording. *Science & Public Policy* 31 (2): 95–105.

Weber, Max. 1968. *Economy and Society*. Bedminster.

Wouters, Paul, and Anne Beaulieu. 2006. Imagining e-science beyond computation. In *New Infrastructures for Knowledge Production: Understanding E-Science,* ed. C. Hine. Idea Group.

Wouters, Paul, and Peter Schroeder, eds. 2003. *The Public Domain of Digital Research Data*. NIWI-KNAW.

Wouters, Paul, and Bas van Heur. 2009. Response to workshop social technology. Social Technology blog (http://socialtechnology.wordpress.com).

Wynne, Brian. 1992. Misunderstood misunderstanding: Social identities and public uptake of science. *Public Understanding of Science* 1 (3): 281–304.

2 WORKING IN VIRTUAL KNOWLEDGE: AFFECTIVE LABOR IN SCHOLARLY COLLABORATION

SMILJANA ANTONIJEVIĆ, STEFAN DORMANS, AND SALLY WYATT

Scholarly work, especially in the humanities and the social sciences, is often seen as solitary. The lone, creative individual, reading and writing while sitting on a chair and gazing out a window, is a powerful image even as it draws attention to the very unglamorous nature of such work. This image of routine, often rather lonely activity contrasts sharply with the much more exciting image of teams of scientists working together in a laboratory, collecting samples, analyzing data, and sharing ideas. But the reality of scholarly work in the humanities and the social sciences has always been otherwise. Scholars in these fields often work together, for example, to conduct multinational and/or longitudinal projects; to turn raw archival and other data into systematic, comprehensible, and usable database records; to comment on colleagues' work; and to prepare publications. Thus, scholars in the humanities and the social sciences routinely engage in collaborative work, and in affective labor stemming from such collaboration, when engaged in the production and distribution of knowledge. The diffusion of information and communication technologies (ICTs) that has occurred in the past few decades offers many possibilities for augmenting or disrupting such collaborative work by shifting the boundaries between visible and invisible tasks, by influencing the division of labor within teams, and by bringing to light various affective underpinnings of scholarly practice. In this chapter, we focus on such affective aspects of scholarly work, and we develop a conceptual framework for understanding the range of affective activities that scholars in the social sciences and the humanities undertake in order to collaborate. We focus particularly on affective activities that may be changed by the incorporation of digital technologies into everyday scholarly practices. Thus, we explicitly address the working practices that are emerging with the use of

ICTs in the production of virtual knowledge, as discussed in the introduction to this volume.

We draw upon three resources to develop our conceptual framework. The first of these resources are theoretical, including the debate about immaterial and affective labor that started with Karl Marx (1861–1863). In recent times, such ideas have been developed as a means of understanding the ways in which ICTs are implicated in processes of globalization and deterritorialization within contemporary capitalist relations of production (Castells 1996; Hardt and Negri 2000; Terranova 2004). Furthermore, the introduction of ICTs into work makes previously invisible elements of collaboration visible, and we pose the question of whether this happens at the cost of affective labor, which may sometimes be best left implicit and tacit. Thus, we also draw upon another theoretical resource, namely literature about invisible work from the sociology of computer-supported work and of health (Star and Strauss 1999). Though there has been much discussion in that literature about technology in relation to both affective labor and invisible work, very little of it has focused on scholarly work. In discussing scholarly work and affective labor, we also draw on theoretical resources in the rhetoric of science (Gross 1990) and on recent studies focusing on affective aspects of scholarly practice (Fraser and Puwar 2008; Gill 2010).

Our second resource comes from empirical research by one of us (Stefan) on international collaboration in the field of social and economic history. In that field, geographically dispersed groups of historians collect data on specific regions and time periods to construct large datasets for international comparative research. (See Olson et al. 2008; Shrum et al. 2007.) In order to enhance access to their colleagues and to each other's data, the historians make use of computing and communication technology.

The third resource is our own experience of working together in writing this chapter. This resource builds on reflexive ethnographic approaches (Haraway 1997; Woolgar 1991; Mol 2002; Anderson 2006; Atkinson 2006; Ellis and Bochner 2000),[1] and it seeks to make visible our work practices related to collaborative writing. Such reflections on our own experiences of collaboration are not only a resource, but also an attempt to contribute to filling a gap in critical analyses of scholarly work, which we discuss throughout the chapter. As Rosalind Gill points out, "for all the interest in reflexivity in recent decades, the experiences of academics have somehow largely escaped critical attention" (2010, 229).

In the first section, we discuss the debates about immaterial and affective labor and how they relate to academic labor. That section ends with an outline of the three categories we use to understand scholarly collaboration: care work, articulation work, and persuasion work. We then introduce our two empirical cases: the collaborations of economic and social historians and our own collaboration. We then discuss each of the previously identified categories more fully in both theoretical and empirical terms, focusing on how they can be used to understand collaboration in situations where digital technologies are omnipresent. We conclude by discussing what our analysis means for the study of scholarly work and for the study of affective labor, suggesting that each could be improved by recognition of the other.

THE CHANGING NATURE OF LABOR AND SCHOLARLY WORK IN THE DIGITAL AGE

The changing nature of labor generated by the increasing use of ICTs in the late twentieth century has been a topic of detailed analysis in sociology, economics, political science, and other fields (Castells 1996; Hardt and Negri 2000; Terranova 2004). Under the umbrella terms *informatization* and/or *digitization*, the ICT-driven transformations of production and labor practices have been identified as causing—or anticipated to cause—the following structural, organizational, and ontological changes: deterritorialization of production processes; abstraction of labor practices, and a shift toward immaterial and affective labor. All of these changes constitute a new type of economy, captured by a variety of qualifiers, such as *post-industrial, information, digital, network,* and *knowledge* (Bell 1973; Negroponte 1995; Tapscott 1996; Castells 1996; Boyett and Boyett 2001; Webster 2002).

In this new type of economy, the network emerges as the dominant organizational model of production, which simultaneously provides and calls for collaborative labor structures organized without physical centers and spatial limitations. Put differently, the network as an organizational model of production facilitates deterritorialization of labor practices. Such a tendency toward deterritorialization is considered to promote the virtualization of labor processes and relations, i.e., to endorse computer-mediated functioning and existence of production sites and teams. Hardt and Negri posit that deterritorialized, virtualized work leads to abstracted cooperation. This arises through a process of homogenization, through which different professional practices become converted into identical operations of manipulating information:

> In previous periods, . . . the tools generally were related in a relatively inflexible way to certain tasks or certain groups of tasks. . . . The computer proposes itself, in contrast, as the universal tool, or rather as the central tool, through which all activities might pass. Through the computerization of production, then, labor tends toward the position of abstract labor. (Hardt and Negri 2000, 292)

Deterritorialized, virtualized, homogenized, and abstracted knowledge and labor in the information economy shift progressively toward virtual labor and immaterial labor.

The term *immaterial labor*, introduced in Marx's *Theory of Surplus Value* (1861–1863), refers to those labor practices in which the product is not separable from the act of production. Marx gives as examples teachers, doctors, priests, and artists. In Hardt and Negri's account (2000), *immaterial labor* refers to the processing of information or to conceptual work, such as problem solving and/or symbolic manipulation, associated with media production, Web design, marketing, and the like. Other recent theoretical descendants of Marx's concept can be recognized in Bourdieu's (1980, 1986) notion of social capital; in Foucault's (1976/1998) idea of biopower; in Deleuze and Guattari's (1980/1987) theorizing on the production of innovations, values, and thinking processes; and in contemporary feminist studies, which have expanded the concept of immaterial labor to the areas of domestic life, biological reproduction, and sex work (Fortunati 2007). Particularly relevant for the analysis of the information economy are the conceptions of immaterial labor presented in the work of new media-oriented scholars, among them Hardt and Negri (2000), Lillie (2006), Coté and Pybus (2007), in which immaterial labor is characteristic of the information-processing jobs that have replaced manufacturing jobs in the information economy.[2]

Scholarly work, the form of immaterial labor analyzed in this chapter, is a distinctive example of an informational occupation. As Frank Webster points out, academic work both includes and opens the door to "the highest level informational occupations, those found at the hub of informational capitalism" (2002, 117). Interestingly, Marx already identified scholars and teachers in his original account on immaterial labor (1861–1863). This early recognition confirms that some professions, such as academic work, involve immaterial labor as their primary mode of production, regardless of technological, economic, and overall societal developments. Some other forms of labor, however, emerge alongside such developments. For instance, the notion of "user labor" is directly associated with Web 2.0 practices related to user-generated content, and it continues to provoke debates about the economic, social, ethical, and other aspects of such a technologically generated novelty (van Dijck 2009; Baym and Burnett 2009; Terranova 2004). Moreover, as Gregg (2011) argues, mobile technologies challenge the affective and immaterial dimensions of both the work and the everyday life of professionals in informational occupations.

Information jobs, including scholarly work, employ information, communication, and affect in their production processes. This type of immaterial labor is bound up with human interaction, and hence with the creation and the manipulation of affects. Hardt and Negri (2000) thus define affective labor as a form of immaterial labor focused on the creation and the manipulation of affect. Similarly, Massumi presents affect as the ability to affect and/ or to be affected, and argues that "affect is central to an understanding of our information-and-image-based late capitalist culture" (2002, 27). Although Massumi identifies affect as central to late capitalism, the significance of this notion can be found in much earlier writings. For instance, in one of the earliest accounts of affect, Aristotle describes affect, the basis of *pathos*, as "all those feelings that so change men as to affect their judgements" (2004, II.1). These words from the fourth century BC portray activities targeted at the creation and manipulation of affect almost identically to how contemporary authors depict and interpret affective labor. Still, Massumi also posits that "our condition is characterized by a surfeit of [affect]," and warns that, despite such a surfeit, "there is no cultural-theoretical vocabulary specific to affect" (2002, 27). We aim to contribute to such a vocabulary by proposing three categories of affective academic work.

Our definition of *affective labor* draws on the literature and on the understanding of the concept that emerged in the course of writing this chapter. In our conceptualization, *affective labor* refers to activities that create, sustain, and/or modify behaviors and judgments.[3] In a scholarly environment, affective labor can be found in formal and informal interactions between scholars, and between them and other social actors. The production of affect is also part of the goal of much academic work, including teaching and the preparation of texts.

In the remainder of this chapter, we explore the notion of affective labor with regard to scholarly practice, aiming to highlight, analyze, and interpret forms and roles of this aspect of academic work in relation to how the use of ICTs mediates processes of scholarly collaboration and knowledge production. In our analysis, we furthermore deploy the concept of invisibility, which is integral to both affective labor and scholarly practice.

Star and Strauss (1999) introduce the concept of invisibility to portray "the ecology of visible and invisible work"; however, they argue that "no work is either inherently visible or invisible" (1). They identify three ways in which invisibility of work is achieved: creating a non-person, disembedding background work, and abstracting and manipulating indicators. "Creating a non-person" refers to situations in which the product of the work is visible but the worker is invisible—for example, people who do cleaning work are often invisible, arriving late at night or early in the morning, but the result of their labor is visible to all. Disembedding background work is almost the reverse—the workers are quite present, but some of the work they do is relegated to the background. For example, in hospitals nurses are very visible but much of the work they do in looking after patients is taken for granted. "Abstracting and manipulating indicators" refers to the ways in which formal indicators are used to make certain tasks invisible. For example, in academic contexts in which productivity is quantified by a set of norms for different teaching, research, and administrative tasks, some of the sub-tasks of care and consideration become invisible. Universities increasingly deploy workload allocation systems based on notional numbers of hours for different tasks in order to balance the amount of work across individuals or across departments. Such systems rarely provide for the types of affective labor discussed here.

The concept of invisible work has been used to powerful effect in analyses of health-care work (Mesman 2008; Mort et al. 2003) and of computer-supported cooperative work (CSCW) (Schmidt and Simone 1996; Suchman 1987). Much of the literature on health care focuses on the invisible work of low-paid medical support staff, such as nurses, and even lower-paid ancillary workers, such as cleaners. More recently (Oudshoorn 2008; Wathen, Wyatt, and Harris 2008), the invisible work of patients and the family members and friends who care for them has received more attention. CSCW research draws upon earlier studies by Anselm Strauss of work and the division of labor. Strauss was concerned to focus on actual work practices and task division rather than on the social division of labor. He also introduced the concept of articulation work to capture particular sorts of invisible work, namely "the meshing of the often numerous tasks, clusters of tasks . . . the meshing of efforts of various unit-workers (individuals, departments, etc.)" (1985, 8). Strauss' concept of articulation work and our own concepts of care work and persuasion work constitute three main categories of the conceptual framework we propose in this chapter, a framework we employ in analyzing the affective elements of scholarly practice.

Star and Strauss (1999) caution against attempts to make everything visible or to formalize all work, arguing that there are good reasons for some work to remain invisible.[4] We accept this point and develop it further in the remainder of this chapter, focusing on the role of ICTs in making various work practices visible. Also, we emphasize that there can be "bad," "unproductive," "unnecessary," and in other ways negative affective labor, positing that those aspects come to the fore with the emergence of technologically mediated visibility.

Based on our analysis of the literature (summarized above), our fieldwork with historians, and our own experience as academics (in general and in this particular instance), we identify three main categories for understanding the affective labor involved in scholarly collaboration. As previously mentioned, the three categories are care work, articulation work, and persuasion work. These are not intended to be either comprehensive or mutually exclusive; they are meant to be used as a heuristic to draw our attention as analysts to those aspects of scholarly work that often remain invisible or unspoken. Affective work is often only mentioned in passing in the literature. In our conceptual framework, affective engagement figures in all three categories. Before defining and illustrating each of these categories more fully, we introduce the empirical cases on which our analysis is based.

INTRODUCING THE CASES: HISTORIANS COLLABORATE AND SO DO WE

As was discussed in the preceding section, scholarly work has long been seen as a good example of immaterial labor. Despite this, as several scholars have commented, scholarly work has remained exempt from critical analysis. (See, e.g., Gill 2010.) This chapter contributes to filling that gap by drawing on fieldwork done in the framework of a research project on "socio-technological aspects of collaboratory projects in social and economic history," and on our own experience of scholarly collaboration in general and of writing this chapter in particular. The fieldwork entailed an ethnographic study of the practices, risks, and opportunities associated with the implementation of the collaboratory model in the field of social and economic history.[5] More precisely, the project analyzed a number of collaboratories related to the International Institute of Social History (IISH) in Amsterdam.[6] These collaboratories included between 20 and 60 members, with varying backgrounds, located around the world. Each collaboratory revolved around a specific research topic, such as labor relations, strikes and lockouts, migrant organizations, life courses, or occupations. In most cases, collaboration focused on harmonizing and sharing existing databases, although some collaboratories built new databases by reinterpreting regional or national censuses and other material. Each collaboratory used computing and communication technology, and they also met a few times a year at conferences and workshops.

The fieldwork covered the period from early 2008 until the beginning of 2010 and combined various ethnographic techniques, among them participant observation, text analysis, and interviewing. An important part of the fieldwork was Stefan's attendance at both formal and informal sessions of international workshops and conferences. In addition, various members of the collaboratories—within as well as outside the IISH—were interviewed.[7] The online interaction among the members of the various collaboratories was studied closely by monitoring and analyzing the use of the collaborative software and the mailing lists. Finally, all the relevant documents on and by the collaboratories, such as funding proposals, guidelines on metadata, taxonomies, code books, minutes of meetings, and position papers, were examined.

Our second empirical example comes from our own experience of scholarly collaboration in preparing this chapter. Our collaboration began in early 2009, when Stefan and Sally individually responded to the call for abstracts for this volume. In the spring of 2009, they began meeting together to prepare a joint extended abstract. Smiljana joined the Virtual Knowledge Studio at the beginning of July, and was invited to contribute to the preparation of this chapter very soon thereafter. Some features of our early encounters are discussed below. The empirical material about our collaboration includes conversations, email messages, earlier drafts of the chapter, and written reflections developed individually at different points during the preparation of the chapter. When we first prepared such reflections, we did not anticipate that they would appear in the final version in a form close to their original form (sometimes edited slightly in order to make them comprehensible for a wider audience). In addition, we considered suggestions and comments made by reviewers in the Virtual Knowledge Studio (Clement Levallois, Stephanie Steinmetz, Charles van den Heuvel, and Paul Wouters), who suggested that their comments could be used in our analysis, and on anonymous reviews obtained by the publisher and the editors of the volume.

Although the idea to use our own experience of producing this chapter was mentioned in the extended abstract prepared at an early stage, it took some time to find an approach that suited our ambitions. The idea of a reflexive approach proved to be very useful, since it enabled us to discuss our personal experiences in academic collaboration and thus to highlight aspects of affective labor that could not be easily included in our discussion of the fieldwork on historical collaboratories for ethical, methodological, and epistemological reasons. We used our own collaboration to help us think through some of the more personal and affective experiences of academic collaboration without compromising the confidentiality and trust relations that Stefan developed with the historians during his fieldwork. Including our own experiences also stems from a more general methodological concern about how to capture emotional and affective processes in scholarly collaboration. In our view, it is highly problematic to attempt to describe the collaborative practices of other scholars as if they were something remote and exotic about which we could know and be objective. To focus on "sense" while denying our "sensibility," as discussed further in the next section, is not only ethically dubious; it also deprives us of an important source of insight.

To illustrate our methodological and epistemological concerns and the use of our reflections, we provide the following example, in which Smiljana reflects on how a remark made during a workshop to discuss early drafts of chapters for this book led her to consider the research process and how to write about it:

I was back on the "S-team"[8] board, both emotionally and intellectually. And isn't it exactly what we are writing about in this chapter? Is it possible to separate emotional and intellectual aspects of academic, especially collaborative, work? Are we and do we want to be professionals who are adding, editing, interpreting the data without adding/editing/interpreting our own and our colleagues' feelings emerging from a professional activity? What if we . . . switched from traditional *Introduction-Theory-Method-Results-Conclusion* structure . . . to a form of academic expression that would stress and encourage reflexive writing? Wouldn't such a shift give us a new lens to observe and understand better theoretical, methodological, epistemological, and other decisions put forward in scholarly texts? (Smiljana's reflection, September 11, 2009)

In addition to illustrating some of our methodological and ethical concerns, this reflection also talks about the importance of care work.

CARE WORK: LOOKING AFTER PEOPLE, DATA, AND TECHNOLOGY

In this section, we introduce the concept of care work, which entails work done in looking after our colleagues, our tools, and our outputs, and which is the first building block of the conceptual framework we propose in this chapter. We provide some additional background to the concept before discussing different instances of care work, namely care in the choice of collaborators and various instances of technically mediated care work, such as care of technology, intellectual property, and/or metadata. We conclude the section by examining the positive and negative aspects of carelessness.

We use the word 'care' deliberately, aware of its double meaning. It can mean "taking care of," thus, it can refer to the ways in which scholars care for their sources, their own data and texts, their colleagues, and their material resources (such as computers and computer programs). 'Care' also means "being careful," as scholars often are with their own claims and those of others. However, by using the word 'care' we do not imply that academic work is necessarily always either caring or careful. Sadly, uncaring and/or careless treatment of data, sources, texts, and colleagues is not unknown in scholarly practice. The advantage of the word 'care' is that it draws attention to how various aspects of scholarly work can be understood from the perspective of affective labor.

In scholarly practice, care work has both formalized and informal aspects. The formalized aspects are exemplified by disciplinary ethical codes, citation styles, peer review processes, promotion committees, and the like. These formalized and visible aspects of academic care work are indispensable elements of socialization into the scholarly community, taught and practiced throughout academic curricula. Informal and commonly invisible elements of academic care work are broad-ranging and often appear under a rather vague umbrella of personal and/or institutional "style of behavior." Along this line, academic organizations are deemed more or less hierarchical, collaborative, considerate of newcomers, open to innovation, and so on.

Similarly, some academics are known to be supportive and careful readers of colleagues' texts; attentive listeners to colleagues' problems; willing to share contacts, sources, and resources; and non-authoritarian. Others are known for exactly opposite behaviors. At an extreme, Gill observes the growing aggression in anonymous peer review, wondering when it became "acceptable to write of a colleague's work, 'this is self-indulgent crap'" (2010, 239).

It is clear that many informal aspects of academic care work are not unique to academia. Other arenas of professional work share similar benefits and/ or difficulties and enjoy relatively high levels of autonomy. Yet the academic community may be especially vulnerable to difficulties arising from this sphere of professional practice, owing to its continuous effort to safeguard itself from affect in any "secular" meaning. Academic "sense," meaning a carefully nurtured, especially self-nurtured, image of scholarly practice, has traditionally been juxtaposed with non-academic "sensibility." Nonetheless, the academic community, focusing on its proclaimed pursuits of rationality and objectivity (even when embodied in anti-positivist, postmodern, and other lines of thought) sometimes falls into fallacy *pars pro toto*, assuming that features of formal academic work warrant analogous features of informal activities. If academics are trained and subsequently assessed on their ability to gather, analyze, and present their findings non-affectively (and here we consciously avoid the word 'objectively'), it is expected that they will engage in other activities in the same manner. But counter-examples are not hard to find. For instance, partners for cooperative research and writing are often chosen, or avoided, not only on the basis of research interests and areas of expertise, but also by virtue of compatible and/or desired status positions, projected institutional and/or individual benefits, personal styles of writing and professional behavior, and other affective reasons. We ourselves did this. We do not work on the same project, and we come from different disciplines, yet our reasons for working together were as much affective as instrumental. Sally wrote the following on the subject of her reaction to the suggestion made by the other editors that she and Stefan work together:

I've done a lot of co-authoring in my career, and I'm becoming increasingly fussy about whom I work with. It's not always an easy process but when it works, it results in something better than I could have done by myself. I liked the idea of working with Stefan—I had liked the style of his PhD very much and he seemed like someone I could work with on a more personal level. So we met. . . . We talked. (Sally's reflection, September 8, 2009)

Stefan was more ambivalent at first, largely as a result of earlier experiences:

> To be frank, I had mixed feelings about this idea [to co-write a chapter with Sally].
> . . . I always envisioned the process of co-authoring as being one of the most inspir-
> ing moments of academic dialogue. In practice, however, my few experiences in this
> field proved to be rather disappointing. No discussions that went on for hours in dark
> pubs, no in-depth engagement with my contributions by the other authors (at least
> not at the level I was hoping for). (Stefan's reflection, September 9, 2009)

Among the historians whose work we analyzed, personal networks and
styles of behavior also dominate the process of selecting collaborators. In
some cases, the collaborations date from before the formation of the actual
collaboratory. One collaboratory, for example, builds on a national data collection project that started in the early 1990s and only became a collaboratory in early 2008. In other instances, the idea to create a collaboratory
was the starting point for finding suitable collaborators. Identifying people
with appropriate expertise and comparable research approaches subsequently
proved difficult, especially since these projects revolved around methodological innovation in the field and thus required a relatively high amount
of trust among the participating historians. A related issue is that the work
is, for the most part, voluntary. Individual participation is not based on financial incentives, but mainly on social bonds and academic opportunities.
Many members are affiliated with the wider network of the IISH, and many
have long experience in cooperating with researchers at the institute. The
fact that the collaboratories are initiated by the IISH is sometimes mentioned
as an additional reason to participate, because of its leading position in social
and economic history.

The most obvious form of care work in computer-mediated collaborations is the care of the technology. At universities and at research institutes,
there has traditionally been a clear division of labor between scholars in the
humanities and the social sciences and members of the technical support staff.
If not antagonism, there is often incomprehension on both sides. In relation
to the discussion above about how invisibility is achieved, technical workers
are non-persons for many scholars. The technicians and the work they do to
ensure a smooth-running infrastructure are invisible. As with cleaning, it is
only by its absence or failure that their work becomes visible to the academics.

In an attempt to overcome the need for technical expertise, the historians chose to use Liferay, a relatively easy-to-use software package for

collaboration. It was expected that future support by technicians would be limited and that researchers would be responsible for (and would take care of) maintaining the software. Aside from the efficiency argument, it was argued that this would ensure that the researchers would engage with the software and would learn how it functioned. But most of the researchers remained reluctant to engage with the software at a technical level, and constantly commented on its minor flaws and on the lack of immediate technical support. Most of the historians kept expecting the software to work effortlessly and viewed the technical support staff as mere service providers. The technical specialists, on the other hand, only rarely engaged in depth with the historians' use of the software in their daily work routines. As part of an interventionist research strategy, Stefan acted as an interface in this process and mediated the interactions between the academics and members of the technical staff. (See the introduction to this volume.)

We too used collaborative software that was being developed and introduced within the Virtual Knowledge Studio contemporaneously with the preparation of this book. All three of us are rather cautious of the virtues of such spaces. Nonetheless, we did use the Virtual Knowledge Studio collaboratory rather intensively, as we reflected during an email exchange:

I already put "my part" of the chapter in the collab, but I am still working on it. By the way, it is interesting to see that our collaborative space—as self-declared techno-skeptics—is the most intensively used of all in [the Virtual Knowledge Studio collaboratory]. (Stefan's email to Smiljana and Sally, October 20, 2009)

This illustrates that academics do not have to be particularly enthusiastic about ICTs in order to use them effectively.

The introduction of technology and the formalization of data bring other questions of collaboration and ownership to the fore. Issues of intellectual property have always been important in research, and there are long-standing systems of copyright and patenting for dealing with them. The development of shared databases raises new challenges, especially for historians who do not have established guidelines for the sharing of data or for the acknowledgment of the work needed to create and maintain shared data. The development of intellectual property arrangements in social and economic history can be understood as formal care work. Since historians are increasingly sharing their data at various stages of the research process, open data licenses are now prominent on the agenda.

Sharing historical data implies sharing knowledge about the process of collecting and analyzing the data. This knowledge is formally created in various ways: historians add metadata to their dataset (the usual list of attributes of the individual dataset), they make annotations in the database (used to specify the process through which the data has been obtained from existing data), and they are supposed to write methodological papers (extended accounts of data collection and analysis). In principle, they can also discuss the research process in their publications, although this is not very common in the field of history and most collaboratories are not yet in the publishing phase. In addition, members of the collaboratories exchange knowledge of the research process during workshops and conferences, via online discussion forums, and via email and mailing lists. The amount of care invested in these processes varies greatly.

As was mentioned earlier, care work is not always positive in intent or outcome, and is sometimes absent in collegial interaction. An example of lack of care—for others' work schedules and needs—is the absence of engagement between members of the historical collaboratories. Very few of them approach this proactively. Most have to be asked repeatedly to contribute their data or the accompanying meta-knowledge. The collaboratory appears to be a low priority, and they only react when asked. Despite the general acceptance of collaborative research in history and in other academic fields, it remains rare for researchers to come together systematically as an interpretive community in which the multiple, situated, and distinctive subjectivities and perspectives of the researchers are exchanged in an "interpretive zone" (Wasser and Bresler 1996, 6). Rather, there is a tendency to decontextualize, reduce, and objectify fieldwork into textual transcripts, with researchers engaging in limited explicit reflexive processes to "put back in" and take into account the contexts, subjectivities, and research relationships through which the texts and the knowledge are produced and made meaningful (Mauthner and Doucet 2008, 977).

In our own experience, we have witnessed acts of carelessness, and of being carefree. We were interested in the ways in which technology might provoke hostility:

We [three of us] returned to the issue of "negative" affective labor—and shared some experiences Smiljana and I had recently had in other contexts—unproductive performance of niceness and the role of email.[9] I doubt we can use such examples as they involve other colleagues but at least they sensitize us to the dark side of affective labor (of course, there are much darker sides in academia—plagiarism, ripping off graduate students). (Sally's reflection, September 21, 2009)

In the same reflection, Sally also discussed a specific act of care, or carelessness, which might be termed "epistemological carelessness":

When Smiljana and I talked on Friday, she asked me if she should do more reading in order to expand the "jottings" document [the first draft of a theoretical section]. I encouraged her to just write—that she probably already knew more than enough to expand that document. Of course, I think my colleagues should read, but sometimes I think in academic work we get too caught up in the literature and sometimes it pays to let oneself go. (Sally's reflection, September 21, 2009)

This injunction to carelessness, or to the importance of being carefree, resonated with Stefan:

Originally I had not planned to work on some more reflections—although we agreed to do—but Sally's reflections inspired some ideas. One of them relates to the last point of Sally's [September 21] reflections, about the advice to "just write." For me, Sally's writing in general and her reflections in particular really inspire me to write without first spending several years with my nose in the books. . . . I always make academic writing much more complicated than it needs to be and then I spend weeks to make the text readable again. (Stefan's reflection, September 22, 2009)

We recognize that our focus on technically mediated care work means that some important aspects of care work, particularly face-to-face interactions with colleagues, are underestimated. We will return to this in the conclusion to the chapter.

ARTICULATION WORK: GOING WITH THE FLOW

The term *articulation work* refers to labor practices that support the articulation and the coordination of distributed work. The notion of articulation work was used in the CSCW literature to refer primarily to the work that gets things back on track in the event of work processes going wrong or not working or simply not having been anticipated by those who designed the system. The concept has been used to argue that designers (and those who study them) should pay attention to "the hidden tasks of articulation work" in order to understand why computer systems work or not (Star 1999, 387). Strauss points out that articulation work is "a kind of supra-type of work in any division of labor, done by the various actors" (1985, 8). Similarly, Schmidt and Bannon emphasize that "articulation work arises as [an] integral part of cooperative work as a set of activities required to manage the distributed nature of cooperative work" (1992, 7). In this section, we discuss coordination work in academic collaboration before discussing what the technical mediation of coordination work in such settings means for the autonomy, the visibility, and the formality or informality of scholars and tasks.

The amount of articulation work needed to coordinate cooperative work varies with the size of the group. The articulation work we did in order to write this chapter is obviously not as substantial as that needed to manage and coordinate the creation of a large database by 40 historians. In all cases, however, articulation work often isn't taken into account in the development of a collaborative project and instead falls in the category of invisible work. In practice, articulation work proves to be one of the most time-consuming activities in a collaboratory. However, since this type of work is rarely visible, extra coordination efforts are often not covered in the budget of a collaboratory, and many funding agencies do not recognize the actual costs incurred—a phenomenon that has also been observed in other academic collaboratories (Cummings and Kiesler 2005).

The size of a group is not the only factor determining the extent of articulation work required. The degree of conjunctive tasks can also play an important role. Conjunctive tasks (Sonnenwald 2007, 646) are tasks that entail contributions by all—or at least the majority—of the group's members. In the case of the collaboratories in social and economic history, such tasks may entail the creation of a common code book, the licensing of data, guidelines for creating and using metadata, or the development of a collectively used taxonomy. The development of a code book, for example, requires a lot of discussion, coordination and, eventually, agreement in order to be useful for the data-gathering process of all members of the group. In general, the collaboratories having the most conjunctive tasks required the most articulation work.

In the collaboratories in social and economic history, most research tasks are carried out individually. Each historian contributes data on his or her own theme, region, and/or time period of expertise. Often such a collaboratory originates from one or more national projects, which try to increase their scope. Adding foreign experts to the project team means that the collaboratory covers more ground, but it also necessitates the coordination of a greater number of individual efforts in order to make comparison of international data possible.

Our own coordination required creating clarity about the expectations we each individually had with regard to the content of the chapter and how to proceed. Since most texts develop their purpose and affect in the creative process of writing, we were fully aware of the limitations of such an endeavor. Still, we extensively discussed the structure and argument of the chapter during various meetings in the canteen, particularly our use of some kind of taxonomy. We also discussed the appropriate word. Instead of 'taxonomy' we could also have used 'classification', 'types', 'sensitizing concepts', or 'heuristic', each of which has slightly different connotations. For Stefan, this discussion showed how one needs to be explicit in collaboration—perhaps even more explicit than one would be if one did not collaborate:

Looking back on our meeting last Thursday it is obvious that I had some problems with the whole concept of a taxonomy. I probably still have them (and I would certainly prefer to call "it" a conceptual framework), but now it seems much more interesting that we actually had such a long discussion on this concept. . . . Normally, when working alone, I would not have bothered to think for long about my discomfort [with the word 'taxonomy']. I would have probably proceeded to work on the chapter without including a taxonomy. But the collaboration required me to be explicit. (Stefan's reflection, September 22, 2009)

This requirement to be explicit about certain aspects of the research process seems to be especially relevant when co-creating large historical databases. The geographically distributed nature of a collaboratory entails that historians are explicit about the collection, the construction, and the analysis of their data. However, traditionally, historians do not elaborate on their research process in their publications or in the information accompanying their data. In contrast to sociologists and other social scientists, social and economic historians do not explicitly and systematically discuss their research process, nor do they consistently monitor how they collect and analyze their data. In part, this can be explained by the discipline's tradition to write both for academics and for a general audience. Historians assume that the general audience is not interested in technical discussions about the research process, and if too much methodological detail is given the audience may lose interest in the study at hand.

Obviously, there are limits to what one can make explicit. Not all knowledge is recordable in easily transferred forms, such as documents (Finholt and Olson 1997, 28), and as a result it is not easily shared across distance. Nevertheless, when co-creating social scientific data one can develop elaborate rules for annotation and metadata. In doing so, one can transfer some of the tacit knowledge about a dataset and thus potentially improve interpretations of data by secondary users (Zimmerman 2008). However, such a system is very time consuming, and it isn't clear whether collaborators think that this extra effort produces enough extra benefits. Moreover, as Michener et al. (1997, 335) argue, there is no end to metadata: "There is no unique, minimal, and sufficient set of metadata for any given data set, since sufficiency depends on the use(s) to which the data are put."

If articulation work is defined as a set of activities required to manage the distributed nature of cooperative work, then coordination is too narrow a concept. Coordination suggests that such tasks are planned and are capable of being planned. The advantage of articulation work as a concept is that it captures both formal, planned coordination activities and all the informal, invisible, *ad hoc*, unplanned work that people do, especially when conducting complex tasks in large organizations distributed across time and space. Such articulation work within academic contexts includes the communication of know-how and tacit knowledge about an academic field and about how systems within the organization work.

The unplanned and informal aspects of articulation work are also closely related to the idea of "corridor talk" and the loss thereof in collaborations without co-location. In a collaboratory, the regular mechanisms of meeting in the corridor and inquiring about work-related or personal matters are absent. The implications of this are difficult to uncover in full, but the loss of common ground and the need to bridge distance are important aspects of articulation work. One common example is the practical organization of face-to-face meetings.

Historians working together to construct shared databases undertake much of the articulation work identified in the CSCW literature on the design of information systems, especially in relation to classification. Communications about tasks, task divisions, timetables, classification, and system design, especially as they are made increasingly public on electronic discussion lists and forums, are also an important part of articulation work. With the wider adoption of collaborative software in academic practice, articulation work increases the visibility of elements of scholars' work that previously may not have been observable.

Another example of making scholars' work increasingly visible through the use of ICTs comes from our own experience of sharing calendars. While we were working on this chapter, all members of the Virtual Knowledge Studio were asked to share our Web calendars with colleagues. Aimed at facilitating the planning of meetings, this request had one peculiar feature: we were instructed not to select a "busy/not busy" option when sharing calendars, although such an option would still serve the goal of facilitating the scheduling of meetings and similar activities. Instead, we were instructed to make the specificities of our engagements visible. Some colleagues noted that their calendars included information about private engagements and thus were not appropriate for sharing, and for that reason they chose the "busy/not busy" option despite the instruction. One colleague, in a private communication, explained why he included his dental appointments in the shared calendar and no other appointments: he "did not like the way it was superimposed." "Corridor talk" went a step further, raising the question of whether scholars really wanted and needed to share all their professional engagements with colleagues. This example illustrates the phenomenon of blurring the boundaries between the public and the private, a phenomenon that is well known to those who analyze blogging, twittering, and other communicative practices prompted by new media. Yet it also illustrates Star and Strauss' observation that, despite the possibilities provided by ICTs, "some forms of . . . discretion activity may often be best left unspecified, and not represented in system requirements" (1999, 9). More fundamentally, the case of shared Web calendars points to the question Star and Strauss propose as a starting point in thinking about CSCW: "What exactly *is* work, and to whom it might (or should) be visible or invisible?" (1999, 10) Indeed, the sharing of calendars has long been of interest within CSCW. In a review of the field in 1993, Bannon and Hughes point to the asymmetry "between the work required and the benefits accrued" (1993, 25), suggesting that senior managers are the main beneficiaries of such systems.

In this section, we have demonstrated how articulation work can expand not only as a result of larger groups working together, as would be expected, but also as a result of the technology itself which seems to require explicit and visible coordination. Not only does articulation work make previously invisible tasks more visible; it can also add to the range of tasks. Also, as the calendar example shows, calls to facilitate articulation work can be ambiguous and can prompt debates on some of the fundamental themes in academic practice, such as scholars' right to autonomy, authority, and confidentiality of work. These aspects of scholarly work are closely related to persuasion work.

PERSUASION WORK: THE GENTLE ART

The rhetoric of science has become an established field of inquiry (Perelman and Olbrechts-Tyteca 1969; Gross 1990; Simons 1990; Gross and Keith 1997; Fahnestock 1999; Ceccarelli 2001; Gross 2006). Yet associating rhetoric with science, and persuasion with scholarly discourse, can sometimes provoke hostility from academic colleagues who regard such ideas as almost blasphemous. This arises from the academic community's previously mentioned efforts to dissociate itself from the field of affect and to establish scholarly work as exclusively logos-based. Yet the beauty of rhetoric lies its two-millennia-old tradition of demonstrating, across historical, cultural, and ideological contexts, that logos, ethos, and pathos cannot be separated.

In the domain of science, a rhetorical approach posits that claims of science are products of persuasion. "Rhetorically, the creation of knowledge is a task beginning with self-persuasion and ending with the persuasion of others." (Gross 1990, 3) But what exactly is the subject of scientists' persuasion and self-persuasion? Gross explains:

[T]he rhetorical view of science does not deny "the brute facts of nature"; it merely affirms that these "facts," whatever they are, are not science itself, knowledge itself. Scientific knowledge consists of the current answers to three questions, answers that are the product of professional conversation: What range of "brute facts" is worth investigating? How is this range to be investigated? What do the results of these investigations mean? Whatever they are, the "brute facts" themselves mean nothing; only statements have meaning, and of the truth of statements we must be persuaded. (4)

Our third category refers to the persuasion work that is part and parcel of scholarly practice. We distinguish three main forms: credibility work, reputation work, and position work. *Credibility work* refers to those elements of scholarly practice captured above by Gross. In this type of activity, scholars' labor is aimed at persuading others (colleagues, peer reviewers, scientific community, funding agencies, general public, and so on), and also at persuading themselves that the phenomena of their analyses are worthy of investigation and that the proposed method(s) of data gathering, analysis, and interpretation best meet the accepted criteria of validity and reliability. Closely related to this, reputation work is aimed at demonstrating that a scholar is capable of producing an analysis that meets those criteria—that is, that the scholar possesses sufficient expertise to produce research findings and conclusions that will be regarded as valid and reliable by his or her academic peers. Finally, *position work* refers to those scholarly activities related to achieving, confirming, and preserving a certain status or position in an academic community. These three subtypes of persuasion work are closely related and commonly appear in the sequence credibility-reputation-position. Put differently, achieving credibility (that is, persuading others of the credibility of one's work) commonly leads to achieving scholarly reputation (that is, attaining and/or confirming the reputation of an expert in a research area). Such an achievement may result in a scholarly position; that is, it leads to attaining, preserving, or losing a specific position in an academic community, both in the scholar's immediate institutional surroundings and in the broader research community.

In the historical collaboratories, the use of ICTs brings elements of persuasion work to the fore in a specific way: it renders various aspects of scholarly work visible, as was discussed above. One problem that historians face in this regard is the difficulty of assessing how explicit the producer of the data has to be so that others can understand the specificities of his or her input and, consequently, assess the credibility of his or her work. Another problem that emerges from the use of ICTs is the fear of outside scrutiny. Through explicating that which was implicit, through making public what was private, patterns of practice become open for scrutiny and contestation (Berg 1997, 1086). In a field in which the research process has always been predominantly implicit, making the research process more amenable to inspection by others can be an obstacle to collaboration. In practice, the obstacles to investing time in sharing knowledge and working together may be too great. Despite being members of teams, many researchers work in individualistic ways. However, some historians also argued that the collaborative projects as such did actually increase discussions among peers, but primarily during face-to-face meetings (as at workshops and conferences) and only rarely via mailing lists or in the forum of the collaborative software.

As Kok and Wouters argue in this volume, the use of ICTs in the creation of large historical databases also created some discussion among peers in the social sciences and the humanities. Among mainstream historians, the increased use of computers and statistical methods by social and economic historians is often frowned upon, partially as a result of a more general

skepticism about quantitative research methods and a preference for persuasive storytelling. The social science community, on the other hand, was
increasingly persuaded by the more nuanced research results of social and
economic historians. Kok and Wouters show how earlier attempts to create and analyze large historical datasets did not always meet the standards of
this community, but more recent efforts are generally considered to be both
credible and persuasive.

The writing of this chapter also included various aspects of persuasion
work, starting with self-persuasion related to the credibility of the selected
topic(s) and method(s). In the course of writing the chapter, we also had
numerous offline and online discussions related to the credibility of various
parts of our work. As was described earlier, Stefan had doubts about the
proposed theoretical and conceptual frameworks, so Sally and Smiljana attempted (ultimately with success) to persuade him of the validity of such an
analytic strategy. Still, some of Stefan's worries remained, as one of Sally's
reflections illustrates:

At our last meeting (3 November) Stefan raised his worries about our insufficiently
sophisticated theoretical framework—worries prompted by his reading of Gill and
Pratt (2008). This got me really worried. But I have had time to read the article and
now I'm less worried. . . . [They] are doing something rather different, and I think we
can actually use parts of it. (Sally's reflection, November 11, 2009)

On the other hand, Smiljana had concerns about the fieldwork data:

What I would like to see related to ethnographic work are very specific examples,
something like "on November 14, 2008 the following message . . . was posted to the
collab on international labor. Immediately after, few historians reacted by posting the
following replies. . . . This example illustrates difficulties in articulation work, which
arise when. . . ." I am making this all up, of course, just to illustrate. In the same way,
we need concrete examples—quotes—from interviews and citations from the documents analyzed. (Smiljana's in-text comments, November 3, 2009)

Our reviewers also had comments and suggestions for enhancing the
argumentation of this chapter. Stephanie said "I have to admit that I am
not sure whether I find the presentation of results as purely narratives very
convincing." Along the same line, Paul asked "Would it be possible to also
have personal quotes / anecdotes from the historical case study?" Clement
suggested that "the defense of the thesis along the whole chapter could be
made more salient." Similarly, Paul observed that "currently, the empirical

stuff is rather loose, but you obviously know this. So I would be interested to see how you will weave the material together into a strong story." These comments clearly illustrate the importance of persuasiveness in scholarly discourse and debate: pure narratives are not *convincing*; the *defense* of the thesis could be more salient; the materials should be woven together into a *strong* story. These expressions used by our reviewers indicate that both the "brute facts" and the statements made about them figure in establishing the credibility of scholarly work and, ultimately, in the processes of creating and validating knowledge.

Persuasion work confirms the importance of affective labor in scholarly practice. However, such a role is rarely visible or stated. One instance of the academic community's disclosure of its "vulnerability to affect" is the institution of blind peer review, which is rooted in an acknowledgment of the possibility of affect's influencing scholars' judgment. Still, even this hallmark of academic work does not always or fully reflect the whole range of scholarly activities susceptible to affect. Fraser and Puwar argue that "emotional and affective relations are *central* to the ways in which researchers engage with, produce, understand and translate what becomes 'research'" (2008, 2, emphasis added).

Those relations, though, stem from different roots. Sometimes affective aspects of academic work get edited out of the scholarly record because they are deemed inappropriate according to the norms of scholarly discourse.[10] More significant, however, is the fact that such "discursive inappropriateness" might undermine academic credibility by pointing at aspects of scholarly practice rejected within an ideal model of modern science:

Laying out the affective details [of research] often seems to detract from academic authority. The sense of adventure, drama, mystery, fear—and sometimes, let's face it, the boredom—which produces research . . . risks revealing, perhaps even "exposing," the so-called unscholarly, anecdotal, irrational and unscientific dimensions of the research process. The very opposition between rational and irrational, analysis and imagination, subjectivity and objectivity, constitutes an important if not a central part of the legacy of an ideal of modern science. (Fraser and Puwar 2008, 4)

Still, losing academic credibility is not an end but rather a beginning of an academic drama that might emerge from disclosing the affective elements of academic work. As was mentioned above, credibility leads to reputation, which further leads to position; and this chain works in both ways, upward and downward. Properly trained agents (as Bourdieu would put it) of scholarly practice are not expected to have emotion while on duty—that is, when collecting, analyzing, and/or presenting "the brute facts of nature." On the contrary, they are trained and expected to "add to the sum of valid, reliable, statistically demonstrated, "objective" knowledge. After which, they would go into the field to witness to their faith, spread their learning and presumably reproduce themselves." (Wander and Jaehne 2000, 214) Not only does challenging such an academic order result in potentially damaged academic credibility; more important, it results in the loss of a scholar's ability to participate in the academic market—in other words, to exchange the products of his or her scholarly labor. Fraser and Puwar write:

[W]hile we [scholars] do not sell our "raw" research data but rather make it an accessible resource to each other, it is nevertheless a commodity in kind which can be translated into (exchanged for) published articles, royalties, esteem-ratings, reputation, status, departmental income, promotion and invitations in the global circuits of academic productivity. (2008, 14)

This summarizes the credibility-reputation-position interplay in scholarly work by highlighting one of the best-kept secrets of scholarly practice: that academic work, just like any other type of labor, strives for profit, whether in the form of affective revenue, such as recognition and reputation, or in the more tangible form of money and other material resources. Still, the image of an idealistic and (nearly) altruistic scholar is so prevalent that even critically oriented authors seem to accept it too readily. For instance, in her recent and worthwhile endeavor to put the academic community under scrutiny, Gill portrays scholars as people "notoriously bad at talking about (poor) pay" who fail to "secure pay deals that even keep pace with inflation," and who are "more likely than any other occupational group to do unpaid overtime," yet are "deeply invested in and passionately attached to their work"—so much so that they "often draw no distinction between [their] work and [them]selves" (2010, 232). Contrary to this, in one of the rare, openly critical accounts of scholarly practice, Philip Wander writes:

Morning after morning, day after day, year after year, I faced arguments based on "science." Then one day in the early 1970s, after about five years of struggle, it dawned on me that what I was hearing was not science. The arguments were not about science; they did not have science as their purpose. They were about hiring, retention, tenure, promotion, chair elections, travel funds, etc. . . . These efforts had less to do with science . . . than with resource allocation. (Wander and Jaehne 2000, 214)

Of course, it would be both cynical and unjust to claim that the allocation of resources constitutes the main part and/or purpose of scholarly practice. Yet concealing this and similar aspects of academic work is equally unjust, as it implies not only concealing the fact that scholarly labor can be unconstructive, negative, and unpleasant but also obscuring the complexity of knowledge production and validation.

CONCLUSION

In this chapter, we have begun to develop a vocabulary for discussing the affective labor involved in scholarly collaboration. We have introduced three categories—care work, articulation work, and persuasion work—in order to understand the ways in which the affective labor of scholars may change as they produce virtual knowledge and work in technologically intensive environments, which are characteristic of late capitalism. We have drawn attention to the ways in which scholars care (or do not care) for their data, their tools, and themselves, and for their relationships with colleagues. We have illustrated the importance of articulation work and the ways in which it is changed with the introduction of collaborative tools, which themselves affect the relative visibility of different tasks. We have also explored how persuasion work figures in scholarly practice, shaping this practice, collaborative academic relationships, and the production of academic works.

There are at least three issues we have not explored fully. The first is non-mediated care work and the importance of direct interaction for affect. The dependence on technology as a collaborative tool renders face-to-face care work even more invisible. Our own reflections are full of examples of face-to-face care work, particularly the pleasure we all had in our meetings that took place in our workplace canteen. But because our focus is on technologically mediated care work, we have not discussed face-to-face care work here. Second, we have not discussed the gendered division of affective labor. Research in other sectors, such as health care, demonstrates that care work is often women's work. In the case of organized religion, on the other hand, much of the (visible) care work is done by men (e.g., imams and priests). Though we expect that gender plays an important role in academic settings, it has not been our focus in this chapter. The third issue we have not discussed is the potential for using technology directly in knowledge production (see chapter 5 below) rather than as a tool for supporting collaboration (as we have done in this chapter). In the case of the Labor Relations Collaboratory, there is a lack of reliable quantitative data about labor relations in the pre-modern period, and so the experts have to construct "guesstimates." The best way of doing this remains controversial among historians, and until now advanced statistical or modeling techniques have not been used to fill gaps in the historical record.

But we have begun to fill some gaps that are of direct interest to us. The literature on immaterial and affective labor has hitherto neglected scholarly work, even though it is one of the paradigm cases of immaterial labor. One advantage of focusing on the affective labor of scholars that might be relevant for other types of work is the double nature of scholarly collaboration in that affect is both the outcome and part of the process. As our discussion of persuasion work demonstrates, producing affect is central to the scholarly process, whereas our discussions of care and articulation work focus more on affect among scholars.

As we mentioned in the introduction to our two cases, one reason we included our own collaboration as a case was that we felt it was easier to discuss our own feelings about working together. It would have been more difficult for the historians to do so, not only because we would have to impute motivation, feeling, and affect but also because we might appear to be judging them in ways we do not want. In retrospect, we are aware that we underestimated the difficulties of using our own experiences in this way—something Hernández et al. (2010, 11) also experienced when they wrote autoethnographic accounts of their academic careers. Our work was influenced not only by the collaboration among the three of us but also by the broader context in which we work, including reviewers of this chapter, other contributors to the book, and other colleagues at the Virtual Knowledge Studio. In order to protect those wider working relationships, we have sometimes exercised a degree of self-censorship in choosing not to include some of our observations or some of our email exchanges. This does confirm, however, that preserving invisibility is sometimes crucial to good care work. Acknowledging the complexities of our collaboration not only confirmed what we already knew about the deeply social nature of scholarly work; it also reinforced our view of affective labor as one of the most important elements of scholarly practice.

Romanticized and stereotypical narratives depicting scholars' work as exclusively logos-based, as aimed at producing knowledge, and as bettering the world conceal the fact that the academic community is not immune to both positive and negative aspects of affective engagement, and that, in fact, those emotional engagements constitute an inevitable element of knowledge production. Therefore, to understand the dynamics of knowledge production more fully, scholarly practice should be rethought and reformulated so as to incorporate the full range of scholarly labor—the practices of care and neglect, the complexities of articulation work, the importance and hidden dimensions of persuasion work, and so on. In short, academic sensibility, with both its positive and negative faces, should become an equal counterpart of academic sense in analyses of scholarly practice and knowledge production.

NOTES

1. Here we have cited a selection of works from the extensive literature of cultural studies, science and technology studies, and post-structuralist anthropology that have embraced self-reflexive styles of writing.

2. The "immaterial labor" debate is largely concerned with the changing nature of labor in late capitalist economies. There is indeed much more to be said about how the changing nature of immaterial and affective labor as experienced by scholars relates to the increased commercialization of universities and publicly funded research more generally. That is beyond the scope of this chapter. For more on this topic, see Fraser and Puwar 2008; Gill 2010.

3. See Krause 2008 for a detailed account of the relationship between affect and judgment.

4. For example, those involved in the so-called caring professions may carry on interacting with students or patients, in a holistic way, under or outside the surveillance of bureaucratic accountability.

5. Bos et al. (2007, 656) define a collaboratory as an organizational entity that spans distance, supports rich and recurring human interaction oriented to a common research area, fosters contact between researchers known to one another and between researchers not known to one another, and provides access to data, artifacts, and tools required to accomplish research tasks.

6. Although the project aimed to understand the impact of the collaboratory model on knowledge production in social and economic history, and thus explored changes in the exchange of tacit and implicit knowledge, the project was not specifically designed to study affective labor.

7. In all, 35 historians, economists, sociologists, and demographers were interviewed. Besides having different disciplinary backgrounds, the interviewees worked in

various countries (the United Kingdom, Russia, the United States, Germany, Turkey, Portugal, Uruguay, Argentina, South Korea, India, the Netherlands, Italy, Spain, Finland, and Brazil). Although more men with high academic status were interviewed, the group of interviewees also included women and scholars in the early stages of their careers.

8. This refers to us. As Smiljana recalled on September 11, 2009, "when Sally submitted the abstract [for the Virtual Knowledge Studio book workshop in August 2009], the first sensation of *ourness* suddenly struck me. What triggered such a sensation was a nickname Sally came up with: "Please find attached a slightly longer outline for the chapter being prepared by the 'S-team,' she wrote, alluding to our first names. So, perhaps symbolically, accidentally, and/or semi-jokingly, the team was born."

9. On the politics and etiquette of email, especially in relation to how email can intensify work, see Gregg 2011.

10. As Fraser and Puwar put it, "it is still more feasible to preserve the affective qualities of an enquiry within a novel than it is within the documentation of fieldwork" (2008, 3).

REFERENCES

Aristotle. 2004. *Rhetoric*. Dover Thrift Editions.

Anderson, Leon. 2006. Analytic autoethnography. *Journal of Contemporary Ethnography* 35 (4): 373–395.

Atkinson, Paul. 2006. Rescuing autoethnography. *Journal of Contemporary Ethnography* 35 (4): 400–404.

Bannon, Liam J., and John A. Hughes. 1993. The context of CSCW. In *Report of COST14 CoTech Working Group 4 (1991–1992)*, ed. K. Schmidt. European Commission.

Baym, Nancy K., and Robert Burnett. 2009. Amateur experts: International fan labor in Swedish independent music. *International Journal of Cultural Studies* 12 (5): 433–449.

Bell, Daniel. 1973. *The Coming of Post-Industrial Society: A Venture in Social Forecasting*. Basic Books.

Berg, Marc. 1997. Problems and promises of the protocol. *Social Science & Medicine* 44 (8): 1081–1088.

Bos, Nathan, Ann Zimmerman, Judith Olson, Jude Yew, Jason Yerkie, Erik Dahl, and Gary Olson. 2007. From shared databases to communities of practice: A taxonomy of collaboratories. *Journal of Computer-Mediated Communication* 12 (2): 652–672.

Bourdieu, Pierre. 1980. Le capital social. Notes provisoires. *Actes de la Recherche en Sciences Sociales* 31: 2–3.

Bourdieu, Pierre. 1986. The forms of capital. In *Handbook of Theory and Research for the Sociology of Education*, ed. J. Richardson. Greenwood.

Boyett, Joseph H., and Jimmie T. Boyett. 2001. *The Guru Guide to the Knowledge Economy*. Wiley.

Castells, Manuel. 1996. *The Rise of the Network Society*. Blackwell.

Ceccarelli, Leah. 2001. *Shaping Science with Rhetoric: The Cases of Dobzhansky, Schrödinger, and Wilson*. University of Chicago Press.

Coté, Mark, and Jennifer Pybus. 2007. Learning to immaterial labor 2.0: MySpace and social networks. *Ephemera* 7 (1): 88–106.

Cummings, Jonathon N., and Sara Kiesler. 2005. Collaborative research across disciplinary and organizational boundaries. *Social Studies of Science* 35: 703–722.

Deleuze, Gilles, and Felix Guattari. 1980/1987. *A Thousand Plateaus: Capitalism and Schizophrenia*. Athlone.

Ellis, Carolyn, and Arthur Bochner. 2000. Autoethnography, personal narrative, reflexivity: Researcher as subject. In *Collecting and Interpreting Qualitative Materials*, ed. N. Denzin and Y. Lincoln. Sage.

Fahnestock, Jeanne. 1999. *Rhetorical Figures in Science*. Oxford University Press.

Finholt, Thomas A., and Gary M. Olson. 1997. From laboratories to collaboratories: A new organizational form for scientific collaboration. *Psychological Science* 8 (1): 28–36.

Fortunati, Leopoldina. 2007. Immaterial labor and its machinization. *Ephemera* 7 (1): 139–157.

Foucault, Michel. 1976/1998. *The Will to Knowledge*, volume 1: *The History of Sexuality*. Penguin.

Fraser, Mariam, and Nirmal Puwar. 2008. Introduction: Intimacy in research. *History of the Human Sciences* 21 (4): 1–16.

Gill, Rosalind, and Andy Pratt. 2008. In the social factory? Immaterial labor, precariousness and cultural work. *Theory, Culture & Society* 25 (7–8): 1–30.

Gill, Rosalind. 2010. Breaking the silence: The hidden injuries of the neoliberal university. In *Secrecy and Silence in the Research Process: Feminist Reflections*, ed. R. Ryan-Flood and R. Gill. Routledge.

Gregg, Melissa. 2011. *Work's Intimacy*. Polity.

Gross, Alan G. 1990. *The Rhetoric of Science*. Harvard University Press.

Gross, Alan G. 2006. *Starring the Text: The Place of Rhetoric in Science Studies*. Southern Illinois University Press.

Gross, Alan G., and William M. Keith, eds. 1997. *Rhetorical Hermeneutics: Invention and Interpretation in the Age of Science*. SUNY Press.

Hardt, Michael, and Antonio Negri. 2000. *Empire*. Harvard University Press.

Haraway, Donna. 1997. *Modest_Witness@Second_Millenium: Female©_Meets_Oncomouse™: Feminism and Technoscience*. Routledge.

Hernández, Fernando, Juana Maria Sancho, Amalia Creus, and Alejandra Montané. 2010. Becoming university scholars: Inside professional autoethnographies. *Journal of Research Practice* 6 (1): article M7 (available at http://jrp.icaap.org).

Krause, Sharon. 2008. *Civil Passions: Moral Sentiment and Democratic Deliberation*. Princeton University Press.

Lillie, Jonathan. 2006. Immaterial labor in the eBay community. In *The eBay Reader*, ed. K. Hillis, M. Petit, and N. Epley. Routledge.

Marx, Karl. 1861–3 (1967, 1970, 1972). *Theories of Surplus Value*. Lawrence & Wishart.

Massumi, Brian. 2002. *Parables for the Virtual*. Duke University Press.

Mauthner, Natasha S., and Andrea Doucet. 2008. Knowledge once divided can be hard to put together again: An epistemological critique of collaborative and team-based research practices. *Sociology* 42 (5): 971–985.

Michener, William K., James W. Brunt, John J. Helly, Thomas B. Kirchner, and Susan G. Stafford. 1997. Nongeospatial metadata for the ecological sciences. *Ecological Applications* 7 (1): 330–342.

Mol, Annemarie. 2002. *The Body Multiple: Ontology in Medical Practice*. Duke University Press.

Mesman, Jessica. 2008. *Uncertainty in Medical Innovation: Experienced Pioneers in Neonatal Care*. Palgrave Macmillan.

Mort, Maggie, Carl R. May, and Tracy Williams. 2003. Remote doctors and absent patients: Acting at a distance in telemedicine? *Science, Technology & Human Values* 28 (2): 274–295.

Negroponte, Nicholas. 1995. *Being Digital*. Knopf.

Olson, Gary M., Ann S. Zimmerman, and Nathan Bos. 2008. *Scientific Collaboration on the Internet*. MIT Press.

Oudshoorn, Nelly. 2008. Diagnosis at a distance: The invisible work of patients and health-care professionals in cardiac telemonitoring technology. *Sociology of Health & Illness* 30 (3): 272–288.

Perelman, Chaim, and Lucy Olbrechts-Tyteca. 1969. *The New Rhetoric: A Treatise on Argumentation*. University of Notre Dame Press.

Schmidt, Kjeld, and Liam Bannon. 1992. Taking CSCW seriously: Supporting articulation work. *Computer Supported Cooperative Work* 1 (1–2): 7–40.

Schmidt, Kjeld, and Carla Simone. 1996. Coordination mechanisms: Towards a conceptual foundation of CSCW systems design. *Computer Supported Cooperative Work* 5 (2–3): 155–200.

Shrum, Wesley, Joel Genuth, and Ivan Chompalov. 2007. *Structures of Scientific Collaboration*. MIT Press.

Simons, Herbert W., ed. 1990. *The Rhetorical Turn: Inventions and Persuasion in the Conduct of Inquiry*. University of Chicago Press.

Sonnenwald, Diane H. 2007. Scientific collaboration. In *Annual Review of Information Science and Technology*, ed. B. Cronin. Information Today.

Star, Susan Leigh. 1999. The ethnography of infrastructure. *American Behavioral Scientist* 43 (3): 377–391.

Star, Susan Leigh, and Anselm Strauss. 1999. Layers of silence, arenas of voice: The ecology of visible and invisible work. *Computer Supported Cooperative Work* 8 (1–2): 9–30.

Strauss, Anselm. 1985. Work and the division of labor. *Sociological Quarterly* 26 (1): 1–19.

Suchman, Lucy. 1987. *Plans and Situated Actions: The Problem of Human-Machine Communication*. Cambridge University Press.

Tapscott, Don. 1996. *The Digital Economy: Promise and Peril in the Age of Networked Intelligence*. McGraw-Hill..

Terranova, Tiziana. 2004. *Network Culture: Politics for the Information Age*. Pluto.

van Dijck, José. 2009. Users like you? Theorizing agency in user-generated content. *Media, Culture & Society* 31 (1): 41–58.

Wander, Philip C., and Dennis Jaehne. 2000. Prospects for "a rhetoric of science." *Social Epistemology* 14 (2–3): 211–233.

Wasser, Judith Davidson, and Liora Bresler. 1996. Working in the interpretive zone: Conceptualizing collaboration in qualitative research teams. *Educational Researcher* 25: 5–15.

Wathen, Nadine, Sally Wyatt, and Roma Harris, eds. 2008. *Mediating Health Information: The Go-Betweens in a Changing Socio-Technical Landscape*. Palgrave Macmillan.

Webster, Frank. 2002. *Theories of the Information Society*, second edition. Routledge.

Woolgar, Steve, ed. 1991. *Knowledge and Reflexivity: New Frontiers in the Sociology of Knowledge*. Sage.

Zimmerman, Ann S. 2008. New knowledge from old data. The role of standards in the sharing and reuse of ecological data. *Science, Technology & Human Values* 33 (5): 631–652.

3 EXPLORING UNCERTAINTY IN KNOWLEDGE REPRESENTATIONS: CLASSIFICATIONS, SIMULATIONS, AND MODELS OF THE WORLD

MATTHIJS KOUW, CHARLES VAN DEN HEUVEL, AND ANDREA SCHARNHORST

Know ye now, Bulkington? Glimpses do ye seem to see of mortally intolerable truth; that all deep, earnest thinking is but the intrepid effort of the soul to keep the open independence of her sea; while the wildest winds of heaven and earth conspire to cast her on the treacherous, slavish shore?

—Herman Melville, *Moby Dick*

The world is not a solid continent of facts sprinkled by a few lakes of uncertainties, but a vast ocean of uncertainties speckled by a few islands of calibrated and stabilized forms.

—Latour 2005, 245

Uncertainty is often explained as a lack of knowledge, or as an aspect of knowledge that implies a degree of unknowability. Such interpretations can result in commitments to acquire more information about a particular situation, system, or phenomenon, with the hope of avoiding further surprises. In addition, in some cases uncertainty is interpreted as evidence that "objective" knowledge cannot be attained. The above quotation from Latour's *Re-assembling the Social* may appear to echo such ideas, but, as Latour admits, "[p]aradoxically, this 'astronomical' ignorance explains a lot of things. . . . We have to be able to consider both the formidable inertia of social structures and the incredible fluidity that maintains their existence: the latter is the real milieu that allows the former to circulate." (2005, 245) Latour suggests taking up this backdrop of fluidities from which more stable and less stable structures coagulate into existence. In other words, rather than reading uncertainty as a deplorable property of knowledge, Latour proposes to recalibrate, or realign, knowledge with uncertainty, and thereby remains open to a productively disruptive aspect of uncertainty.

In this chapter, we continue to trace the lines of inquiry suggested by Latour's notion of an "ocean of uncertainties." We do so by looking at how uncertainty can be a source of knowledge that can disrupt categories that provide epistemological bearing, much like the "solid continents" Latour mentions. We ask how new forms of knowledge production dealt with the challenge of uncertainty in the past, how they tried to reduce or capture uncertainty, and in what instances they produced new uncertainties. We undertake these excursions into science history with new virtual-knowledge practices in mind and with the aim to discover what lessons can be learned. Owing to their innovative nature, the new practices of knowledge production characterized and analyzed in this book imply uncertainty. They are also supposed to alter our understanding, and they almost always occur at the boundaries between different disciplines. What is at stake here is whether different sciences want to keep their feet firmly on solid ground or whether they are open to new insights offered by oceans of uncertainties. We argue that having a strong inclination to *either* islands (which provide epistemological bearing) *or* oceans (which set objectivity adrift) puts researchers at risk of not tapping into uncertainty as a source of knowledge. This may be tantamount to developing a closed system of explanations that leaves a *particular* (and potentially *restricted)* arena for knowledge production.[1] An emphasis on both forms of knowledge is necessary, which implies a balancing act between relying on firm epistemic grounds and carefully broadening one's scope so that new avenues of knowledge can be explored. In terms of virtual knowledge, persistent attention to uncertainty opens up potentials otherwise veiled. Put somewhat provocatively, what we consider to be problematic about problems is the ways in which they invite solutions. As the historian of cartography John Brian Harley has argued, "[i]nstead of just the transparency of clarity we can discover the pregnancy of the opaque." (2001, 159)

Ideally, it is the dynamic interplay between the two forms of knowledge production that is needed. In practical terms, however, this interplay is not free of tensions, fights, and struggle. This dialectic relationship can be found at all levels of knowledge production, whether inside a specialty or across disciplines. We want to emphasize the creative potential of embracing uncertainty by looking into ambitious research projects in the history of science. Recalling examples from the past, we also wish to emphasize that uncertainties that can be associated with current forms of virtual knowledge are not new. The production of virtual knowledge implies a necessity to increase awareness of elements of uncertainty. This applies to all periods in which foundations of scholarship are subjected to change. In phases of profound reorganizations of academia—cognitive and epistemic, as well as social and organizational—we would like to call for carefulness, thoughtfulness, and a certain modesty when embracing new media, new techniques, and new concepts. (See the introduction to this volume.) Knowledge production is a path-dependent process. Current fractures and controversies cannot be understood without mapping the networks of evolving schools of thought (Collins 1998; Börner and Scharnhorst 2009) and specialties in science. (See chapter 7 below.) Science history is an indispensable source of knowledge about how to judge, evaluate, and moderate current controversies. Last but not least, the current emphasis on visual elements in the production of virtual knowledge can be related to our historical cases. (See chapter 4 below.) The use of visual elements in the design and development of the theoretical models of the selected cases, in their application to practice, and in their final presentation provides another link to current debates about the relationship of uncertainty and visual representations of knowledge.

We begin by discussing some of the ways in which the natural sciences, the humanities, and the social sciences have engaged issues of uncertainty. Discussions pertaining to uncertainty in science and technology studies have often focused on research practices in the natural sciences. We show how various authors in the humanities and the social sciences have problematized this focus on practices of the natural sciences when it comes to analyzing research practices in the social sciences, and how they emphasize the need for approaches that distance themselves from the natural sciences, or seek to augment the natural sciences with more qualitative methods. However, we do not wish to advocate either the scientific methods used in the natural sciences, those used in the social sciences, or those used in the humanities as proper epistemological approaches for embracing uncertainty. We conclude the first section by discussing why we think a degree of cross-fertilization between these areas is necessary.

To support the claims that uncertainty can be a source of knowledge while acknowledging that this source can best be utilized through a combination of elements from the humanities, the social sciences, and the natural sciences, we present three historical examples in the second section. Rooted in a variety of disciplines (namely the emerging science of documentation and information, architecture, and the then-new field of cybernetics and operations research), each of the three examples shows a certain drive to provide knowledge about the world. This goal is highly appealing but hard to reach. All three cases departed from "solid continents of facts" to find their (representation of the) world. We take this goal of "total" or "all-encompassing" knowledge of the world as an attempt to provide a "complete" system in which the world is framed, and ask to what extent this still leaves room for an appreciation of a "vast ocean of uncertainties." The examples were chosen to show historical precedents to present-day notions about uncertainty, to ask whether and how approaches to uncertainty have developed over time, and to indicate what can be learned from history. They concern the role of data and classification, the design of interactions, and the inclusion of dynamics in formal approaches to complex systems. By means of these examples we want to show how uncertainty can lead to new knowledge, and how the feature of uncertainty is addressed, as well as partly suppressed or lost, in attempts to develop complete theories of the world. Straddling serendipity and formalization, our historical examples show to what extent disruptive dimensions of uncertainty have been taken up in attempts to provide explanations of the world. In addition, we continue our review of existing approaches to uncertainty by showing how approaches informed by the natural sciences already contain ideas emphasized in the humanities and the social sciences. Rather than claiming victory for one particular approach, we invite the reader to think about possible interactions between different ways of approaching uncertainty.

Finally, we draw lessons from the historical cases and assess their effects on several aspects of current and future e-research. We believe that our historical studies of classifications, designed interactions, and models can inspire future e-research. Our case studies reveal differing approaches to dealing with uncertainty. Each has important implications for the way knowledge is codified. Science history can help us to understand this variability. E-research brings codification of knowledge to a new level, and this makes it even more important to have a firm understanding of the way researchers are dealing with uncertainties in practice. (See chapter 2 above.) We hope that our analysis will provide ways for researchers, particularly those pursuing e-research in the humanities and the social sciences, to engage uncertainty and appreciate its productive (and disruptive) effects.

To summarize, our discussion of the potential value of uncertainty with regard to knowledge representations revolves around three questions: In what ways can uncertainty be a source of knowledge, and how does appreciating this dimension of uncertainty require a combination of natural sciences, humanities, and social sciences? How can historical examples of knowledge representations of the world provide insights into ways of thinking about uncertainty as a source of new knowledge? How can these examples inform present-day approaches to uncertainty in e-research in the humanities and the social sciences?

UNCERTAINTY IN THE NATURAL SCIENCES, THE HUMANITIES, AND THE SOCIAL SCIENCES

Although uncertainty has been a subject of scrutiny throughout the history of the natural sciences, it has received less attention in the social sciences and the humanities. Although the body of work on uncertainty in the humanities and the social sciences is fragmented, a number of authors working in these fields have recently explored uncertainty and risk from a multidisciplinary perspective (Bammer and Smithson 2009). It can be argued that the characteristics of data and scholarly practices in the humanities and the social sciences warrant paying more attention to uncertainty. For example, the highly ambiguous meaning of data in the humanities (American Council 2006, 6) was already an object of study in 1824, when Leopold von Ranke tried, in his *History of the Latin and Teutonic Nation*, to separate historical facts from fiction, myth, and legend in order to create an objective historical science. This view was challenged a century later by historians (among them Benedetto Croce and Carl Becker) who emphasized the role of interpretation and argued that the present desires, fears, and anxieties of historians shaped their understanding of the past. This longstanding debate about whether there is sufficient historical evidence to enable us to know the "truth" of the past has later been framed using the concept of uncertainty. It is "part of historians' stock in trade, yet historians differ enormously in how uncertain they are" (Curthoys 2009, 127; also see chapter 7 below).

Within the humanities, only a few studies try to link scholarly practices with aspects of uncertainty. For example, in their study on spatial vagueness and uncertainty in the computational humanities, Kemp and Mostern (2001) observed that the traces created, defined, and shaped by communities cannot easily be reduced to quantitative data. They therefore proposed to follow the example of environmental modeling implemented in GIS applications of the 1980s and the 1990s by "asking scholars to change their methods to suit technology, rather than making the technology work for them," thereby reducing uncertainty (ibid., 1). Jack Owens turned the question about the demands of technology around by asking "What do historians want from GIS?" However, Owens still proposed that historians (in collaboration with mathematicians) experiment with the use of algorithms and fuzzy logic. By doing so, they would be able to acquire more rigor in the methods they use to handle ambiguity and uncertainty in historical records and the complexities of history, particularly world history (Owens 2007a, note 42; Owens 2007b, 2030; Coppola, Owens, Szidarovszky 2008; Owens 2009). These approaches show a commitment to reducing uncertainty, and display a tacit endorsement of ideals pertaining to knowledge production from the natural sciences, which points to the need to do away with a multitude of interpretations and lack of objectivity.

We argue that it is characteristic of the humanities and the social sciences to come across uncertainty in the form of heterogeneity and ambiguity, and that this is due, at least in part, to differences in scholarly practices in the humanities and the social sciences. According to Latour, defining and ordering the social should be left in the first place to the actors themselves after having characterized the full range of controversies, rather than leaving it to analysts to impose order beforehand. "Re-assembling" the social in this way is a time-consuming process in which the movements of the actors "will be constantly interrupted, interfered with and dislocated by . . . uncertainties" (Latour 2005, 23). Uncertainty should not necessarily be lamented. It can also be understood as an aspect of knowledge that might be appreciated more positively. Uncertainty may point to knowledge otherwise downplayed or ignored, and it may encourage scholars to assess their own understanding, knowledge, and intuitions.

We argue that recent work on the subject is able to open up such features of uncertainty. Its ability to do so relates to the fact that such work unsettles well-established boundaries between the natural sciences, humanities, and the social sciences.

Brugnach et al. (2008, 11–12) make the important observation that "uncertainty cannot be understood in isolation, but only in the context of the socio–technical–environmental system in which it is identified." They suggest developing a relational concept of uncertainty, which "involves three elements: 1. an object of perception or knowledge (e.g. the socio–technical–environmental system); 2. one or more knowing actors (e.g. a decision maker) for whom that knowledge is relevant; and 3. different knowledge relationships that can be established among the actors and the objects of knowledge." (ibid., 5) In this framework, there may be three causes of uncertainty. First, we may be dealing with systems whose behavior can only be predicted to some extent. Second, we may have incomplete knowledge of the system in question. Third, there may be different or even incompatible frames of reference for the system in question. In the case that Brugnach et al. consider (that of adaptive strategies in water management), uncertainty is also approached as a potentially fruitful aspect of knowledge: "Handling uncertainties shifts from elimination toward exploring other options by reconsidering our relation to the water management situation and the other actors involved." (ibid., 13) Although this communicative approach to uncertainty is devoid of the desensitization that occasionally accompanies other approaches in the natural sciences, it leaves a number of issues unaddressed.

A first objection is that the aforementioned authors do not carefully distinguish between epistemic and ontic uncertainties. Whereas epistemic uncertainty is a consequence of incomplete or fallible knowledge, ontic uncertainty is a claim about intrinsically indeterminate or variable properties of systems (Petersen 2006, 52). However, ontic uncertainty may turn out to be epistemic uncertainty—new means of knowledge production may become available as a result of technological, institutional, economic, and socio-political factors. This shifting boundary between ontic and epistemic uncertainties means that distinctions between these types of uncertainty may (or may not) change over time. In other words, the claim that epistemic and ontic uncertainties cannot be distinguished is itself an uncertain statement. What should be studied are the dynamics between these two types of uncertainties and the extent to which different groups of actors agree or disagree about such demarcations.

Second, in the approach of Brugnach et al. it is difficult to assess the sources of uncertainty. Petersen (2006) distinguishes a number of locations of uncertainty in the case of climate models. Uncertainty may be due to conceptual and mathematical models. In other words, the way in which systems have been schematized and formalized may introduce simplifications that leave insufficient room for detail. Also, the model inputs may be a source of uncertainty. What is more, the technical implementation of the model may introduce uncertainties, for example, in the form of coding errors that may or may not be debugged.

Third, the processed output and interpretation can be a source of uncertainty. The resulting typology is displayed in figure 3.1. Although this typology warrants more explanation, we emphasize its value in finding the source of an uncertainty. Typologies of this kind are necessary in attempts to find out to what extent uncertainties can be explained.

A final and related objection is that the focus of Brugnach et al. (2008) on multiple frames of reference tends to ignore the role of knowledge instruments in facilitating knowledge about uncertainty. Access to uncertainties is, to some extent, shaped by technological practices, which at least partly constitute the conditions under which similarities and dissimilarities between various frames of knowledge are observed.

Petersen's work is relevant to our discussion of uncertainty not only because it encompasses quantitative and qualitative aspects of uncertainty but also because Petersen creates an analytical space in which both aspects can be studied. For example, value diversity can affect model inputs as much as statistical uncertainty. Petersen's approach makes it difficult to adhere to a rigid division of the natural sciences, the humanities, and the social sciences, and can thereby inform studies of uncertainty. This important work also highlights problems with *a priori* distinctions between quantitative and qualitative approaches to uncertainty. Our examples further reveal how making such distinctions beforehand can be problematic. This will lead to recommendations for present-day e-research to refrain from clinging to either quantitative or qualitative methodologies exclusively.

EXAMPLES: UNCERTAINTY IN REPRESENTATIONS OF THE WORLD

We discuss uncertainty in relation to representations of the world because such representations concern an enormous number of components and a dense fabric of interactions, which are very likely to lead to some degree of uncertainty. We discuss three historical cases of representations of knowledge of the world, and elaborate on their ability to tap into the disruptive and productive potential of uncertainty.

First, we discuss Paul Otlet's attempt to develop a system of universal classification, focusing on aspects of uncertainty in the organization of

Sorts of uncertainty

UNCERTAINTY MATRIX Location/source of uncertainty ↓	Nature of uncertainty		Range of uncertainty (inexactness/imprecision or unreliability/inaccuracy)		Recognized ignorance	Methodological unreliability	Value diversity
	Epistemic uncertainty	Ontic uncertainty / indeterminacy	Statistical uncertainty (range+chance)	Scenario uncertainty (range of 'what-if' options)		• Theoretical basis • Empirical basis • Comparison with other simulations • Peer consensus	• General epistemic • Discipline-bound epistemic • Socio-cultural • Practical
Conceptual model							
Mathematical model — Model structure							
Mathematical model — Model parameters							
Model inputs (input data, input scenarios)							
Technical model implementation (software and hardware implementation)							
Processed output data and their interpretation							

FIGURE 3.1

Typology of uncertainty in simulation. Source: Petersen 2006, 50. Reprinted with permission.

knowledge systems and their interfaces. Our second case is Buckminster Fuller's World Game, a simulation of the world in the form of a game. Here we concentrate on the interaction of users with data that takes places within the parameters of a pre-designed environment, and whether this designed interaction allows users to question their means of interaction. Third, we look at Paul Forrester's development of a mathematical model that deals with world equilibrium. This case explores the limitations and possibilities of using formal, mathematical language and computer-based simulations to emulate complex features of the social world.

We claim that each of these three engagements with uncertainty (classifications, designed interactions, and modeled landscapes) has its own problems of uncertainty. In our discussion of these engagements, we talk about quantitative (completeness, exactness, accuracy) and qualitative (evidence, authority) aspects of data. In addition, our case studies elaborate on the ability of the representation in question to tap into the potentially disruptive dimensions of uncertainty. In the third and final part of this chapter, we ask how our discussion of historical representations of the world can inform approaches to uncertainty in e-science.

OTLET: A VISUAL CLASSIFICATION OF UNIVERSAL KNOWLEDGE OF THE WORLD

One geometry cannot be truer than another; it can only be more convenient.

—Henri Poincaré (1952, 50)

The Belgian "utopist" Paul Otlet (1868–1944) is considered a pioneer of modern information sciences. In his *Traité de documentation* (1934), Otlet attempted to formulate a theory of documentation that, as Boyd Rayward has pointed out, has several characteristics in common with modern information science. He also introduced new disciplines that are still relevant for modern information science, such as "bibliometrics" (Rayward 1994). Otlet is often mentioned as a forerunner of the World Wide Web. Although we want to avoid the suggestion of a causal historical relationship, similar characteristics can be recognized in Otlet's theory on documentation and in the more recent concepts of the Internet, hypertext, the World Wide Web, Web 2.0, and the Semantic Web (Rayward 1994; van den Heuvel 2009, 2010). In the context of this chapter, Otlet is of particular interest because of how he organized knowledge, because of his quest to reveal scientific "facts," and because of the inclusion of uncertainty in his model.

Otlet is probably best known for his Universal Decimal Classification (UDC), based on Melvil Dewey's Decimal Classification. For Otlet, the UDC was a tool for the organization of documents that in their totality form a "graphic memory of mankind, the material body of our sciences and our knowledge" (La Fontaine and Otlet 1908, 177). According to a process referred to as the "Monographic Principle," documents of whatever content or medium can be reduced to the most elementary "items of information with [their] own identity" and re-ordered into new combinations (Rayward 1990, 1). The UDC was crucial in this process, as becomes clear from Otlet's metaphor of "mapping": [I]t allows us to find a place for each idea, . . . for each part of a document. Thus it allows us to take our bearing in the midst of the sources of knowledge, just as the system of geographic coordinates allows us to take our bearing on land or sea. (Rayward 1990, 153) However, the UDC would not only allow for navigation of a vast array of knowledge; Otlet also thought it would enable "special classification to group facts into scientific laws" (ibid., 12). In *Monde: Essai d'Universalisme* (1935), Otlet tries to capture the complete reality of the world in one equation. According to Otlet, the synthesis of the world is the product of object and subject, but also, importantly, of the unknown. Figure 3.2 shows how this synthesis is expressed, first in words and then in a letter code based on the first letters of the words. In order to make this equation independent of language, Otlet proposed a numerical annotation of decimal fractions.

Figure 3.3 shows two spheres. The outer sphere represents the objects—(0,1) things (nature, man, society and divinity), (0,2) space, and (0,3) time. The inner sphere represents the subjects—(0,5) Creations, (0,6) Expressions), and (0,7) the Unknown and Mystery—circling around the central globe representing (0,4) the Self. This representation of Monde as a whole, indicated with the numerical code (0,8), is visualized on one page of an oblong folder in which all eight elements are represented separately and, in the last one, turn in circles around the world documentation center (0.9) Mundaneum. On this representation of the World, Otlet wrote: "The equation of the world develops like this. It is at the same time its classification." Ducheyne (2009, 234) uses this representation to underline Otlet's attempt to connect the microcosm of human beings with the macrocosm of the universe so that all knowable elements of reality and the relations between them could be overseen, comprehended, and contemplated.

At first sight this interpretation of Otlet's use of the universe metaphor as a macro- and microcosm in which every aspect of reality (and the unknown)

This equation will be even more concise if one expresses it
with the first letters of the terms

$$W = \begin{cases} T(N+M+S+D) \\ S \\ T \end{cases} \quad \begin{cases} S(k+s+a) \\ C(s+h+o) \\ E \end{cases} \quad \begin{cases} (x+y) \end{cases}$$

$$1 = \begin{cases} 0.1\,(0.11+0.12+0.13+014) \\ 0.2 \\ 0.3 \end{cases} \quad \begin{cases} 0.4 \\ 0.5 \\ 0.6 \end{cases} \quad 0.7$$

Then these letters are replaced by their numerical symbols all
preceded by zero (0).
This is followed by the custom to simplify the notation by the
suppression of zero […].
Thus:

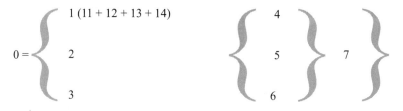

FIGURE 3.2
Otlet: Equation of the World, *Monde* 1935, pp. XXI–XXII. Translation by Charles
van den Heuvel from Otlet 1935.

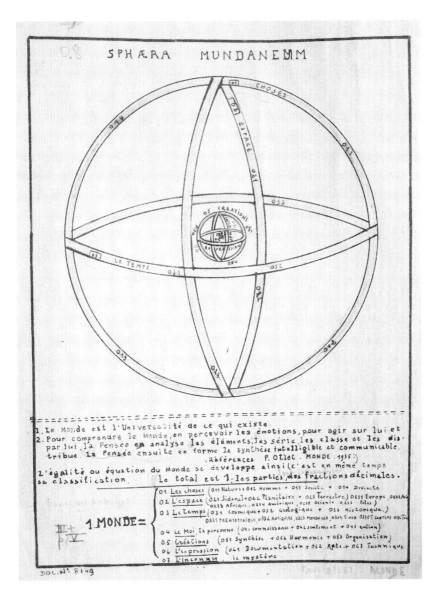

FIGURE 3.3

Otlet: Sphaera Mundaneum (July 31, 1937). © Mons, Mundaneum EUM 8149.

has a clear and designated space seems coherent, but a comparison with other representations reveals a picture that is less clear. Uncertainty is not restricted to the place to which Otlet had assigned it, a fact of which he must have been at least somewhat aware. He made many different representations of the world, some spherical, some cubic, and some attempts to combine the spherical and the cubic. Whereas uncertainty is visible in the spherical representation, it remains unclear where uncertainty is located in the cubic representation. The three visible faces of the cube show the domains, the sectors, and the instruments of Otlet's plan of the world, but we cannot see which sort of information he projected on its three other faces, and whether these included a representation of uncertainty.

The consequence is what Petersen has referred to as an unclear distinction in the distribution of ontic and epistemic uncertainty, which we addressed above. However, this is not just a matter of representation; it is also a matter of scalability. Otlet expresses a clear-cut distinction between time and space in his visual representation of the world, giving them separate classification numbers. But in the text of *Monde, essai d'universalisme* he writes: "Substances, Movement, Space and Time are . . . the four most fundamental categories that constitute for us the World. These categories are not separable but occur simultaneously." (Otlet 1935, vi) This means that matter-energy and space-time cannot be separated into clear-cut categories. Otlet seems to be aware of this scalability problem: "the laws applicable to macro-physical objects are not applicable to micro-physical objects" (ibid., 30).

In this case, Petersen's exploration of the source of uncertainty is of interest. He refers to a dimension in the location of uncertainty that owes its existence to conceptual and mathematical models and data input. Otlet's input of simplified concepts, such as matter, energy, space, and time, here results in uncertainty. Otlet believes that the problem can be solved by mathematics, which in his view not only had become "an instrument to realize a higher level of abstraction: it becomes 'thought' (*la pensée*) itself. . . . Mathematics is not just a translator of concepts, but a producer of concepts." (ibid., 31) However, by giving the same decimal codes to concepts that differ in meaning, Otlet's mathematics merely bypasses these differences, and at the same time introduces complexity and uncertainty to the implementation of his model. Finally, there is the problem of mediation between knowledge representation and users/producers located around it. Ducheyne focused on images that positioned the individual in the center of Otlet's representation of knowledge in spheres. However, there are many representations of Otlet's *Monde* in which the human being is an observer from the outside, which creates a different perception of the world. When the person is in the middle, that person is surrounded by his or her own complete knowledge universe (including uncertainty). However, the external observer, together with other viewers, gets an outside, often partial view of the world in which the location of uncertainty is not always clear.

Several sketches of eyes in Otlet's knowledge representations allude to the fact that he tried to map how the world could be perceived. The importance that Otlet attributes to perception becomes clear in his *Monde*, where "The Conception of World" is discussed: ". . . the world presents itself before our eyes as a multiplicity and variety. . . . Placed before the panorama of things—the most general expression to indicate these particular elements of which the whole is composed—we perceive substances, beings, phenomena, viewed either by themselves or in their environments." (Otlet 1935, v)

The position of the human being has consequences not only for the perception but also the production of knowledge within this model. Otlet was thinking of mechanical and manual data enrichment in a universal network of documentation (Rayward 1983; van den Heuvel 2009). In his view, scholars would work together, assisted by machines for complementary operations of analysis and synthesis, to extract desired elements mechanically (van den Heuvel 2008, 2009, 2010). The UDC is an important instrument in this process. An important difference between the UDC and purely topical classification schemes is that the former does not just order subjects or topics in classes by numeric codes. Through its auxiliary tables or connector signs, the UDC also enables linking to additional information, such as place, language, and/or physical characteristics. On a technical level, the classification system made it possible to link annotations to specific documents, or parts of (interrelated) documents, that, following the Monographic Principle, were (re)composed around a classification number. The linkage characteristics of the UDC not only allowed the connecting of various classification systems but also created a space for contributors around documents. The latter could annotate documents ranging from simple additions to comments that express various points of view.

The process seems at first sight similar to Wikipedia, in which the involvement of many people who add and edit certain lemmas aims to improve those lemmas in particular and the digital encyclopedia in general

(Wright 2007). However, Otlet's knowledge system and collaboratory is more top-down than Wikipedia. For Otlet, the producer of knowledge is first and foremost an outsider to the system whose contribution would be recognized only after a long process of editing. Such experts would nowadays be called domain experts (van den Heuvel 2009, 2010). In his plea for digital disorder, Weinberger states that "the real problem is that any map of knowledge assumes that knowledge has a geography, that it has a top-down view, that it has a shape" (2007, 63). However, Weinberger's assumption that the World Wide Web does not have a shape or a hierarchy is not completely correct. (See Barabási 2003, 236–237.) Weinberger's "power of the new digital order" has (implicit) hierarchical relationships as well.

This brings us to another aspect of uncertainty, which Petersen labels as uncertainty at the source of the output and interpretation. If users cannot see implicit hierarchies, and cannot see who or what is accountable for this output, how should the results be interpreted? There is no doubt that Otlet's attempt to come to an objective classification to structure the world stands in a positivist tradition. It displays a certain degree of ignorance, and the components of Otlet's atomist architecture of knowledge do not always fit. This chapter questions the correctness of Otlet's visualizations of hierarchical relationships between knowledge classes, but also his designs for protocols to regulate the various forms of data enrichment. Otlet's orders of knowledge and protocols have a higher degree of accountability than Weinberger's new digital order, in which "everything is miscellaneous." As such, Otlet's visualizations might be usefully investigated in discussions of the role of accountability and authority in distributed authorship.

Still, this will take place in a different way than Otlet intended. As we have already noted, Otlet had tried to design places for the unknown and for mystery, putting them next to everything he considered to be known. Formalized in this way, these factors could not really disturb the static model. However, Otlet feared tensions at the fringes of his model of classification. At the nodes of the auxiliary tables, which are at the interfaces between the hierarchical order of the classification system and the disorder of data enrichment by machines and human beings, there was a higher risk of uncertainties interfering with his model (van den Heuvel 2009; van den Heuvel and Rayward 2011). Otlet tried to control these by developing protocols for updating the UDC, accepting that it would be temporarily out of control before a new zenith of stabilization was reached. "The ideal resembles a regular, but elastic sphere. Deformed and compressed, the sphere forms itself according to the pressures on it. Thus, the ideal can only regain its integral form when the circumstances that caused its deformation are eliminated." (1935, 363)

We stated that uncertainty is not necessarily problematic and that it may even open up new vistas of thought and serendipity. Rather than follow Otlet's protocols that streamline and even silence the input of uncertainties by uncontrolled or partially controlled data enrichment, we could analyze, and extrapolate from, these frictions. In the visualizations of knowledge objects, Otlet is not bypassing problems of data integration; he is, quite literally, facing them in a creative way. The study of incompatibility and inoperability might lead to a better understanding of the forms of uncertainties that need either to be prevented or to be cherished as new creative solutions in knowledge production (van den Heuvel and Rayward 2011). Or, as Randall Collins put it in his attempt to discover a universality of patterns of intellectual change, "[c]reativity is the friction of the attention space at the moment when the structural blocks are grinding against one and another hardest" (1998, 76).

FULLER: SIMULATING THE WORLD IN A GAME

Otlet's classification scheme is data driven and sees human interaction as a necessary (albeit disruptive) activity, although some human intervention is needed to update data and to fine-tune existing classification schemes. In the context of Fuller's World Game, users come to the foreground as (among other things) a source of uncertainty: users may have completely diverging beliefs about the amount of data that is sufficient to support an interpretation or theory, even whether model validation and verification is needed at all. The interaction enabled by Fuller's World Game hints at empowerment: playing the World Game supposedly increases awareness of world issues, their complexity, and the need to approach them in a holistic fashion. However, we argue that the determination of these experiences by underlying design issues and the differing appreciations of users should also be taken into account. In order to study these aspects of uncertainty, the case study of Fuller's World Game mainly looks at design-related decisions, which is where Fuller's modernist view of the roles of design and technology in society comes into play.

In 1963, in an attempt to counter ecological, economic, and political problems facing humankind, Fuller set out to collect all knowledge he considered relevant to the future of the Earth by creating a World Resources Inventory of Human Trends and Needs. He then combined this inventory with the so-called Dymaxion World Map—a map of the world projected onto a polyhedron, resulting in a depiction of the continents as nearly contiguous land masses.[2] Fuller's work led to the development of the World Game Integrative Resource Utilization Planning Tool in 1971. A year later, Fuller and others established the World Game Institute, which developed "the world's largest and most accurate map of the world, one of the most detailed and substantive databases of global statistics available anywhere and educational resources designed to teach interdependence, collaboration, respect for diversity, and individual participation in a global society" ("Global Simulation Workshop," O.S. Earth, at http://www.osearth.com).

The World Game was also proposed as an alternative to another form of gaming that was dominant at the time: war games. In the World Game, the process of governing the world is simulated in debates in which solutions to problems are negotiated with other players. Players need to engage with issues such as hunger, illiteracy, and environmental damage. As a result, players are expected to develop critical insights that will enable them to truly address and solve these problems on a global scale. Thus, Fuller explicitly takes the entire world as his object of study. We need, he argues, to study societal problems at a global scale, so that we do not limit our reasoning to "local-focus hocus-pocus" (Fuller 1963, 272).

The environment in which Fuller developed the World Game was very much shaped by the intellectual traditions of cybernetics and systems theory, which emphasized the need to study the functioning and the design of systems on a macro scale for the purposes of understanding, control, and regulation. Fuller's own background in architecture and design aroused an intellectual commitment on his part to deliver instruments or tools for improving systems that would contribute to holistic understandings of such systems.

The World Game can indeed be seen as a tool, though one more oriented toward delivering knowledge by enabling people to explore complex systems and issues. The World Game aims to fill a knowledge gap that Fuller considers extremely problematic: people are unaware of some of the causes of environmental and economic problems that continue to plague the Earth, and as a result they are not equipped with the knowledge to act. The word 'game' was used to make this rather daunting task as accessible and appealing to as many individuals as possible. Fuller was firmly convinced that the problems mankind faced could only be dealt with in a participatory manner. This required insight into the collective dimensions of existence that the World Game was meant to instigate. Fuller formulated this as follows:

I am certain that none of the world's problems—which we are all perforce thinking about today—have any hope of solution except through . . . society's individuals becoming thoroughly and comprehensively self-educated. Only thereby will society be able to identify, and inter-communicate the vital problems of total world society. Only thereafter may humanity sort out and put those problems into order of importance for solution in respect to the most fundamental principles governing man's survival and enjoyment of life on Earth. (1971, 1)

Fuller celebrates what he sees as the computer's empowering potential, which is related to its ability to manage data and to present complex problems in a reliable and accessible manner: "the computer will keep constant track of where the resources are geographically located or where they are travelling" (Fuller 1981, 221). Moreover, the computer was expected to extend human senses in an empowering manner: "the natural and physical, and human resource data thus made available, will expand the decision makers' awareness of all possible alternatives for resource utilization, and can lead to better solutions and clearer directions in achieving national goals" (221). Fuller's definition of models is also based on his idea of making explicit the means for acquiring efficiency and optimization: "Models: the graphical, functional and mathematical orderings and simplifications of the omni-complicated and inter-related processes of the World. The conceptual simplifications of 'reality' into the vectors of an interacting process which can be dealt with on a scientific basis." (104) The game's goal is thus to provoke a process of self-education through which society will be able to "identify, and inter-communicate the vital problems of total world society" (Fuller 1971, 1).

The World Game provides the means to articulate clearly the consequences of better, more advanced designs by making explicit the collective consequences of actions by individuals playing the game. Winning the game involves "making the world work, making mankind a success, in the most efficient and expeditious way possible" (Fuller 1981, 95). Equipping users with the means to gain these insights requires that the tools used to produce knowledge be accessible to everyone, that knowledge be updated and presented in real time, and that the produced knowledge be easily disseminated.

In that sense, functionalities attributed by Fuller to the computer played an important role: its efficiency in handling data was considered to be crucial for the optimization of the World on a scientific basis.

The Dymaxion world map is a visual representation of the world that serves an important rhetorical purpose in Fuller's work, since it helped underline the idea that humanity is a collective enterprise. The map is chosen because it projects the Earth as a collection of adjacent continents, thereby emphasizing the fact that humanity co-exists rather than being dispersed over different, insulated continents.

Fuller tried to get universities to incorporate the World Game in their curricula, and in 1964 he proposed it as a contribution to the 1967 International and Universal Exposition in Montreal. Since 2000, the World Game has been facilitated by O.S. Earth, a company co-founded by Fuller, which organizes "workshops" at which participants can play the World Game (albeit without maps). The organization claims that the older version of the global simulation was a series of guided activities combined with lectures, and that participants mainly listened passively instead of being engaged in a more interactive fashion. More emphasis is now put on the perceived need for "authentic" and "personal" experiences of the individual players. Interactive experiences are ensured by making extensive use of negotiation, which enables "experiential learning" in which "participants proactively shape their own identities within the world and, in fact, the state of their entire world."[3]

Concerns related to time and money may seem trivial, but they do show how differing priorities can eventually shape the content and the experience of the game. In fact, Fuller may not have appreciated the high priority given to the fast-paced, more entrepreneurial experience that O.S. Earth emphasizes. Earlier versions of the World Game came with the advice that, to be able to fully understand and appreciate the intent and scope of the World Game, users should submerge themselves in the work of Fuller: "[F]or any group or individual who wishes to pursue his or their interest in Design Science exploration and the World Game, the most powerful place to begin is with the writings of Dr. Fuller. All of his books plus the World Design Science Decade documents are first priority." (Fuller 1971, 97) In the worst case, simply allowing uninformed people to play a World Game could, in Fuller's view, lead to wild and rampant imaginings and unfounded speculations regarding the future of humanity.

Though the underlying sources of information about the world's resources and population are constantly updated, and the World Game provides calculations according to scientifically developed models, it bears a suggestive and not a literal relationship toward the world it portrays. The use of data, the calculations, and the platform on which the game is played are largely aimed at incorporating the user's findings into a designed domain of exploration. Fuller expected that playing the World Game would develop the ability of the general public to come to more politically defined deliberations based on values incorporated into the World Game. This strong bond between intention and representation is something that the World Game shares with war games, a form of gaming that Fuller disdained. In her study of war games, Sharon Ghamari-Tabrizi makes clear that the purpose underlying such games is not to bear objective semblance to reality. Her analysis of war games shows how they center around narrative, partly based on lived experiences and expertise of military personnel, but also relies on the "demand of realism" as part of the dramatization (Ghamari-Tabrizi 2000, 199). The demand for realism can also be found in Fuller's World Game—it frames the world in a particular way, which is shaped by data, calculations that process data, interactional principles that reflect a highly political worldview, and a visual-interactional component that supposedly opens up issues that plague the world to users. So how does this lead to uncertainties?

One form of uncertainty is related to the use of data in the World Game. In his writings, Fuller does not reflect on how data are collected, on their availability, or on their quality. The possibility of collecting and managing data is taken for granted, which may introduce uncertainties into the process of playing the World Game—through incomplete or fallible datasets or inaccurate calculations. The game's intention was never to give a completely accurate description of the world's problems, though Fuller does claim that its underlying models have a "scientific" base. These models involve approximations (in varying levels of detail) of more specific situations, and are far from innocent. These models mobilize epistemic authority in the sense that they are expected to be able to answer questions the designer of the model deems relevant.

Another form of uncertainty comes from the differences between individual users' experience and knowledge. This issue also applies to more recent "serious games." Since the World Game fulfills the aforementioned "demand for realism" by being constructed in a certain manner, its users straddle discovery and manipulation: by playing the game, they may expand their knowledge of the world, and thereby incorporate Fuller's political ideas into their thinking. However, the World Game offers a particular view of the world. Even though there is the possibility for interaction, this occurs according to designed parameters that limit the scope of users' experiences.

The design principles incorporated into Fuller's World Game constitute the means by which users engage with issues, but whether playing the World Game indeed changes or informs their worldview remains in question. We believe that expertise on the part of model users is also important. However, the emphasis on immersive game experiences, which can be found in Fuller's World Game as well as in other present-day "serious" games, can lead users away from the principles underlying their experience of such games. The question is whether there can be such a thing as user reflexivity and engagement in the face of opaque or authoritative simulation technologies. The development and use of games and simulations is not exclusively a technical matter; it also should take into account users' perceptions, desires, and capacities. Approaching interaction design as an exclusively technical matter risks ignoring these crucial aspects of users' experiences. Fuller's World Game attempted to provide a practical solution to the problem of accessing specialized, isolated, and scattered knowledge, normally available only to well-educated experts. Though the need for a "comprehensive approach" to problem solving and the need for wide public participation are undisputed, it is questionable whether an "institution" such as the World Game is the ultimate answer. There is arguably a tension between in-depth and specialized knowledge and the ability to operate on a more general level that allows knowledge exchange between very different forms of knowledge acquisition. Obviously, there is neither a single nor an easy way to achieve that—as we will also see in the next case. Nevertheless, Fuller's experiment should at least be seen as encouragement to strive for forms—both inside and outside an academic environment—that allow learning and knowledge production through user interactions.

FORRESTER: WALKING THROUGH DYNAMIC LANDSCAPES
With each downpour,
more than ever, Your dear valley changes too:
In the self-same stream you'll never, Swim again,
I promise you.

—Goethe (1950, 512)[4]

The two representations of the world discussed above dealt with uncertainty in different ways. Otlet's classification was an attempt to order all possible available knowledge of the world in designated places, reduce factors of uncertainty, and extract the most elementary "facts." Fuller's World Game created a space in which actors could play out scenarios related to issues facing the Earth. In this section we discuss a model that creates a playing ground for the exploration of scenarios: the "world model" of Jay Wright Forrester.

Forrester's model is based on a systemic approach in which knowledge about actors, interactions, and spheres of action (such as the economy, politics, and the natural environment) are acquired by empirical observation. Once the main relevant variables are identified, the well-defined, isolated units are recombined again. System dynamics (Sterman 2007)—to which Forrester's model belongs—departs from simple assumptions about cause and action and embraces insights into the presence of various feedback cycles, which make social processes anticipative, adaptive, self-empowering, and therefore partly unpredictable. Using advances in mathematics and computing, a complex systemic "machinery" is built to model the world. The resulting model gives space to uncertainty in the form of producing a variety of possible scenarios and allows the user to test hypotheses about causalities and correlations. At the same time, it contains the same sources of uncertainty that Petersen (2006) classified: ambiguity of the modeling process in terms of the extraction of the "right" processes, lack of knowledge about processes and data needed to validate the model, and the principal unpredictability of some complex processes.

In 1971, Forrester attended a meeting of the Club of Rome, a "think tank," consisting of academics, entrepreneurs, diplomats, and politicians, that dealt with problems related to the rapid growth of the world's population, such as famine, pollution, and water shortages. One of the results of this encounter was the proposal to use a model approach of system dynamics developed at MIT to create a "world model." Its main aims were to address uncertainty, to counter crisis, and to minimize risks in the world in a "scientific" manner. The decision—comparable to Fuller's World Game initiative—must be seen in the light of attempts within the field of cybernetics to formulate solutions to global problems. (Wiener 1954; von Foerster 1984)

In Forrester's model, the world was seen as a system modeled by a network of processes, which he organized in workflows:

By "world system" we [mean] his social systems, his technology, and the natural environment. These interact to produce growth, change, and stress. It is not new to have great forces generated from within the socio-technical-natural system. But only recently has mankind become aware of rising forces that cannot be resolved by the historical solutions of migration, expansion, economic growth, and technology. (Forrester 1971, 1)

The visualization of Forrester's world system model shows the world as a large set of variables, which change. Change is caused by a network of positive and negative influences (feedback loops). The size of the population, the availability of natural resources, the current capital investment, the development of agriculture, and pollution are the main areas for which variables are defined. The variable "quality of life" is introduced to measure the performance of the world system. The availability of food is its main factor, followed by material standard of living, effects of pollution, and crowding (figure 3.4).

Forrester tries to map the complexity of the world in ways similar to the work of Otlet, since he tries to identify the main relevant factors for human development, analogous to the identification of the main components or streams of knowledge. However, Forrester's approach is more dynamic, and focuses on processes and flows rather than the exact designation of potentially relevant categories that Otlet had in mind. Whereas Otlet develops a generic but adaptive language to describe all knowledge, and Fuller developed a setting in which humans can appropriate and alter knowledge. Forrester develops a plot describing how, in a given, pre-defined situation, the world would develop based on the best available knowledge. With newly acquired knowledge this plot might alter. The modular structure of Forrester's model allows for such adaptations. But social dynamics entail other feedback loops. Knowing the plot and the scenarios, people might change their behavior as depicted in the model. In other words, we can change the plot. Although Forrester is aware of this, such options are not encapsulated in the model:

Forrester expects that new knowledge and understanding (including learning from the World Model) can alter the decision making of mankind, leading to a different course of events than those described by the World Model. Such consequences are not included in the model. Therefore the book does not incorporate the possible changes in human aspirations and values that might come from widespread recognition of the predicament facing mankind. (Myrtveit 2005, 15)

Once developed as a computer program, this plot produces long-term forecasts for the "quality of life," for the population, and for natural resources.
Forrester represented such forecasts in growth curves of such variables as size
of population, capital investment, and pollution (figure 3.5).

For Forrester it was important to demonstrate that his model contradicted
theories of unlimited growth, a very timely consideration during a period
when the dominant credo was (as it still is) unlimited consumption as the
driving economic force. Instead, Forrester set out to examine "some of the
forces that will become barriers when growth goes too far" and "the changes
that can arise to stop exponential growth" (Forrester 1971, 5). As a result,
Forrester hoped to study "the transition from a world of growth to a world
of equilibrium" (ibid., 5).

One should not imagine this "equilibrium" as an inevitable static final
stage. A more accurate understanding is the notion of *Fliessgleichgewicht*
(equilibrium in flow), a term coined by Ludwig von Bertalanffy (1949, 42)
to characterize a steady state in biological systems. It means that the system is
stable (in homeostasis) but also open, and that internally processes take place
continuously.. The idea of limited growth was not new. Forrester himself
pointed to Malthus and explained that his model was just richer in the processes it included:

This book examines the structure of the countervailing forces at the world level
when growth overloads the environment. The world will encounter one of the several possible alternative futures depending on whether the population growth is
eventually suppressed by shortage of natural resources, by pollution, by crowding,
and consequent social strife, or by insufficient food. Malthus dealt only with the latter, but it is possible for civilization to fall victim to other pressures before the food
shortage occurs. (1971, 8)

The idea of equilibrium warrants more attention. First, equilibrium is a
state of relative stability in which processes either stop or enter a cycle of
reproduction. Since this equilibrium is a moment captured in the flow, this
state is not the end of the process. Second, equilibrium can be seen as a quasi-
stationary state, and can be interpreted as a specific location in a hypothetical
landscape. For some systems, this landscape can be defined or measured in
advance. Think, for example, of the energy landscape for a mechanical system, which explains why a ball always rolls downhill. Mathematical theories
of dynamic processes provide connections between dynamic processes of

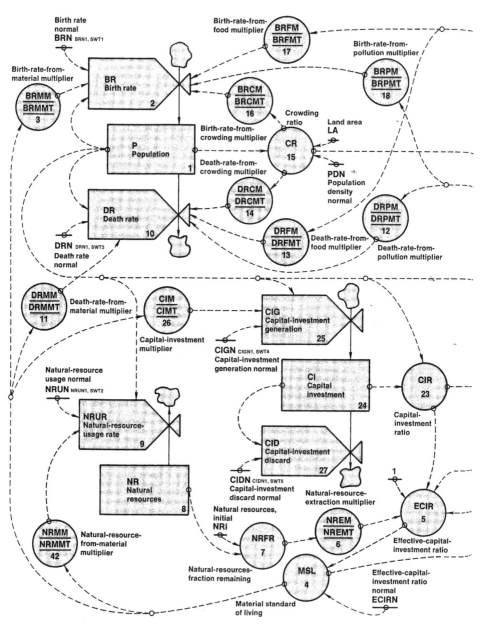

Complete diagram of the world model interrelating the five level variables — population, natural resources, capital investment, capital-investment-in-agriculture fraction, and pollution.

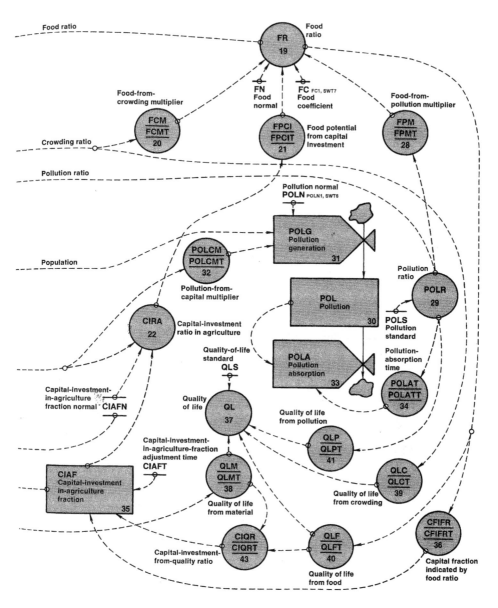

FIGURE 3.4

Forrester's diagram of the world as a mapping of processes. Adapted from Forrester 1971, 20–21. Reprinted with permission.

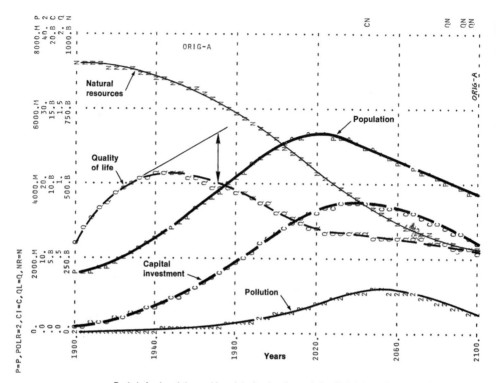

Basic behavior of the world model, showing the mode in which industrialization and
population are suppressed by falling natural resources.

FIGURE 3.5

Forrester's visualization of one possible behavior of the world model expressing
limits to growth. Adapted from Forrester 1971, 70. Reprinted with permission.

change at the micro level and the search of the whole system for a balance.
This can take the form of an ordered state, or an equilibrium, but only for a
limited period in time. Just as a river always descends, the system develops in
such a way that it finally reaches a low point in such an imaginary landscape
(Scharnhorst 2001).

Functions that shape the system's landscape have to be found within the
system description itself in the form of principles which govern its dynamics. Simulations are tools to explore the model. It has been argued that the
advantage of simulation over thought experiment is the higher speed of calculations or the higher accuracy (Myrtveit 2005). However, a simulation is
never only a tool or method; it is also, at the same time, a process of problem

solving and negotiating epistemic stands (Beaulieu, Ratto, and Scharnhorst, 2011). From a mathematical point of view, numerical simulations are a way to obtain results if no closed analytic treatment of the system's dynamics is possible—in other words, if the possible solutions cannot be obtained *a priori,* as is the case in Forrester's world model. Once all correlations between variables are fixed and parameters are set, a computer is able to calculate the mutual dependencies of variables and their correlated temporal change. This computer simulation is used as an approximation for exact solutions, but also as a tool to explore the possible landscape of scenarios. However, the idea of a specific stable state that will be reached still guides the explorative search through different computer scenarios. Thus, Forrester's "world in equilibrium" can be seen, using the metaphor of the landscape, as a moment of rest in a "fertile valley," which has been reached after a dangerous journey over icy mountains and through hot deserts. It is a state that is stable and that promises stability (although the stability may be temporary).

In general, two different approaches to complexity can be differentiated: "as complex as required and as simple as possible" and "as complex and complete as possible" (Scharnhorst, Marz, and Aigle 2009). In the first case, a reduction is made to extract laws needed to reproduce complex phenomena, leaving aside all disturbing details. The second, contrasting approach constructs a model that is as complex as possible and contains all information available, all the while assuming that any detail overlooked by the first approach might just be significant to the overall functioning of a model. Concerning uncertainty, neither of the two approaches is privileged. In the first case, the uncertainty about scenarios entailed by the model is reduced, but it is the selection of the few constitutive mechanisms that carries most ambiguity. In the second case, empirical evidence might be found for most of the influences and correlations taken on board, but the space of possible developments might be infinite, never to be fully explored, which creates ambiguity toward the relevance of the simulated scenarios. The world model of Forrester, though criticized for oversimplifications and for largely leaving out social and political elements, belongs more to the second approach.

Furthermore, Forrester's model is an example of how different epistemic traditions can meet at a trading zone of models, where thought experiments, observations, and concepts meet. The model is, in principle, open to any insight into human behavior. It relies on insights of psychology, sociology, economics, political sciences, and cultural studies. However, the use of mathematics as a language creates a barrier to participation. This does not apply to Forrester's model exclusively; it applies to any encounter between domain sciences and computer sciences. In spite of possible mappings between mathematical principles and natural language, some expertise in formal approaches is needed to avoid misunderstanding and misinterpretation. Here the comprehensive education required by Fuller, with the aim of avoiding restriction of the world to closed-circle "experts," becomes relevant again. Such a comprehensive approach to problems requires recombination of isolated knowledge streams and creative use of the ambiguous nature of knowledge. Otlet's language for describing the world's knowledge offers the possibility to at least mark (or classify) objects of knowledge in such a way that ambiguity can be addressed. This concerns, in particular, the use of facets and auxiliaries. It is the envisioned mixing of various epistemic traditions in all three world models that makes them so interesting in relation to current challenges to crossing epistemic boundaries in e-research and e-science.

STRATEGIES FOR E-RESEARCH AND THE NEED FOR EXPERIMENTS WITH INTERFACES, INTERACTIONS, AND MODELS

How can our discussion of the role of uncertainties in the previous three historical examples lead to more affirmative and multi-disciplinary approaches to uncertainty? Our case studies demonstrate that the inclusion of uncertainty is often a result of design decisions in knowledge production that can remain implicit. Otlet tried to reduce the complexity of the world by designating places for all factors he deemed relevant, such as uncertainty, but at the same time he suppressed inconvenient and complicating factors. The interfaces between the various components of Otlet's knowledge system can be observed to study how his system can lead to an appreciation of uncertainty. We saw how in Fuller's World Game players could develop scenarios of interaction and thus get a firmer grip on uncertainties. However, the possibilities of these interactions were largely determined by Fuller's design. Such analyses are important for understanding previous forms of interaction and games, since in both cases underlying processes of framing issues and narrative forms embedded in the user experience may remain hidden or opaque. It can be argued that some reflexivity on the part of the user is needed for a meaningful interaction with simulations and serious games, though we also showed that designers can play an important facilitating role in this respect. Forrester's World in Equilibrium is both exclusive and inclusive of uncertainties: exclusive in the sense that potentially important political and social factors are left out, with the risk of oversimplifying the world's reality, but inclusive in the sense that Forrester's mathematical model strives for a complete set of parameters needed to calculate possible future scenarios based on complex phenomena. In line with our three historical cases, we now look further at present-day examples of interfaces, interactions, and modeling future scenarios.

INTERFACES

A present-day example of interfaces is the tagging of cultural artifacts by non-professionals in online collections in the *steve.museum research* project, which enhances access to cultural heritage collections and engages users with museum objects (Trant 2009). Similar experiments are needed in which researchers shape the classification of data and conceptualize tools that provide access to various forms of knowledge organization. However, such experiments should not be aimed at a smooth transition of data between expert-generated and user-generated content, but should allow for an extrapolation of tensions and frictions in order to better understand the meaning of uncertainty in the social sciences and the humanities. The design of such experiments and their execution should be objects of analysis at the same time.

INTERACTIONS

As the recent work of Noah Wardrip-Fruin (2009) shows, computer games that remain sufficiently open allow users to enter into a productive dialogue with these designed interactions. Games designed according to this principle "create a surface-level experience that will make it possible for audiences to build up an appropriate model of the system internals" (ibid., 300) and thus express "the evolving state of the underlying system." (415) This so-called SimCity Effect (named after a popular computer game that is representative of the kind of interaction Wardrip-Fruin discusses here) "leads to audience understanding of the operations of an underlying system." (420) This raises the question whether Wardrip-Fruin is perhaps positing a free-floating Cartesian user that will be able to tap into the potential of the SimCity Effect. Although his design proposals may lead to enhanced interactions of users with computer systems, we argue that Wardrip-Fruin cannot simply assume these designs lead to or improve user empowerment, and that he reasons too much from the perspective that well-designed applications will automatically yield solutions and profound experiences for the users. (See chapter 1 above.)

MODELS

In a recent volume on issues regarding the modeling of complex systems, McDaniel and Driebe (2005) argue that models can fulfill a crucial role in appreciating uncertainty. The behavior of complex systems will inevitably introduce what they call "the unexpected," though they urge that such surprises are both inevitable and upsetting (ibid., 9), They suggest that a "different attitude" is needed, "one that enables healthier responses" (9). Common responses to uncertainty emphasize that more information should be acquired, and that methods of measuring and observation should be improved, which leads to an avoidance of surprise (3). In this regard, McDaniel and Driebe admit: "Uncertainty challenges us and often upsets us. Our natural desire to have the world a predictable place and to be in control of situations as they unfold can lead to dysfunctional responses to uncertainty. . . . We are in the process of finding out what does and does not work. Wisdom is an essential tool to have in the face of uncertainty and wisdom is an attitude rather than a skill or a body of knowledge." (9) What does this "healthy attitude" consist of? We emphasize again that "models" are not restricted to certain mathematical apparatus, but rather encompass a variety of concepts and theoretical approaches ranging from thought experiments to data models and predictive models. It is important that both the advantages and the limitations of such models be made explicit whenever they are applied. For the humanities, it is important that models not reduce the uncertainty usually present in these areas, but are used to complement traditional methods through unexpected innovative perspectives. Ideally, these models are not primarily problem solvers but intellectual troublemakers.

EPILOGUE

An important lesson to be learned from the Modernist examples of exploring uncertainty in knowledge representations, as we described them in this chapter, is that history appears to repeat itself in terms of how uncertainty is approached. Although e-research is sometimes hailed as a new paradigm that will radically transform scientific practice, it also reproduces the often-celebrated and often-performed distinction among the natural sciences, humanities, and social sciences. This is not to say that collaborations in e-research among scientists, social scientists, and humanist scholars in handling uncertainty cannot be beneficial; we just need different strategies. The three explorations (one of interfaces, one of interactions, one of models) serve as a conclusion to our chapter by exploring the question of how uncertainty can be appreciated, and what design principles can facilitate that appreciation.

As our case studies demonstrated, social scientists and humanities scholars took a particular approach to handling uncertainty: they were inclined to adopt approaches developed within the natural sciences to reduce uncertainty, in order to make their methods more rigorous. On the other hand, natural scientists are confronted with the tension of extracting relevant processes without ignoring the historicity, the contextuality, and the anticipatory nature of human actions. A comparative analysis of approaches to uncertainty from multidisciplinary points of view suggests that certain disciplines emphasize the positive effects of this concept, such as serendipity, creativity, artistic freedom (visual arts, music), stock-in-trade (history), preference of ambiguous agreement (psychology), engagement (theology), and accepting the impossibility of truth finding (law) (Bammer and Smithson 2009, 306).

On the basis of these potential effects of uncertainty in the humanities and the social sciences, we claim that these disciplines might have something to offer the natural sciences. We can even go a step further. Without taking into account the experiences collected and the epistemic strategies developed by scholars in the social sciences and the humanities to deal with a plurality of perspectives, the influence of history (path dependency), and the ephemeral sources of creativity, the natural sciences will not be able to deal with complex phenomena. This will apply especially to cases about the social world. Rather than favoring approaches from the natural sciences as more rigorous and desirable, the question is how potential positive tradeoffs among the natural sciences, the humanities, and the social sciences can be facilitated. Institutional support and funding might lead to broader engagements with e-research in the humanities and the social sciences in the long term. Changes in curricula are also required. However, in the short term, we need experimental interventions in which critical analysis is combined with design. Apprehension that institutional support and funding based on an expected outcome might nip creativity and innovation in the bud calls for careful managing of expectations (Beaulieu and Wouters 2009, 61–63).

NOTES

1. We speak of knowledge production, not of acquisition of knowledge. In a Latourian framework, knowledge is not something ready-made that may subsequently be acquired; it is (in Latour's own terms) a product of chains of actors who perform translation: "chains of translation refer to the work through which actors, modify, displace, and translate their various and contradictory interests" (Latour 1999, 311). As a result, knowledge can only be explained by a rigorous focus on practice: "[S]cience studies is not defined by the extension of social explanations to science, but by emphasis on the local, material, mundane sites where the sciences are practiced. . . . What has been revealed through the study of practice is not used to debunk the claims of science, as in critical sociology, but to multiply the mediators that collectively produce the sciences." (Latour 1999, 309) Thus, a focus on practice reveals the various elements of chains of translation, or mediators, whose performances and persistence articulate "knowledge."

2. For examples of the Dymaxion World Map, see the enhanced publication website of this book.

3. "Introducing the New Global Simulation" (at http://www.osearth.com).

4. Johann Wolfgang von Goethe, *Sämtliche Werke in 18 Bänden*, Band 1: *Sämtliche Gedichte* (Artemis, 1950: 512); English translation by Nigel Cooper.

REFERENCES

American Council of Learned Societies Commission on Cyberinfrastructure for the Humanities and Social Sciences. 2006. *Our Cultural Commonwealth* (available at http://www.acls.org).

Bammer, Gabriele, and Michael Smithson, eds. 2009. *Uncertainty and Risk: Multidisciplinary Perspectives*. Earthscan.

Barabási, Albert-László. 2003. *Linked: How Everything Is Connected to Everything Else and What It Means for Business, Science, and Everyday Life*. Plume-Penguin Group.

Beaulieu, Anne, and Paul Wouters. 2009. E-Research as intervention. In *E-Research: Transformation in Scholarly Practice*, ed. N. Jankowski. Routledge.

Beaulieu, Anne, Matt Ratto, and Andrea Scharnhorst. 2011. Learning in a landscape: Simulation-building as reflexive intervention. Preprint (available at http://arxiv.org).

Bertalanffy, Ludwig von. 1949. *Vom Molekül zur Organismenwelt: Grundfragen der modernen Biologie*. Athenaion.

Börner, Katy, and Andrea Scharnhorst. 2009. Visual conceptualizations and models of science. *Journal of Informatrics* 3 (3): 161–172 (available at http://arxiv.org).

Brugnach, Marcela, Art Dewulf, Claudia Pahl-Wostl, and Tharsi Taillieu. 2008. Towards a relational concept of uncertainty: About knowing too little, knowing too differently, and accepting not to know. Ecology and Society 13 (2) (available at http://www.ecologyandsociety.org).

Collins, Randall. 1998. The Sociology of Philosophies: A Global Theory of Intellectual Change. Harvard University Press.

Coppola, Emery A., Jack B. Owens, and Ferenc Szidarovszky. 2008. Fuzzy rule-based modeling of degrees of trust in cooperation-based networks: Close Research collaboration among domain experts (historians) and mathematical modellers. Presented at TECT strategic workshop on Visualization and Space-Time Representation of Dynamic, Non-linear, Spatial Data in DynCoopNet and Other TECT Projects, Universidad Politécnica de Madrid.

Curthoys, Anne. 2009. Historians and disputes over uncertainty. In Uncertainty and Risk: Multidisciplinary Perspectives, ed. G. Bammer and M. Smithson. Earthscan.

Ducheyne, Steffen. 2009. To treat of the world. Paul Otlet's ontology and epistemology and the circle of knowledge. Journal of Documentation 65 (2): 223–244.

Forrester, Jay Wright. 1971. World Dynamics. Wright-Allen.

Fuller, Richard Buckminster. 1963. Ideas and Integrities: A Spontaneous Autobiographical Disclosure. Macmillan.

Fuller, Richard Buckminster. 1971. The World Game: Integrative Resource Utilization Planning Tool. World Resources Inventory.

Fuller, Richard Buckminster. 1981. Critical Path. St. Martin's.

Ghamari-Tabrizi, Sharon. 2000. Simulating the unthinkable: Gaming future war in the 1950s and 1960s. Social Studies of Science 30 (2): 163–223.

Harley, John Brian. 2001. Deconstructing the map. In The New Nature of Maps: Essays in the History of Cartography, ed. P. Laxton. John Hopkins University Press.

Kemp, Karen K., and Ruth A. Mostern. 2001. Spatial vagueness and uncertainty in the computational humanities. Presented at First COSIT Workshop on Spatial Vagueness, Uncertainty and Granularity, Ogunquit, Maine (available at http://www.geokemp.net).

La Fontaine, Henri, and Paul Otlet. 1908. L'Etat actuel des questions bibliographiques et l'organization de la documentation. IIB Bulletin 13: 165–191.

Latour, Bruno. 1999. Pandora's Hope. Harvard University Press.

Latour, Bruno. 2005. Re-assembling the Social: An Introduction to Actor-Network-Theory. Oxford University Press.

McDaniel, Reuben R., and Dean J. Driebe, eds. 2005. *Uncertainty and Surprise in Complex Systems: Questions on Working with the Unexpected.* Springer.

Myrtveit, Magne. 2005. The World Model Controversy. Working Paper WPSD 1/05, System Dynamics Group, University of Bergen (available at http://folk.uib.no).

Otlet, Paul. 1935. *Monde, Essai d'Universalisme: Connaissance du Monde, Sentiment du Monde, Action Organisée et Plan du Monde.* Editiones Mundaneum.

Owens, Jack B. 2007a. What historians want from GIS. *ArcNews* 29 (2): 4–6.

Owens, Jack B. 2007b. Towards a geographically-integrated, connected world history: Employing Geographic Information Systems (GIS). *History Compass* 5 (6): 2014–2040.

Owens, Jack. B. 2009. Laxenburg TECT Conference: Reflections on a Literature That GIS Scientists and Historians Do Not Know (available at http://idahostate.academia.edu).

Petersen, Arthur C. 2006. *Simulating Nature: A Philosophical Study of Computer-Simulation Uncertainties and their Role in Climate Science and Policy Advice.* Uitgeverij Maklu.

Poincaré, Henri. 1952. *Science and Hypothesis.* Dover.

Rayward, W. Boyd. 1983. The international exposition and the world documentation congress, Paris, 1937. *Library Quarterly* 53 (3): 254–268.

Rayward, W. Boyd, ed. 1990. *International Organisation and Dissemination of Knowledge: Selected Essays of Paul Otlet.* Elsevier.

Rayward, W. Boyd. 1994. Visions of Xanadu and hypertext. *Journal of the American Society for Information Science American Society for Information Science* 45: 235–250.

Scharnhorst, Andrea. 2001. Constructing knowledge landscapes within the framework of geometrically oriented evolutionary theories. In *Integrative Systems Approaches to Natural and Social Sciences—Systems Science 2000,* ed. M. Matthies, H. Malchow, and J. Kriz. Springer.

Scharnhorst, Andrea, Lutz Marz, and Thomas Aigle. 2009. Designing survival strategies for propulsion innovations (available at http://arxiv.org).

Sterman, J. D. 2007. Exploring the next great frontier: System dynamics at fifty. *System Dynamics Review* 23 (2–3): 89–93.

Trant, Jennifer. 2009. Tagging, folksonomy and art museums: Early experiments and ongoing research. *Journal of Digital Information* 10 (1) (available at http://journals.tdl.org).

van den Heuvel, Charles. 2008. Building society, constructing knowledge, weaving the web: Otlet's visualizations of a global information society and his concept of a universal civilization. In *European Modernism and the Information Society: Informing the Present, Understanding the Past*, ed. W. Rayward. Ashgate.

van den Heuvel, Charles. 2009. Web 2.0 and the semantic web in research from a historical perspective: The designs of Paul Otlet (1868–1944) for telecommunication and machine readable documentation to organize research and society. *Knowledge Organization* 36 (4): 214–226.

van den Heuvel, Charles. 2010. Web archiving in research and historical global collaboratories. In *Web History*, ed. N. Brüggen. Peter Lang.

van den Heuvel, Charles, and W. Boyd Rayward. 2011. Facing interfaces: Paul Otlet's visualizations of data integration. *Journal of the American Society for Information Science and Technology* 62 (12):2313–2326.

von Foerster, Heinz. 1984. *Observing Systems*. Intersystems.

Wardrip-Fruin, N. 2009. *Expressive Processing: Digital Fictions, Computer Games, and Software Studies*. MIT Press.

Weinberger, David. 2007. *Everything Is Miscellaneous: The Power of the New Digital Disorder*. Holt.

Wiener, Norbert. 1954. *The Human Use of Human Beings: Cybernetics and Society*. Doubleday.

Wright, Alex. 2007. *Glut: Mastering Information through the Ages*. Joseph Henry.

4 VIRTUALLY VISUAL: THE VISUAL RHETORIC OF GEOGRAPHIC INFORMATION SYSTEMS IN POLICY MAKING

REBECCA MOODY, MATTHIJS KOUW, AND VICTOR BEKKERS

A number of authors, among them John Berger (1972), Jean-François Lyotard (1993), William Mitchell (1992), Stuart Hall (1997), and Laura Mulvey (1973), have argued that we live in a visual culture: that societies rely more and more on the use of visual material, and the importance of visual material appears to be increasing accordingly. One reason for this is the increasing ubiquity of media and technologies that have enabled the creation and diffusion of images in unforeseen ways. Another reason behind the importance of visual material relates to its rhetorical aspects: the perceived ability of visual material to illustrate, to mobilize authority, and to communicate knowledge. The ubiquity of the visual and of visual rhetoric can affect policy making.

In this chapter, we ask how the relationship between policy making and visual cultures can be understood. We focus on the use of geographic information systems (GIS), which feature a strong visual component that is often used in policy making. The ability of GIS to visualize information is often seen as a way to make complex information easier to understand. We assess this claim by looking at the influence of the visual component of GIS on how organizations, ideas, and actors are integrated. We do not simply assume that policy making has been changed by GIS and their visual component. Our analysis is more contextual. In addition to examining GIS and their visual components, we examine the influence of institutions and socio-political factors on GIS. We ask how and to what extent GIS affect the topic studied, thereby potentially also shaping the institutions and the socio-political contexts in which GIS operate.

Our main questions are these: How do GIS influence the integration of organizations along different dimensions? How does the visual component

of GIS contribute to this, in the case of public policy making? In addressing
these questions, we bridge two often separate lines of inquiry: policy studies and studies of visual culture. We propose a zigzagging between these:
studies of visual culture bring into focus qualities attributed to the visual
component of GIS, while insights from policy studies can show how the
actual implementation of GIS affects both organizational structures and GIS
themselves. We argue that studying the relationship between GIS and policy
making in this manner provides an understanding of how technology plays a
mediating role in visual culture. Along the lines of the discussion of "virtual
knowledge" that recurs throughout this book, we discuss GIS as potential
agents of change and ask whether they are capable of producing new forms
of knowledge and unsettling existing power relations. More specifically,
our study of the organizational aspects of GIS-related practices allows us to
show whether and how practices surrounding GIS are affected by vested
and emerging interests. Thus, our chapter bears a resemblance to that of
Beaulieu, de Rijcke, and van Heur (chapter 1) in that we attempt to show
the influence of pre-existent institutional elements in terms of their ability
to shape epistemic authority. The epistemological promises attributed to the
visual also feature in the chapter by Kouw, van den Heuvel, and Scharnhorst
(chapter 3), whose discussion of uncertainty and knowledge production often alludes to the value attributed to visual representations of knowledge.
Ultimately, we wish to contribute to the critical and contextualized approach to new media, new techniques, and new concepts proposed by the
editors in the introduction to this volume.

We first discuss the notions of visual culture and visuality. Subsequently,
we focus on GIS and examine their potential to integrate organizations,
ideas, and actors. We then proceed to construct a conceptual framework
based on work about policy design, which we use to analyze three policy
issues: contagious livestock diseases, flood risk, and particulate matter. Based
on these cases, we then assess the influence of GIS. We conclude by suggesting directions for future research regarding the relationship between studies
of visual culture and public policy making.

VISUAL CULTURE AND VISUALITY

The study of visual cultures does not look exclusively at the content of images, but also examines the different origins and roles that visual images and

visual experiences have within cultures. This includes researching cultural, political, economic, and technical dimensions of visual material that are particular to different times and contexts. Studies of visual cultures provide important insights relevant to our discussion of the relationship between public policy making and visual material. In this section, we discuss how studies of visual culture show how seeing and perceiving contain historically variable relations and therefore are not free of political motives. Studies of visual culture also examine the role played by the technologies involved in the production of visual material. The next section focuses more on the role of technologies in visual cultures, which, in our case, involves a discussion of geographic information systems.

Examining what constitutes and shapes the activities of "seeing" and "perceiving" requires us to look not only at the kinds of signifying systems, languages, skills, and techniques employed within a certain culture but also at the ability of that culture's members to make sense of visual information. Although seeing and perceiving can be explained as neutral and purely cognitive, studies of visual cultures show how perception involves historical and political specificities that influence what it means to "see" or to "perceive." According to Jonathan Crary, "vision and its effects are always inseparable from the possibilities of an observing subject who is both the historical product and the site of certain practices, techniques, institutions, and procedures of subjectification" (1992, 5). This implies that social environments and perception cannot be understood independently, a concept that studies of visual cultures identify as "visuality":

Within visual culture studies, the term 'visuality' stands for the way that vision and the various modes of attention that we commonly identify—seeing, looking, gazing, spectating, and observing—are historically variable. It reminds us that vision is an active, interpretative process strongly governed by communities and institutions, rather than an innocent openness to natural stimuli. (Alpers et al. 1996, 68)

Apart from studying the spectator, studies of visual culture also provide critical readings of authorship of visual representations. Studies of visualizations often emphasize their potential to disclose important properties that usually are not read, or that cannot be read simply from complex datasets (Ware 2000, 2). Various sciences now feature strong visual components that arose in the late 1980s when computation and data storage became more accessible and scientists had to confront the vast amounts of information that were becoming available as a result (Wright 2008, 78). Edward Tufte discusses the role of the information visualization designer, heralded as an individual who has the ability to create an optimal fit between dataset and visualization (2001). However, designers increasingly embrace the idea that data can be represented in a multitude of ways. In an edited volume on cartographic visualizations, Abrams and Hall (2006) take up the possibilities of new visualization tools to address questions of meaning, objectivity, and interpretation in visualizations: "To design is to invent strategies for visualizing information that make new interpretations possible." (2006, 1) A notable example of a new means for visualizing data is the open-source platform Processing, developed by Casey Reas and Ben Fry (2007). Echoing a critical perspective often encountered in open-source communities, Reas and Fry express a desire to "facilitate designers' taking control of their own tools" (ibid., xxv). But since no visualization is free from the idiosyncrasies and choices of its creator, questions related to authorship remain important: Why is a particular visualization seen as thorough, optimal, or eloquent? For whom is this important?

In this chapter, we take a critical perspective by studying whether visualizations indeed enhance communication, participation, accessibility, and transparency. We use contextual approach in which we not only look at technologies but also at their social context. According to Martin Lister et al., "the capacity to see is educated and disciplined, habituated and interested, and primed to be alert or dominant in one way or another; ways that are specific to culture and history. Thus, there are different ways of seeing at different times and in different cultures that are shaped by the ideas, interests, social institutions, and technologies of an era or culture." (2003, 101)

GEOGRAPHIC INFORMATION SYSTEMS

In the previous section we argued that visual information is shaped by social, political, economic, and cultural factors that not only contribute to its acceptance but also create a demand for it. In addition to deconstructing practices of seeing and perceiving, studies of visual culture look at how technologies shape seeing and perceiving. In order to understand the relationship between geographic information systems and public policy making, we examine how GIS are used in creating, manipulating, and distributing visual images. Before assessing how GIS affect the process of public policy making within visual culture, we first explain what functionalities and qualities are commonly attributed to GIS.

Geographic information systems involve computerized systems that, like other ICTs, can order, manage, and integrate large quantities of data. Policy makers often argue that GIS present this data in a manner in which complex information becomes comprehensible for non-experts. GIS make it possible to visualize spatial distributions of social entities and their characteristics. Through GIS, dynamics of these entities can be visualized, and correlations between different social entities can be displayed. Furthermore, GIS can follow the accumulation in spatial terms of societal issues (Snellen 2000; Meijer 2002; Greene 2000). GIS support public policy making and decision making by presenting information visually—for example in the form of a map, a movie, or a virtual world. As a result, the expectation is that this opens up the variety of possible decisions in policy making: complex data now can be understood by a large group of people who would not have understood the data had they been presented in the form of a spreadsheet (Lips et al. 2000; Moukomla and Poomchatra 2004; Carver et al. 2000; Overchuk et al. 2005).

Although the ability of GIS to produce visualizations is often emphasized, other functionalities of GIS should not be pushed to the background, since they influence the content of GIS applications and how these are used.

First, GIS can be used for calculation. By using different calculation techniques, input values, and models, GIS enable the development of a scenario-based form of "if-then" reasoning. GIS thereby gain the reputation of being less fixed and more thorough than other forms of analysis. For example, in the case of an outbreak of avian flu in Thailand, GIS made it possible to base predictions related to the spread of the flu virus on the mobility of infected animals (Moukomla and Poomchatra 2004).

Second, GIS enable control through correlation in organizations by linking different datasets to one another. This can make visible issues that had been unknown or inaccessible, and thus can create new knowledge. Work procedures can thus be standardized, and standardization makes greater control over such procedures possible. For example, in California in the mid 1990s, GIS helped to make sure that federal funds were distributed in such a way that schools with large numbers of children from low-income families received more funding. Data about low-income families, school districts, and school attendance were stored in different databases. GIS helped to integrate these databases and calculate which schools should receive extra funding (Greene 2000).

A third and related quality attributed to GIS is their ability to enhance transparency. In the example of schools cited above, decisions about the allocation of funding were made in a way that was transparent for different public administrators. Such processes of decision making can be standardized, and the course of the policy processes can be studied. As a result, the process of decision making can become more transparent. As was detailed above, the ability of GIS to visualize different possible approaches to an issue may increase the accessibility and transparency of policy issues. What is more, combining datasets may yield new insights (Lips et al. 2000; Moukomla and Poomchatra 2004; Carver et al. 2000; Overchuk et al. 2005).

GIS can offer a means of communication through which different organizations can share data and see how other organizations look at policy issues. This can aid in the integration of such organizations: GIS provide a way for organizations to communicate with one another on how a particular policy issue is best approached. Another form of integration concerns the ability of GIS to integrate different datasets and thereby to make new information visible. We hasten to add that such advantages and disadvantages ascribed to the integration of actors and data should not be taken at face value. Rather, we ask exactly what aspects of policies and processes of deliberation make GIS so attractive to those involved with policy making, for example by endowing policy making with a degree of transparency, and whether this shapes policy making in some way (Bekkers and Zuurmond 2004).

POLICY DESIGN

Our conceptual framework of policy design is based on the institutional analysis and development framework of Ostrom et al. (1994). Our framework enables an analysis of integration in our case studies. In this theoretical approach, institutions structure action through rules. This framework distinguishes the "action arena" as the social space in which individuals interact about the policy issue at stake. All actors in the action arena have agendas of their own and aim for policies that fits their respective values and norms. As a result, groups of actors might come into conflict in trying to promote their values and norms within the policy design, thereby pushing values and norms of other actors to the background (Dror 1968; Etzioni 1967;

Lindblom 1959). Those who manage to push their values and norms forward most successfully see these norms reflected in the final policy design, which may exclude other actors. This is where the integration of organizations becomes relevant, since the ties of communication between these groups can influence the outcomes of conflicts they might have.

We approach power in terms of interaction, in the course of which the perception of power is most important. Actors and coalitions act on the basis of how much power they believe other actors and coalitions to have. Therefore, the power relations within the action arena can only be explained by reference to the perceptions of the actors themselves. When other actors see one actor as very powerful, that actor behaves in a dominant manner, and others react accordingly. Within the action arena there are also groups that try to hinder certain proposals and alternatives from being taken into the policy design. Their degree of success varies, depending on the relative amount of power wielded by such groups (Etzioni 1967). Therefore, the group with the largest amount of perceived power will see most of its values and beliefs reflected in the proposal. We not only discuss the influence of GIS in this process, but also outline the specific influence of the visual component of GIS on the process of integration.

We would like to emphasize that the actions and interactions within the action arena do not only depend on the power relations of actors within the arena and their values; actions and interactions are also influenced by formal institutions, regulations, and laws. The actions taken in the action arena have to fit within the legal system. Formal institutions thus determine the scope of the actions and interactions possible within the action arena (Ostrom et al. 1994). Formal institutions are not shut off from the action arena, however, and they can be influenced by actions in the action arena. For example, new legislation may be passed and new institutions formed in the action arena.

In addition to formal regulations, we also examine informal rules or "rules in use" (Ostrom et al. 1994). For example, some organizations always choose to work together because of past relationships, even though they are not legally obliged to do so. Through actions in the action arena, rules in use may change, new alliances may be made, and new actors may be included. Leading values and norms may also restrict the possibilities for actors (Bachrach and Baratz 1970; Cobb and Elder 1972; Birkland 1998).

Below we describe the case studies along the lines of the power relations within the action arena, according to the contextual variables such as the formal and informal rules, and according to the leading values and norms in society. On the basis of these descriptions, we look at the influence of the visual component of GIS. Do these visual components influence the power configurations among individual actors and among organizations? In addition, we analyze how organizations might be integrated, thereby changing the formal institutions, the rules in use, and the leading norms.

CASE STUDIES

LIVESTOCK DISEASES

Germany has a long history of dealing with contagious livestock diseases, having suffered many outbreaks in past centuries. Because of this history, financial resources are available to prevent and contain contagious livestock diseases. The outbreak of contagious livestock diseases, such as swine fever or foot and mouth disease, can have major economic and societal impacts. The GIS application used in Germany for managing livestock diseases is called TSN, which stands for Tierseuchen-Nachrichten (meaning, in English, Animal Disease News). TSN has been in development since 1993. It establishes a computerized nationwide alarm and evaluation system for outbreaks of infectious livestock diseases. Additionally, it demonstrates what course of action should be taken to evaluate whether the correct action has been taken and to learn from outbreaks. Moreover, it functions as a database for research in the areas of contagious livestock diseases. All people and organizations that are granted access to TSN are able to access this database through a Web browser. In addition, TSN includes an intranet application that enables veterinarians to find addresses of particular farms and statistics about them. A map server integrates all the data stored in TSN and enables those data to be represented in the form of maps.

In the case of each outbreak thus analyzed and represented, it becomes clear where exactly the outbreak has occurred, when it was found, what the history of the diagnosis is, and what measures were taken to cure the animals or to prevent the outbreak from spreading. This allows for follow-ups on the measures to be taken. In the case of an epidemic, others can see what actions have been taken. The GIS application calculates how fast the disease will spread, taking into account such variables as the presence of other farms in the vicinity of the infected farm, the presence and density of related (and possibly infected) animals living in the wild, the mobility of people in the area, and wind speeds (relevant in cases where the disease is airborne). The application can then predict the speed and the scope of the spread of the epidemic. This can be viewed on a map and in the form of animations. The application is able to calculate where a restricted area and a buffer zone should be created, and how large these should be.

The German government has appointed the Friedrich-Loeffler-Institut (FLI) to operate TSN. The FLI is funded by the national government and runs and operates TSN and functions as a center of expertise for infectious animal diseases. It is the primary organization responsible for informing policy makers in the German government about these issues. In the case of an outbreak, it establishes a diagnosis of the disease and tells the government what measures are needed to prevent further outbreaks. The government grants the FLI the power to operate TSN and to decide on all matters regarding TSN. In practice, this means that TSN is the sole repository of the data concerning farms, outbreaks, wildlife, and diseases. The FLI also has a monopoly position in providing information to government policy makers regarding the status of prevention. Therefore, the FLI is the only organization that advises the government on matters of infectious animal diseases and their consequences.

The information provided by the Friedrich-Loeffler-Institut to the government is communicated mostly in the form of maps or animations showing a simulation of the effects of measures taken. This is seen as an appropriate way of presenting data, since understanding the original data requires expert knowledge on the subject. In interviews, representatives of both the FLI and the government have said that they are very pleased with this form of communication.[1] Respondents from both the FLI and the government argue that issues are far more "clear" when so represented. Respondents from the government in particular emphasize that they are happy to have one organization that they can trust provide them with accurate and up-to-date information.

However, there are two problems with this assertion of clarity. First, the original data have a margin of error, since wind and mobility cannot be predicted without error. The margin of error is visible in the original programming, and is also acknowledged by scientists at the Friedrich-Loeffler-Institut. However, visual representations of livestock diseases do not inform the viewer of this margin of error. Experts on livestock diseases believe this error cannot be communicated, since that would make it difficult for policy makers to understand the model. According to these experts, images containing margins of error would no longer be unambiguous. As a result, policy makers in the government are often unaware of these margins of error, and assume the image is the unambiguous truth.

Other organizations involved in the management of contagious livestock diseases are less pleased with the role of the FLI. These organizations include research institutes such as universities and organizations dealing with the meat industry, with environmental organizations, and with activist organizations advocating animal rights. (See note 1.) These organizations argue that containment and prevention should be dealt with in a manner different from the approaches suggested by the FLI. However, they are unable to communicate their ideas to the government for two reasons. The first is that they do not have any data. The second is that they do not have the power or the authority to communicate their ideas to the government.

The previously mentioned organizations have accused the Friedrich-Loeffler-Institut of embedding its own values in its programming, which is based on algorithms that reflect the norms on prevention and containment held by the FLI. (See note 1.) As a result, universities, animal-rights activists, and research institutes without access to TSN claim that other views are excluded from the application. In this way, especially in the eyes of organizations for animal rights, not all alternatives for policy creation, such as the alternative of diminishing the number of livestock farms as a measure for prevention, are being communicated to the government. They consider the alternatives that are communicated to be biased, since these reflect the values of only one actor. This is revealed in visual representations as well: when certain possibilities are excluded from the underlying calculations, they will not show up in the image. An example often given by universities and by animal-rights activists is that it seems to be impossible to ever obtain an outcome in which killing the animals would be the best alternative: any set of parameters entered in the application yields an image showing that vaccination of animals would yield the best results.

In the past, all involved organizations negotiated a solution. Since the emergence of TSN, that is no longer the case. Only some actors are invited to negotiate. The excluded actors claim that only actors that share the views of the Friedrich-Loeffler-Institut are invited to negotiate. According to them, they no longer have access to the databases, simply because they hold other norms and values. They find no chance to negotiate their issue(s), for they have no data with which to substantiate their point. The FLI admits that some actors are excluded for the sake of privacy of farmers, whose personal data cannot be given to any organization. (See note 1.)

There has been some integration among organizations. The application allows for organizations to work together, to share data, and to make sure that all information stays up to date. However, some organizations that hold opinions different from those of the Friedrich-Loeffler-Institut feel left out of the process of negotiation and argue they have no means of bringing their ideas and policy proposals to policy makers. The fact that the FLI has been able to position itself as the only organization responsible for communicating with the government on matters related to livestock diseases has further reinforced this situation.

People in the German government appear to believe that visual representations are very helpful. They are convinced they now have the means to understand issues in ways previously unavailable, and they argue they can actually see the consequences of different policy alternatives. Previously they were not able to understand consequences of measures, since this information was provided to them in lengthy documents written in technical language they were not able to understand. Policy makers consider the visual representations sufficient to make the situation clear, since they believe the representations in question are unproblematic and complete. In their opinion, this makes choosing the best alternative much easier. However, since these images do not allow for the display of margins of error, the "truth" attributed to them is not as straightforward as policy makers think. Furthermore, universities, animal-rights activists, farmers, and other actors not involved in TSN claim that the application and its calculations are manipulated to serve the interests of the FLI, and that this manipulation affects the content of the visualizations made available to the government. They believe that the government, on the basis of the "manipulated images," will not make decisions that don't serve the interests of the Friedrich-Loeffler-Institut.

HIS AND FLIWAS

The Netherlands, with a long coastline, many rivers, and a large part of the country lying below sea level, has a long history of dealing with water management. The floods of 1993 and 1995 led to a desire to speed up the development of applications for the purpose of monitoring water levels and as a means to communicate risk in case of flooding and to create operational warning systems. As a result, a number of applications to deal with these matters were developed.

First, an application named HIS (standing for Hoogwater Informatie Systeem, which means High-Water Information System) was developed. In 2001 the first version of HIS was launched. A geographic information system, HIS can be accessed through a website. The aim of HIS is to prepare for disasters. It monitors water levels, places them in a logbook, and is able to communicate this data to other organizations, to governmental bodies, and to stakeholders. Users of HIS may use the application to create scenarios related to flooding, which may then be displayed on an interactive map in the form of an animation. On the basis of predictions of flooding, HIS can be used to calculate flood-related damage in economic terms and also in terms of the environment, loss of landscape, numbers of victims, and plans for evacuation.

HIS has now been integrated into FLIWAS (Flood Information and Warning System), a larger application that also includes Infraweb, an application that was developed mainly for purposes of communication. The aim of FLIWAS is to develop and implement an application of flood management on a transnational level with Germany, thereby increasing knowledge about the risks of flooding and playing an important role in alerting the public to the risks. FLIWAS incorporates all the features of the applications described above, but also includes the additional feature of acquiring geographical data by satellites.

The Dutch have a long history of dealing with water management on the administrative level. In the field of Dutch public administration, several organizations are responsible for water management. Collectively known as the public water sector, they include the Water Boards (which deal with water management in their appointed territory) and the national Ministerie van Verkeer en Waterstaat (currently called the Ministry of Infrastructure and the Environment, after a recent merger).

The water sector had hoped to use the visual representations created by means of HIS to inform the public of water management and flood risks. However, the Ministry of Infrastructure and the Environment had to decide whether the public should be aware of the risks of flooding or not. The experts in the water-management sector were very much in favor of putting the animations and maps of the risks of flooding on the Web so that citizens could see whether their surroundings were at risk and how fast and how high the water would be coming. The experts argued that citizens had the right to know, but also argued that more citizen awareness would bring attention, and thus resources, to the water-management sector. The Ministry of Infrastructure and the Environment eventually decided that the public should not be allowed to see this information, and established this by law. The position of the Ministry was that citizens would become over-sensitized to the issue as a result of watching the animations (interview with informant, Ministry of Infrastructure and the Environment, July 2008). Additionally, the Ministry argued that the property market would collapse if this information were to be made visible and accessible to citizens.

The initiative to implement FLIWAS was aimed at integrating different institutions operating within the water sector. In this way, the various agencies dealing with the weather, with water levels, with climate, and with landscape data could work together by means of a single application. These organizations have indeed worked together, thereby increasing knowledge of water management. In addition, FLIWAS enables these organizations to influence policy making as a block, and to confront the municipalities in negotiations.

In some cases, the municipalities and the water sector have conflicting interests. Where municipalities would like to build on their territory, the water sector claims space for water management. Because of the use of visual representations generated by HIS and FLIWAS, the water sector can graphically illustrate to municipalities the consequences of their building plans. The municipalities cannot bypass these perceived consequences. However, policy makers in municipalities are not always willing to change their development plans, and are not always happy with what they see as interference from organizations in the water sector.

Before HIS and FLIWAS, according to our respondents from the Ministry and the Water Boards, it was very difficult for policy makers to understand what was actually going on, or to what extent citizens were at risk. Policy makers regarded the information provided by water-management organizations as vague and too technical. Now the water sector can communicate this information to municipal policy makers far more easily. Visual representations are perceived as making visible what will happen if a certain property is built, what the resulting pressures on a dike would be, and how high the water would be in case of a breach of the dikes (and how quickly such an incursion might happen). As a result, visual representations of prognoses are perceived as representations of what will *actually* happen once certain conditions are met. Both policy makers and experts in the water-management sector claim that this way of communicating ensures that policy makers understand what they are dealing with. Because the scenarios are represented on maps, they appropriate a higher degree of "reality": policy makers can relate to the physical environment on which the scenario is projected, which thereby becomes more closely related to reality itself for them.

A first example is the case of the village of Lent, where the municipality wanted to build a new neighborhood and the water-management sector wished to broaden a river at the same location. A conflict occurred, and each party pushed its idea forward. Animations were used to visualize what would happen if the river were not broadened, which could, for example, result in an increased chance of flooding. In these visual representations, flooding occurred with such a speed that it would become impossible to evacuate citizens in time. In the face of such graphic depictions of flooding in this particular manner, the municipality reconsidered its policy and decided not to build a neighborhood there.

In another example, the town of Gouda wanted to build a neighborhood on the flood plains of a river. The water-management sector resisted this fiercely for the sake of the safety of citizens. In the end the municipality prevailed. The animations of the water sector had not impressed the municipality sufficiently.

These examples show that the battle between the municipalities and the water sector is ongoing. Before the implementation of HIS and FLIWAS, municipalities were usually able to carry out their plans unabated. Since the water sector has wielded the ability to mobilize visuals through the GIS applications, however, they have become a force to be reckoned with. Often the Water Boards challenge the municipalities' plans and force them to re-assess their options. The municipalities no longer have to negotiate with just one actor dealing with water management, or only a few; now they are confronted with a coalition backed by an impressive package of information.

In conclusion, a lot of organizational integration has occurred. Because of HIS and FLIWAS, the organizations dealing with water management and the organizations holding information relevant to water management now cooperate and therefore form a power bloc with extensive up-to-date information. This has ensured that the policy interests of the water sector

can be aggressively promoted. The water-management sector has thus secured its place at the negotiating table. The power that sector has achieved
from promoting its information has clearly increased. Because of visual applications, the water-management sector has become able to communicate
consequences, costs, and benefits to policy makers in a way they are able to
understand. In several instances this has caused spatial development plans to
be altered in favor of the ideas of the water-management sector.

PARTICULATE MATTER[2]

The case of particulate matter deals with air quality and public health. In
contrast to the previous cases, the Netherlands does not have a long history of dealing with this issue. Particulate matter is material that remains
suspended in air or liquids and which has a detrimental effect on health. It
originates from several sources, some human (traffic, industry, agriculture)
and some natural (dust, sea salt). Particulate matter can cause heart and lung
diseases, cancer, acute or chronic bronchitis, and asthma. The Netherlands
and the European Union have implemented a number of rules and regulations regarding particulate matter, such as norms that determine boundary
values—the maximum concentration of particulate matter allowed in the
air. Health risks posed by particulate matter were the main reason why regulations were negotiated in the European Union during the 1990s. In Dutch
national law, these directives have been implemented. In areas where the
norm is exceeded, the Dutch government, a province, or a municipalities
can implement a program to improve air quality. Concentrations of particulate matter are measured by means of remote sensing. The Rijksinstituut
voor Volksgezondheid en Milieu or RIVM (National Institute for Public
Health and Environment), the organization dealing with public health and
environmental issues, uses a geographic information system to process the
data acquired by these means. After calculations are made, the data are presented in the form of a map

After 1996, municipalities in the Netherlands became responsible for measuring the air quality in their territory, and improving it when necessary. This
proved problematic for two reasons. First, local government policy makers
were not very happy to discover that the norm was apparently exceeded
across a wide area, which precluded them from building anything there. Second, local governments acknowledged that they were not sure how to measure concentrations of particulate matter. There was the question of where to

measure, and it wasn't clear how large the measuring areas should be. In addition, it wasn't always evident which substances should be measured. Some specialists on particulate matter argued that sea salt didn't count, since it was a "natural" substance; others claimed that excluding sea salt required lowering the norm. In any case, the results of the measurements are published on the Internet by the RIVM. However, most maps of concentrations and visualizations of scenarios (i.e., representations of concentrations in the case of a new road or a new building project) are not made public.

The national government wishes to reduce concentrations of particulate matter, but without damaging building projects. Municipalities wish to build, and are very unhappy with the strict regulations on concentrations of particulate matter. In contrast, environmental organizations wish to reduce particulate matter even further. Because it is so unclear what (and how) to measure, as respondents from environmental organizations argued, local governments were able to manipulate the data. As a result, some projects were allowed to be built, but should not have been built. This was achieved by manipulating maps, for example by enlarging the scale of the area or by placing the measuring poles in a different location. In both cases, the resulting image seems to show that a project is allowed. In reaction to this, environmental organizations have created their own applications for measurement. However, governmental organizations accused environmental organizations of manipulating data in order to make sure that projects that were really legal would be stopped. On a number of occasions, the judge responsible was unable to decide whether a project could or could not continue, since the methods of measurement and the calculations were so ambiguous and opaque that a decision could not be made.

This confusion regarding calculations and measurements stems from two sources. First, uncertainties in the calculations mean that the visualizations on which decisions are based have a large margin of error, though the images do not show and explain this. Second, there is no agreed-upon standard of measurement. As a result, local governments are still able to change the positions of the measurement points, and to enlarge or downscale areas for measurement.

In short, all actors agree that the data and the results of calculations are worthy subjects for discussion. In the case of a conflict, a judge will have to decide whether a building plan may continue (in case the norm is not exceeded by the realization of the plan) or not. Because municipalities often

want to build, the data, simulations, and visualization they provide to the
judge will support their claims. Environmental organizations generally want
to stop construction plans, and provide the judge with their own data, simulations, and visualizations. Therefore, a judge has multiple scenarios from
which to choose. According to respondents from the RIVM as well as municipalities and environmental organizations, decisions concerning whether
a plan can continue seem to rely on the toss of a coin.

In contrast to the previous cases, there is not just a single application;
rather, different groups (with different interests) have developed the skills to
use their own applications. The outcome of the calculations in an application can be manipulated in favor of the group producing it. The environmental organizations are now actors to be reckoned with. In the past they
only had the power to protest, but now they have a tool that can actually
assist them in judicial hearings, and maybe even sway the balance.

Since the start of legislation on particulate matter, the relationships among
the actors can be characterized as distrustful. Each actor accuses the other actors of manipulating the data for their own interests; however, since no actor
has the formal power to promote its information as being more accurate or
legitimate than the information of any other actor, distrust has continued to
fester. Here we can see that the use of GIS has not integrated organizations.
The fact that different organizations use different applications has only led to
more animosity and conflict between organizations.

In the cases of infectious diseases and water management, the potential
of visualizations made with GIS to enhance communication has shown that
communication between experts and policy makers has indeed been made
easier. In the case of particulate matter, however, such is not the case. Different organizations have used different calculations, which result in several
conflicting visualizations. A judge has to confront these conflicting visualizations, and is thereby unable to decide which one is right, since there is
no golden standard or unambiguous and perceivable truth against which
the visualizations in question can be judged. The visualizations have given
environmental organizations more power to negotiate their causes. Previously, municipalities made decisions and the environmental organizations
could not protest on scientific grounds. Now, however, the environmental
organizations are actually able to demonstrate (by means of visualizations)
the consequences of building plans, which might cause a judge to rule in
their favor.

ANALYSIS

The case studies have a number of similarities and differences. First, we find that the power relations between the actors involved have changed in all cases. In the case of TSN, the position of the experts on contagious livestock diseases with access to TSN has improved at the expense of other experts and farmers. The experts without access have been excluded from the organizational structure and are unable to use the data of the Friedrich-Loeffler-Institut or even to voice their opinion. The experts with access to TSN have the power to promote policy proposals on contagious livestock diseases, which they do in a very successful manner. TSN gives the experts who have access to it the power to negotiate with national and European policy makers. These experts have all the information, and they are able to communicate this information in a way that policy makers understand: in the form of a map and/or animations.

In the case of HIS and FLIWAS, all actors now perceive the water sector to have acquired a powerful position. Because of the visual component of HIS and FLIWAS, they can communicate their knowledge more easily. They can communicate with other organizations, but they can also communicate more easily with policy makers, since they are able to create visualizations. As a result, they can illustrate why, for example, a dike should be reinforced. This new-found power of the water sector has caused some friction with the municipalities, since the local authorities feel they are losing power over their territory. This fear relates to the fact that the water sector now has all available information at its disposal, which suggests a degree of completeness according to all respondents. Furthermore, this information can be communicated by means of images in a way the policy makers consider more convenient.

In the case of particulate matter, interactions are complicated by a great deal of conflict between municipalities and building corporations on one side and environmental organizations on the other. Where municipalities and building corporations would still like to build, environmental organizations want to prohibit them from doing so for reasons related to air quality. Both opponents ground their arguments in the inaccuracies of the applications, and both publish images and maps that are supposed to show that they are right. A large number of actors have access to applications that measure particulate matter, and are thereby able to present their information in the form of a map. However, this information is easily manipulated. In this case, the authority attributed to these images by the various stakeholders only reinforces the conflict. All parties expect to gain power by means of the visualizations they can present to a judge. In practice, however, the visualizations of one actor fundamentally conflict with the visualizations of another actor, and therefore do not lead to a straightforward conclusion.

A second point relates to the role attributed to GIS, including their visual component. The use of visual material in the three cases described reveals a certain flexibility of visualizations as epistemic authorities, which suggests a rhetorical dimension, also discussed in studies of visual culture. In the case of TSN, not all parties agree on what TSN actually entails. Those with access, namely policy makers and politicians, agree that TSN is a tool for providing up-to-date information, and that it is very valuable in making calculations and simulations so that policies can be designed. Others, however, believe TSN to be a tool for exclusion. Here we see that the potential of GIS to integrate organizations is used in the opposite way: organizations are denied access to the data. Furthermore, some believe that TSN is used to push certain ideas forward using seductive and persuasive visualizations, since the application can be manipulated. The water sector sees HIS and FLIWAS primarily as tools for calculation and visualization, while policy makers perceive them primarily as tools for visualization and communication. In the case of particulate matter, the applications used to measure, calculate, and present data on concentrations of particulate matter are mostly seen as calculation devices. Furthermore, all involved actors and coalitions agree that the application is an important source of power. Each coalition accuses other coalitions of using the application in such a way that data can be manipulated and outcomes are skewed in favor of a particular purpose.

Third, with respect to organizational integration, GIS provide a means for different organizations to communicate with one another (and share their data in the case of water management). In this way, these organizations and the actors working for them have become more integrated. This does not seem to apply in the case of particulate matter, where integration of organizations has not taken place, and in the case of infectious diseases, where some organizations have been excluded.

CONCLUSION

Whether the way organizations are integrated is altered by the use of GIS remains in question, as does the influence of the visual component of GIS on this process of integration. We draw several conclusions concerning the case studies.

First, the ways in which organizations are integrated (how they communicate, whether and how they share data) is altered by the use of GIS in all three cases. In addition, the way actors communicate with one another in public policy making has changed. GIS can integrate organizations by providing new means of communication and ways of data sharing. These new connections and lines of communication have become more widespread and in some instances are even included in the formal institutional features. This ensures that in the future these lines of communication will indeed be followed. However, the opposite can be found as well: the case of TSN shows that actors were excluded. Another change in the way organizations integrate by means of GIS can be found in the case of particulate matter. Here there is not one single application; there are many actors, each of which uses its own application. Even though the GIS applications ensure that all involved actors can communicate their information, the information is not trusted and is seen as manipulable. This tension points to the fact that communication between different groups now has become possible through the use of GIS, but that the political relations between the groups have not improved. Thus, geographic information systems do influence the way organizations are integrated and connected, in terms of communication and data sharing. But what form this influence takes depends on the way the application in question is implemented, and on its context. This affects not only the number of organizations that are integrated with one another, but also their relations. In terms of public policy making, this can have a profound impact. Organizations with access to applications obtain more power than other organizations, since they have a monopoly on information. Furthermore, new information can emerge when data are shared, and the process of policy making can be enhanced by newly formed connections. These connections can ensure that policy issues are communicated with more stakeholders, and may also account for different policy outcomes. What the effect of this will be cannot yet be predicted.

Second, we conclude that the use of GIS and their visual components have a considerable effect on how organizations are integrated. We found several occurrences of this. First, the relations and connections between organizations change as a result of the visualization function of GIS. Within policy domains, organizations have always worked together. This has mostly included experts in a policy field and policy makers. Before the use of GIS, communication between the two was often difficult. Policy makers were sometimes unable to interpret and understand the data presented to them by experts. Because of the visual component of GIS, in our cases, experts are able to demonstrate effects of policy ideas to policy makers in the form of a map or animation. As a result, policy makers may be better equipped to understand these effects in a way they could not before, since they purportedly did not understand the data presented to them. This alters the relations and connections between organizations, not only because communication becomes less complex, but also because experts gain power in policy making because they are now seen as a serious partner. This is due to the observation that it is possible (at least in principle) to present predictions of the consequences of each proposal in a manner more accessible to policy makers.

Studying the values and power relations at work within visualization remains necessary to do justice to the intricacies of the actual implementation of visualizations. Echoing insights from studies of visual culture, our case studies show that visual representations need to be studied in context to understand how they influence public policy making. The visual component of GIS plays a large part in the alteration of the connections between organizations. We have shown this in terms of who is included, since information is now "opened up" and "transparent," but also in terms of who is excluded. Additionally, relations have been altered by the visual component of GIS. Experts working with GIS grow in stature through the use of visualizations, and thereby have a greater influence on the policy issue at stake. Visual representations are not neutral, and their underlying values need to be taken into account. There is no straightforward answer to the question whether GIS alone bring about the actualization of potentials, nor to the question whether they are responsible for the creation of new potentials. Regarding such potentials, our chapter proposes ways to study whether and how GIS unsettle vested interests and shake up patterns of interlocked technologies, practitioners, and institutions. We invite both policy makers and those studying the use of visual representations in public policy to examine perception and visualizations critically. In many cases, seeing and perceiving involve power relations: the observer holds some degree of power over the seen, and it is possible for one social group, class, or gender to exercise power over others through the use of visual images.

In that sense, claiming that visualizations are devoid of political motives is a very political move indeed.

NOTES

1. Interviews were held in relation to TSN and policy making with several respondents in different organizations in Germany between September and December of 2008. Owing to arrangements for anonymity established before the interviews, the content of these interviews cannot be cited, quoted, or linked to.

2. Interviews were held in relation to particulate matter issues and policy making with several respondents in different organizations in the Netherlands between April and July of 2008. Owing to arrangements for anonymity established before the interviews, the content of these interviews cannot be cited, quoted, or linked to.

REFERENCES

Abrams, Janet, and Peter Hall. 2006. Where/abouts. In *Else/Where*, ed. J. Abrams and P. Hall. University of Minnesota Design Institute.

Alpers, Svetlana, Emily Apter, Carol Armstrong, Susan Buck-Morss, Tom Conley, Jonathan Crary, Thomas Crow, et al. 1996. Visual Culture Questionnaire. *October* 77 (Summer): 25–70.

Bachrach, Peter, and Morton Baratz. 1970. *Power and Poverty: Theory and Practice.* Oxford University Press.

Bekkers, Victor, and Arre Zuurmond. 2004. Achtergronden en eigenschappen van ICT. In *ICT en openbaar bestuur: Implicaties en uitdagingen van technologische toepassingen voor de overheid*, ed. M. Lips, V. Bekkers, and A. Zuurmond. Lemma.

Berger, John. 1972. *Ways of Seeing.* Penguin.

Birkland, Thomas. 1998. Focusing events, mobilization, and agenda setting. *Journal of Public Policy* 18 (1): 53–74.

Carver, Steve, Andy Evans, Richard Kingston, and Ian Turton. 2000. Accessing geographical information systems over the World Wide Web: Improving public participation in environmental decision making. *Information Infrastructure and Policy* 6 (3): 157–170.

Cobb, Roger, and Charles Elder. 1972. *Participation in American Politics: The Dynamics of Agenda-Building.* Johns Hopkins University Press.

Crary, Jonathan. 1992. *Techniques of the Observer.* MIT Press.

Dror, Yehezkel. 1968. *Public Policy-Making Reexamined.* Chandler.

Etzioni, Amitai. 1967. Mixed-scanning: A "third" approach to decision-making. *Public Administration Review* 27 (5): 385–392.

Greene, R. W. 2000. *GIS in Public Policy: Using Geographic Information for More Effective Government*. Esri.

Hall, Stuart. 1997. The work of representation. In *Cultural Representations and Signifying Practices*, ed. S. Hall. Sage.

Lindblom, Charles E. 1959. The science of "muddling through." *Public Administration Review* 19 (1): 79–88.

Lips, Miriam, Marcel Boogers, and Rodney Weterings. 2000. Reinventing territory in Dutch local government: Experiences with the development and implementation of GIS in the Amsterdam region. *Information Infrastructure and Policy* 6 (4): 171–183.

Lister, Martin, Jon Dovey, Seth Giddings, Ian Grant, and Kieran Kelly. 2003. *New Media: A Critical Introduction*. Routledge.

Lyotard, Jean-François. 1993. *The Postmodern Explained*. University of Minnesota Press.

Meijer, Albert J. 2002. Geographical information systems and public accountability. *Information Polity* 7 (1): 39–47.

Mitchell, William J. 1992. *The Reconfigured Eye: Visual Truth in the Post-Photographic Era*. MIT Press.

Moukomla, Sitthisak, and Amonpan Poomchatra. 2004. Rapid response spatial information systems: Avian influenza in Thailand. In *Building Asia: Enabling G-Lateral Ties*, Proceedings of the Map Asia 2004 Conference at the Beijing International Convention Center, Beijing (available at http://gisdevelopment.net).

Mulvey, Laura. 1973. Visual pleasure and narrative cinema. *Screen* 16 (3): 6–18.

Ostrom, Elinor, Roy Gardner, and James Walker. 1994. *Rules, Games, and Common-Pool Resources*. University of Michigan Press.

Overchuk, Alexey L., Lennart Hansen, and Niels Henrik Hansen. 2005. "Developing a farm land distribution model in Russia." In *Proceedings of Regional Workshop on Land Consolidation and Territorial Organization*, Prague (available at http://www.fao.org).

Reas, Casey, and Ben Fry. 2007. *Getting Started with Processing*. MIT Press.

Snellen, Ignace T. M. 2000. Territorialising governance and the state: Policy dimensions of geographic information systems. *Information Infrastructure and Policy* 6 (3): 131–138.

Tufte, Edward. 2001. *The Visual Display of Quantitative Information: Cheshire*. Graphics Press.

Ware, Colin. 2000. *Information Visualization: Perception for Design*. Morgan Kaufmann.

Wright, Richard. 2008. Data visualization. In *Software Studies: A Lexicon*, ed. M. Fuller. MIT Press.

5   SLOPPY DATA FLOODS OR PRECISE SOCIAL SCIENCE METHODOLOGIES? DILEMMAS IN THE TRANSITION TO DATA-INTENSIVE RESEARCH IN SOCIOLOGY AND ECONOMICS

CLEMENT LEVALLOIS, STEPHANIE STEINMETZ, AND PAUL WOUTERS

With enough data, the numbers speak for themselves.

—Chris Anderson (2008)

What are the implications of the emergence of new data sources for scientific and scholarly research? In 2008 this question was provocatively raised in an article by Chris Anderson, editor in chief of the journal *Wired*. He claims that scientists need no longer rely on hypothesis or experimentation. Increasingly, we will all be children of "The Petabyte age." According to Anderson, "at the petabyte scale, information is not a matter of simple three- and four-dimensional taxonomy and order, but of dimensionally agnostic statistics." This calls for "an entirely different approach," one that no longer aims for visualization of data in their entirety. Anderson pleads the case for approaching data streams mathematically first, and establishing a context for them later, rather than starting with trying to understand the data. In short, according to Anderson, we no longer need theory, at least not in the traditional sense of the word. "Out with every theory of human behavior, from linguistics to sociology. Forget taxonomy, ontology, and psychology. Who knows why people do what they do? The point is they do it, and we can track and measure it with unprecedented fidelity. With enough data, the numbers speak for themselves."

Anderson has accurately captured an emerging enthusiasm for data floods. Although his article (to which many have responded in print and on the Web) exaggerates the actual developments in some ways, the basic argument is highly relevant, particularly in the case of computational research. For example, in March 2009 the journal *Science* published a similar article by computer scientists from Microsoft Research and Johns Hopkins University, titled "Computer science: Beyond the data deluge." In it, Gordon Bell, Tony Hey, and Alex Szalay (2009, 1297) argue that "today, some areas of science are facing hundred- to thousand-fold increases in data volumes from satellites, telescopes, high throughput instruments, sensor networks, accelerators, and supercomputers, compared to the volumes generated only a decade ago." This increase in the amount of data is, according to Bell et al., a serious challenge to a variety of disciplines. Not merely an incremental change, it represents a new research paradigm. According to Gray and Szalay (2007), this new "fourth paradigm" is supposed to succeed three older paradigms: the experimental, theoretical, and simulation paradigms. Within computer science it means that the term *e-science* is not primarily concerned with faster computation, but with more advanced database technologies. Astronomy was the first field to make the shift to data-intensive research by collecting all observational data in a global data infrastructure accessible through Web services.[1] High-energy physics, genomics, and oceanography are expected to follow. According to the Microsoft Research team, "data-intensive science will be integral to many future scientific endeavors, but demands specialized skills and analysis tools" (Bell et al. 2009, 1298). The examples they discuss are all based on data-producing technologies, such as digital telescopes, sensors, and particle accelerators.

The postulate of a "fourth paradigm" is further elaborated in a book titled *The Fourth Paradigm: Data-Intensive Scientific Discovery*, edited by Hey, Tansley, and Tolle (2009). The main argument of *The Fourth Paradigm* is that "if we are to achieve *dramatic* breakthroughs, new approaches will be required. We need to embrace the next, fourth paradigm of science." (Mundie 2009, 223) This collection of essays, co-authored by computer scientists and "domain scientists" in the areas of environmental and health research, spells out the implications of large datasets for scientific research and for research infrastructures. It is based on work by the late Jim Gray, a computer scientist who is celebrated as a visionary. Gray defines the fourth paradigm as follows:

The world of science has changed, and there is no question about this. The new model is for the data to be captured by instruments or generated by simulations before being processed by software and for the resulting information or knowledge to be stored in computers. Scientists only get to look at their data fairly late in this pipeline. The techniques and technologies for such data-intensive science are so different that it is worth distinguishing data-intensive science from computational science as a new, *fourth paradigm* for scientific exploration. (Gray, cited in Hey, Tansley, and Tolle 2009, xix)

According to Gray, we are seeing the evolution of two branches in every discipline: a computational branch and a data-processing branch. For example, in ecology there is now "both computational ecology, which is to do with simulating ecologies, and eco-informatics, which is to do with collecting and analyzing ecological information" (xix).

How will the social sciences be affected by these developments? This chapter aims to contribute to a better understanding of the implications of data-intensive and computational research methodologies for the social sciences by focusing on two social science fields: sociology and economics. We address the implications of this debate for sociology and economics by uncovering what is at stake here. Although different kinds of "new data" are collected by both disciplines (transactional versus brain data), they serve as good examples to demonstrate how disciplines are responding to the availability of new data sources. Moreover, contrasting the two fields provides insight into the subtle but relevant differences among various forms of data-intensive research. This comparative study also shows how the notion of "data-intensive research" is actually defined. It is clear that there is no consensus as to when data are massive or complex enough to count as the basis for data-intensive research. A dataset of a few terabytes would certainly count as huge in sociology, but less so in astronomy. As a preliminary definition, we propose to define *data-intensive research* as research that requires radical changes in the discipline. If new, possibly more standardized and technology-intensive ways to store, annotate, and share data are needed, we see this as a case of "data-intensive research." This means that the concept may point toward quite different research practices and computational tools.

We address the following questions for each discipline: Who is making claims on behalf of new sources of data, and what kind of evidence is presented in each case? Are these instances framed as opportunities, or as threats? What kind of resistance, if any, arises from among the challenged orthodoxies? What kinds of questions are these different approaches seeking to answer? What implications can be drawn concerning the conduct of research in, and the societal role of, the social sciences and the humanities?

In 2007, two prominent British sociologists, Mike Savage and Roger Burrows, raised the alarm in their article "the coming crisis of empirical sociology" in *Sociology*, the flagship journal of their profession, published by the British Sociological Association (Savage and Burrows 2007; see also Savage and Burrows 2009). They argue that "transactional data," the data generated by the daily use of networked communication systems by millions of people, will render the survey methodology—one of the cornerstones of the field of sociology—increasingly obsolete. In its place, research groups in private companies have been able to circumvent the survey and are currently exploiting the huge data flow of their companies' operations. This enables them to analyze exhaustive population data without the need for sampling techniques. How does this fit with the data-flood revolution announced in computing and natural science? Who are the new actors in this empirical challenge to sociology, and to what extent is academic sociology really obliged to adapt to this new type of data-driven research?

Basically the same questions arise in economics, which is challenged by yet another radically new type of data: neuroimaging data. Neuroeconomists use functional magnetic resonance imaging (fMRI) scans to provide a new kind of empirical evidence concerning economic decisions. Particular types of behavior can be related to the activation of specific brain areas, leading some to suggest that a fundamental level of explanation has been achieved. Why do we behave as we do, and how? Once measured, emotional states and drivers of decision making provide a more realistic account of behavior, which theoretical constructs in economics have not yet been able to create. Economics has long been ambivalent about the empirical relevance of its sophisticated mathematical theories. These doubts re-emerged when it became clear that the 2008 financial crisis had taken most economists completely by surprise. The emerging subfield of neuroeconomics, which brings together economists, psychologists, and neuroscientists, aims to identify the neurological foundations of human decisions in order to improve the empirical validity of the theoretical decision-making models. As is the case in the debate within sociology, it remains to be seen whether the importing of new datasets will have a significant impact on how academic science is conducted, and on its boundaries. This is the central question explored in this chapter.

We start by re-contextualizing the empirical tradition in sociology and economics. Both disciplines have routinely dealt with relatively large datasets and, indeed, created them. We take this as the background for a critical re-evaluation of the claims that data-intensive research represents a radical novelty, threatening theoretically oriented social sciences. How are the new datasets different from the existing empirical material available in sociology and economics? We then present the responses within the scientific communities. If voices oppose this predicted trend, what is their counterproposal, and from which corners of sociology and economics do they originate? Here, clear differences are highlighted between the two cases, showing that it is indeed necessary to go beyond the simple observation of an era of data-intensive research and to assess each case in terms of its particular historical dynamic and balance of internal intellectual currents. Moving away from the (often confrontational) responses to new forms of data-intensive research, we try to achieve a more balanced view of the implications for the two disciplines. Is the "end of theory" a likely outcome? What (if any) reconfigurations of the fields can be expected in terms of boundaries, expertise, and institutions? Finally, we reflect on a possible alternative scenario which can be discerned in economics as well as in sociology. In this scenario, theoretical reasoning will not be "pushed aside" by the ascendance of data-driven research. Rather, theory work will prosper from the availability of a greater amount of raw data. In the concluding section, we reappraise the lessons that can be learned by the social sciences.

NEW FORMS OF DATA COLLECTION AND ANALYSIS IN SOCIOLOGY

First, we examine whether technological innovation and increasing possibilities to collect vast amounts of data render obsolete theoretical and methodological foundations in empirical sociology. As was mentioned at the beginning of this chapter, this topic has been addressed by Savage and Burrows (2007), who posit a "coming crisis of empirical sociology," and by Anderson (2008), who developed the "end of theory" scenario. Both articles have led to debate in scholarly journals and Internet forums.[2] However, as sociology can hardly be considered a unified field, answering the question of whether theory is becoming obsolete is a challenging task. A look at the diverse topics and methods addressed by the 55 research committees of the International Sociological Association in 2011 throws light on how differently the question might be answered even within those groups. Against this background, a reflection on the empirical tradition in sociology is required to obtain a deeper understanding of the implications of new data forms.

THE EMPIRICAL TRADITION IN SOCIOLOGY: BACKGROUND

At the end of the nineteenth century, sociology emerged as an academic response to the challenges presented by industrialization and rationalization. During this phase of "becoming a science" (Zald 1991), the dominant methodological approach was to treat the discipline in broadly the same manner as natural sciences. An emphasis on empiricism (positivism) served to provide the foundation for sociological claims and, more important, to distinguish sociology from less empirical fields, such as philosophy (Comte 1848; Durkheim 1895). This prospect of empirical social analysis was questioned by various intellectuals. Karl Marx rejected Comtean positivism in favor of dialectic analysis, arguing that appearances ought to be critically examined rather than simply documented. Nevertheless, Marx endeavored to produce a science of society grounded in the economic determinism of historical materialism (Marx 1847). At the turn of the twentieth century, the first wave of German sociologists, including Max Weber and Georg Simmel, introduced sociological anti-positivism, arguing that the appropriate objective for sociological endeavor should be a hermeneutic (interpretative) understanding, rather than law-like generalization. That methodological paradigm formed and shaped the discipline for several decades and led broadly to two contrasting models of sociological research and theorizing: the positivist/quantitative and the interpretative/qualitative.[3] The positivist tradition reached its peak of popularity in the "quantitative revolution" between the 1950s and the 1960s, whereas the qualitative tradition became less important in that period and began to regain recognition in the 1970s. Even though some researchers have proclaimed an end to this paradigmatic quarrel, it can hardly be denied that it still is the main divide within the discipline.[4]

Empirical sociology has an even longer history.[5] Agricultural and trade statistics, as well as censuses, were already developed in ancient China, Egypt, and the Roman Empire (Schnell et al. 1995). The first inquiries of empirical social research are primarily socio-graphic rather than sociological. Usually, their main purpose was to increase bureaucratic efficiency (Bethlehem 2009).[6] Political arithmetic, founded by John Graunt, William Perry, and Edmund Halley (Diekmann 2008), gave a strong impulse to empirical social research and statistics in Great Britain. It can be seen as the forerunner of quantitative analysis of social phenomena as the basis for causal explanation of social conditions. Political arithmetic dominated statistical thinking up to the beginning of the nineteenth century. Gradually it turned into a new field of social statistics ("social calculus"). From 1830 to 1849, in the so-called "era of enthusiasm" (Westergaard 1932), the foundations for modern social statistics were laid. Central statistical bureaus, statistical societies, conferences, and statistical journals were established soon after that period (Kern 1982; Diekmann 2008).

To summarize, the early development of empirical social research was mostly independent of the growth of academic sociology. The founding of several institutes for empirical social research, the founding of market-research and opinion-research institutes, and the founding of research institutions related to evaluation and policy research were important developments.[7] As sociological research became increasingly employed as a tool by governments and businesses, new types of quantitative and qualitative research methods were developed in the second half of the twentieth century, displacing (and often delegitimizing) the older forms of empirical research. Particularly at a time when social data could not be easily collected, stored, and manipulated (Brunt 2001; Bulmer et al. 1991; Osborne and Rose 1999, 2004), the new generation of empirical sociologists perceived themselves as methodological innovators as a result of the invention of the sample survey, the early adoption of the principles of statistical inference, and the codification of the in-depth interview. Because this still-dominant form of empirical sociology has been challenged by "data-driven research," we focus our analysis on that aspect of the discipline in particular.

IS THERE A CRISIS, AND WHO IS AFFECTED?

Savage and Burrows (2007) make claims about a "coming crisis of empirical sociology" and a radical change in the significance of empirical research. They argue that empirical sociologists, instead of keeping pace with the latest developments in the online environment, are beginning to lose their "innovative" role in collecting and analyzing social data. As they frame it, empirical sociologists "occupy an increasingly marginal position in the huge research infrastructure that forms an integral feature of what Thrift (2005) characterizes as "knowing capitalism": "circuits of information proliferate and are embedded in numerous kinds of information technologies" (Savage and Burrows 2007, 886).

This crisis affects three dimentions of academic sociology: who qualifies as a legitimate knowledge producer, which methods are validated as "scientific," and what counts as proper data. The commercialization of empirical sociology via the Internet enables new and powerful social agents, including private firms and institutions, to collect huge amounts of data on complete (sub)-populations as a by-product of their daily transactions.[8] Furthermore, private entities are developing sophisticated methodological techniques for "mining" traces left by digital transactions on the Web or on mobile phone networks. Savage and Burrows (2009) claim that the preferred tools of empirical sociology—the in-depth interview and the sample survey[9]—will therefore become less relevant.[10] The third aspect of the proclaimed crisis of empirical sociology relates to the very nature of what is a sociological variable. The electronic footprints left by the activities of individuals engaged in online shopping or social networking have become a more important proxy for sociological information than the personal and social attributes of the individual "transactor," such as education, gender, age, race, and class, which have been the central variables in sociological research for almost a century.

RESPONSES BY THE SCIENTIFIC COMMUNITY

The idea of a "coming crisis" has dawned upon the scientific community rather slowly, and it has been mainly discussed in the context of British sociology. Savage and Burrows (2007) conclude that empirical sociologists (quantitative as well as qualitative) need to rethink their methodological practices in a radically innovative way. Instead of getting caught up in internal disputes, sociologists will have to become more attentive to the deployment of new methods seeking to describe different forms of the "social." With this line of reasoning, empirical sociologists have two options: they can ignore new forms of social data by invoking their academic superiority and sophistication in social theory, or they can critically engage with research on transactional data by questioning classifications, assumptions, and procedures. In the words of Savage and Burrows, they "could seek to get their hands dirty by exploring the potentials of such new methods and the issues posed by their use" (2009, 766–767).[11]

Rosemary Crompton (2008) reacted to Savage and Burrows' recommendations by emphasizing that the "old" paradigms were still present in contemporary sociology. In her opinion, empirical sociologists should not choose one party (qualitative or quantitative). As these paradigms are inter-dependencies rather than binaries, sociologists have to develop the capacity to work across what appear to be conflicting approaches. This also means that they will have to develop an understanding of a range of different empirical research methods. Consequently, Crompton critiques the suggestion to embrace the "new methodological turn" with its preference for description and classification rather than causal explanation. She suggests that Savage and Burrows remain caught within the binary opposition of the qualitative versus quantitative tradition, and sees this as dangerous. In her opinion, "we need to describe, interpret and understand but we should also be concerned with causes" (ibid., 1223). In this context, Crompton acknowledges that sociologists should be sensitive and responsive to methodological innovation. Her main concerns are related to the possibility that the suggestions by Savage and Burrows could be seen as an argument by sociologists to avoid the study of quantitative methods.

Further rebuttals to the "coming crisis of empirical sociology" were raised in a special edition of the 2009 *European Journal of Social Theory* in which several authors discussed the paradoxical emergence of a crisis of empirical sociology and a return to the empirical within the field. The contributions of Adkins and Lury (2009), Clough 2009, and Savage (2009) show that there is a shift in the very nature of the empirical that requires the reconsideration of the relations between fact and value. In this debate, the crisis of the empirical is not so much understood as the decoupling of sociological expertise and the academic sociologist (a decoupling that might be remedied through greater methodological creativity and innovation). Rather it is perceived as a necessary and productive destabilization of the role of empirical research in shaping the characteristics of sociology as a discipline.

In addition to the responses to Savage and Burrows, Anderson's hypothesis also triggered a lively debate that is directly relevant to the "crisis in empirical sociology." Interestingly, this debate involved intellectuals with no particular allegiance to academic institutions, who provided an alternative angle to the "academic" viewpoint. (See also the discussion at the homepage of edge.org, an eclectic group of intellectuals). For instance, Kevin Kelly (a science writer and a co-founder of *Wired* magazine) guesses that "this emerging method (correlations) will be one additional tool in the evolution of the scientific method. It will not replace any current methods (sorry, no end of science) but will compliment established[,] theory-driven science. . . .

It is not the end of theories, but the end of theories we understand." Similarly, Daniel Hillis (chairman and chief technology officer of Applied Minds, a knowledge-based company) writes: "I do not see why large amounts of data will undermine the scientific method. We will begin, as always, by looking for simple patterns in what we have observed and use that to hypothesize what is true elsewhere. . . . We will extrapolate from the data first and then establish a context later. This is the way science has worked for hundreds of years." These arguments demonstrate that, to some, newly emerging data floods do not signify the end of "the scientific method," by which they mean the basic deductive-nomological model of explanation. On the contrary, it seems that these authors perceive the current developments in data-driven research as a kind of "natural cycle" in the scientific world, leading to methodological innovations and new theorizing without banishing the traditional approaches.

Against this background, it seems that Savage and Burrows' proclamation of a "crisis" succeeded in compelling sociologists to think about and discuss their discipline and changes occurring within it. In this respect, the arguments listed above show that new forms of (transactional) mass data have raised awareness of the necessity for change and adaptation in some theoretical and methodological aspects. However, this need not be perceived as a threat to the field. Newly emerging tools developed both inside and outside academia will not necessarily lead to the abandonment of traditional approaches. They were not born in isolation from other methods and approaches; rather, they developed in a stepwise process of confronting "the old" with "the new." Long before the articles about a crisis in sociology were published, social scientists discussed the impact of the Internet on their practices (Hine 2006; Schroeder and Fry 2007). For instance, the creation of the Association of Internet Researchers in the year 2000 and the comments in the Social Sciences Week Blog of 2005 show how quickly social scientists recognized the Internet both as a research tool offering new research methods for collecting, analyzing, and disseminating data and as a social phenomenon worthy of study in itself.[12] The possibilities offered by new technologies are generally regarded as an enrichment rather than an impoverishment of academic knowledge production.[13] Furthermore, the reactions of social scientists to the development of data collection via the Internet[14] also demonstrate that it is unjustified to chastise sociologists for their ignorance of new methodological challenges. Even though online surveys were mainly a tool for commercial marketing agencies, survey methodologists had already begun to examine their advantages and disadvantages at the end of the 1980s. This resulted in several attempts to improve the methodological tools for online data collection and analysis (Couper 2000; Fricker and Schonlau 2002; Vehovar and Manfreda 1999).[15]

WHAT ARE THE IMPLICATIONS FOR THE FIELD?

Is there a crisis in empirical sociology or not? Should academic sociologists give up on their traditional methodologies, or should we believe the more moderate commentators who play down the significance of the change? We propose that a useful perspective in this debate is to see the recurring cycles of a feeling of crisis in sociology as a fundamental characteristic of the discipline rather than as something external (Hollands and Stanley 2009). Robert Michels (1932, 123–24) characterized sociology as "largely demoralized" and undergoing "an intense spiritual self-criticism." More than 40 years later, Robert K. Merton (1975, 22) commented that sociology "has typically been in an unstable state, alternating between planes of extravagant optimism and extravagant pessimism." One of the most influential articulations of a "crisis" in sociology was expressed by Alwin Gouldner (1970, 1979, 1985). In his view, sociology had become too monolithic, accompanied by a lack of reflexivity with respect to its theories, its methods and its relationship to research and a failure to engage with the changing world. In the subsequent discussions during the 1990s and across the millennial years, concerns were expressed repeatedly about the discipline's decline due to diversity and fragmentation (Turner and Turner 1990; Horowitz 1993; Esping-Anderson 2000; Cole 2001; Berger, 2002)[16] and its future in connection with "public sociology" (Burawoy 2004; Acker 2005; Aronowitz 2005; Ghamari-Tabrizi 2005; Urry 2005).

Against this background, Savage and Burrows' (2007) appeal seems to be a continuation of this "crisis" tradition. The claim of a coming crisis is a metaphor for a perceived need to reflect on the discipline and its internal changes brought about by social, economic, and technical innovations. In this context, the arguments regarding the implications and challenges of the emerging data floods for the field of sociology seem to be both methodological and theoretical. First, it seems worthwhile for empirical sociologists to reflect on their methodological approaches more critically. This includes a change in their own assessment as well as a fresh look at new approaches and more complex methods of data analysis. The collection of new forms of mass data on human behavior, societies, and economies will stimulate the use of advanced computing in sociology. Furthermore, the informed use of innovations in grid computing, visualization techniques, and other novel analytical methods will be necessary to achieve a complete understanding and meaning of the patterns detected. This will require a willingness to team science and novel computational methods. (See chapter 2 above.) First steps in this direction have been undertaken by social scientists in "complexity research."[17] (For more details, see Fischer et al. 2008, 533.) This interdisciplinary and multi-disciplinary field bridges most of the traditional divides that have evolved in social science, such as reductionist/non-reductionist, aggregated/disaggregated, and micro/macro. However, how empirical sociologists will take advantage of this potential will depend on their individual openness to new methods as well as on the acceptance and institutionalization of these methods within the discipline. It seems likely that many empirical sociologists will continue to "do empirical sociology" in more traditional ways.

New technologies are also creating opportunities for new substantive theory. As Blank (2008, 538) argues, these "new theoretical opportunities come in part from the new social forms and new communities created by online technologies." Moreover, online research casts new light on older social formations. New impulses may also arise from the new mass of data. Social network theory is a good example of a theoretical development that, though its roots can be dated back to Simmel and Durkheim, was recently fostered by major advances in computing and methodological tools (Moody and White 2003). These effects will continue, but it is hard to predict which other theories will benefit. After all, the relationship between data and theory is complex. As Blank (2008, 543) underlines, even though the new data promise a remarkably fine-grained, detailed picture of people in all kinds of social situations, this will not necessarily lead to a more advanced understanding of the social. As Bulmer (1984) emphasized, "the scientific method is not understood simply as a meticulous and painstaking collection and analysis of data, but involves a concern with theoretical problems and an urge to explain social phenomena through theoretical work." In this respect, doing social research necessarily involves theory as well as the strategies and techniques of empirical investigation. The collection of large amounts of data alone is not sufficient to guarantee useful research results explaining social phenomena.

NEUROIMAGING DATA IN ECONOMICS

Neuroeconomics is an emerging subfield at the intersection of economics, biology and psychology. Concerned with the elucidation of the neural basis for decision making, it represents an effort to confront data and theories from different fields across the traditional border between natural and social science, displaying a degree of interdisciplinarity rarely witnessed before (Glimcher et al. 2008). Economics received a rather bad press after 2008 because it failed to foresee the global financial and economic crisis; it is even suspected of having played an initiating role in it. This has created a dispute about fundamentals within the field of economics itself. In a widely read essay on the collective failure of the economics profession to predict the financial crisis, Paul Krugman claimed that "economists, as a group, mistook beauty, clad in impressive-looking mathematics, for truth" (2009). Is this discussion comparable to the discussion within sociology? In other words, will new, neurologically plausible models, being considered more relevant due to their supposed proximity to "reality" or "truth," replace mathematical economics? Just as the traditional survey in empirical sociology is threatened by massive amounts of transactional data, traditional theoretical economics is challenged by a new type of empirical material. Neural data generated by neuroscientists in collaboration with psychologists and economists are increasingly accepted in publications with a bearing on economic decision making. To appreciate the meaning of this evolution, let us put this in historical perspective.

THE EMPIRICAL TRADITION IN ECONOMICS: BACKGROUND

In the first three decades of the twentieth century, economics progressively abandoned all references to the biological sciences. This was part of a larger trend in the social sciences, partly inspired by the ambition for professional status on a par with the natural sciences. Culture was seen as independent from a biologically defined human nature. Analyses of cultural behavior were to be self-referential, without the need for physical or biological foundations. This development precluded the use of natural science data. Biometrics, psychophysiological measurements, and population censuses based on biologically inspired definitions all rapidly disappeared from economics. Henceforth, data in economics would be extracted from the body politic (Ross 1991; Degler 1991; Leonard 2005).

Indeed, in the 1930s, major economic datasets were created. Keynesian-ism provided the rationale for the development of national accounting, an information system collecting data on economic variables relevant for mac-ro-policy. With the Great Depression and the transition to a war economy, it became central to the definition of an economist's job to collect, interpret, and predict figures of unemployment, inflation, or investment, all culminat-ing in the measurement of the ultimate index of economic activity: Gross Domestic Product, measurement of which started during World War II in the United States and Great Britain (Mitra-Kahn 2011).

Although data exchange between economics and biology decreased strongly, biological concepts kept percolating through economics. Follow-ing Armen Alchian's article on economic natural selection (1950), the ana-logical comparison between economic competition and natural selection provided the foundations for evolutionary economics, which eventually became a major field in heterodox economics. Pursued in a different form, this analogy also inspired Chicagoan economics, analytically developed by George Stigler (1968) in a "survival principle" in industrial economics. These were mere analogies in the sense that no correlation with biological data was implied by the economic selection models. Only the logical struc-ture of the model was explicitly transferred.

The 1970s saw the first cracks in this strict separation of social science data from biological data. In *Sociobiology: The New Synthesis*, the biologist Edward Wilson (1975) challenged evolutionary biology and social science to check their models and conclusions against the latest biological theories supported by new empirical findings. Provocatively, Wilson wrote that philosophers should revise all their conclusions on human nature, since the seat of their own mind was located in the brain—a biological organ under the influence of emotions. The controversy (the "sociobiology debate") ensuing thereaf-ter in biology and in economics and the rest of the social sciences testified to a fundamental incommensurability between natural and social sciences: data drawn from the biological body could not legitimately inform the social or the cultural sciences. Genetic fitness, the biological variable postulated by the theories of social evolution developed in *Sociobiology*, did not feature in further investigations of economic behavior. However, the debate laid the foundations for a renewed interest in applying insights from the life sciences to understanding complex social behaviors in human societies. With neuro-economics, biological (neural) data on human behavior eventually found a receptive audience in economics. A number of economists see neurological data as a potentially fatal threat to the fiction of *homo economicus*, the rational "utility maximizer" central to microeconomic theories. Neural data shows that individuals exhibit consistent biases in their choices. Humans are "hard-wired" in a manner that seems to contradict the axioms of choice taken for granted in microeconomics and seems to suggest that advances in the science of decision making will come from experimental investigations in neurobi-ology rather than from mathematical refinements of the economic models based on the assumption of rational utility maximization.

IS THERE A CRISIS, AND WHO IS AFFECTED?

The wealth of physiological data provided by functional magnetic reso-nance imaging (fMRI)—a brain imaging technology, developed in the late 1980s, that claims to allow visualization of how neural activity correlates with precise mental states (see Beaulieu 2000 for an analysis of these devel-opments)—created considerable excitement among economists.[18] Human subjects placed in a scanner can perform experiments similar to those usually conducted in a behavioral lab, such as an ultimatum game or an exercise in financial decision making, and their behavioral responses can be compared against the neural states recorded while the task is being performed. Data from such observations make it possible to supplement the verbal accounts of the subjects with an understanding of how their decisions are made at a subconscious level, beyond the reach of *post hoc* justifications by the sub-ject. This empirical connection differs from the various Darwinist or organic analogies, which previously linked economics to biology. Results produced in experimental settings by neurobiologists inform economic models by re-placing the usual normative sets of economic axioms with neurologically validated behavioral assumptions. This suggests that neuroeconomics might displace or even render irrelevant much of mainstream economic theoriz-ing. In this regard, and in response to Krugman's criticism of mathematically oriented economics, some neuroeconomists believe that they can provide new economic models based on behavioral assumptions validated by neuro-logical data. Whereas neoclassical economics postulates a chimerical utility maximizing individual, neuroeconomics would provide a "real" model of a decision maker based on the accumulation of empirical findings in cognitive neuroscience. We illustrate this with an example.

Alan Sanfey's 2003 paper "The neural basis of economic decision making in the ultimatum game" represents an empirical challenge to theoretical economics in several respects. Investigating a paradigm of behavioral game theory, it shows that even in a two-person simple game with monetary reward some participants display altruistic behavior whereas others enforce punishments (at a cost to themselves) when confronted with an unfair partner. These behaviors question the validity of neoclassical economic models based on the assumption of "the self-interested agent." The fMRI study confirms that specific brain areas are selectively activated if a certain type of behavior is displayed. For example, the rejection of an unfair offer is correlated with an activation of the anterior insula, which in previous studies had been associated with subjects experiencing feelings of disgust. This suggests that economic decision making can be associated with emotional states, and it further suggests an empirical research program in neurology concerned with interactions between emotional states and cognitive control. This would threaten the purely axiomatic study of decision making currently practiced in economics.

HOW DID THE SCIENTIFIC COMMUNITY RESPOND?

Behavioral economists, whose research programs provide psychologically rich accounts of economic decision making, are among the most vocal promoters of neuroeconomics.[19] They claim that, in addition to the psychological data gathered in behavioral experiments in labs, neurophysiological data challenge the ethereal theories of decision making developed by mainstream economics—theories built on axiomatic foundations. Psychological bias in decision making, such as framing or endowment, would have a demonstrable neural substrate, and the wiring of the brain does not allow for the perfect rationality postulated by neoclassical economists (Breiter et al. 2001; Knutson et al. 2008).

A manifesto by leading figures of behavioral economics argues that "feelings and thoughts *can* be measured directly now, because of recent breakthroughs in neuroscience," and that "if neural mechanisms do not always produce rational choice and judgment, the brain evidence has the *potential* to suggest better theory" (Camerer, Loewenstein, and Prelec 2004, 556). This challenge is fundamental. It would require economists to supplement their methodology (consisting of axiomatic representations of choice, optimization techniques, and statistical analysis) with very different methods: behavioral experiments (which have already found their place in many economics departments) and the use of animal models, brain imaging, patient studies, and neuropharmacological experiments. That economists will abandon their core competence and convert en masse to biodata-collecting methodologies is improbable, however.

A recent counter-manifesto criticized the boldest claims of neuroeconomists. The economists Faruk Gul and Wolfgang Pesendorfer wrote a long defense of economics as traditionally practiced, denying the relevance of experimental neurological data to explain economic choices:

> Economics and psychology address different questions, utilize different abstractions, and address different types of empirical evidence. Neuroscience evidence cannot refute economic models because the latter make no assumptions and draw no conclusions about the physiology of the brain. Conversely, brain science cannot revolutionize economics because the former has no vehicle for addressing the concerns of economics. We also argue that the methods of standard economics are much more flexible than it is assumed in the neuroeconomics critique and illustrate this with examples of how standard economics deals with inconsistent preferences, mistakes, and biases. (2008, 3)[20]

This argumentation for the separate and independent paths of academic fields rests on a combination of Samuelsonian and Friedmanian methodologies. According to the "revealed preference" theory, advocated by Paul Samuelson in *Foundations of Economic Analysis* (1947), economists have no concern for the psychological antecedents underlying an individual's choice. The task of economists consists of analyzing the market consequences of individual decisions to consume or produce, consequences interpretable in terms of changes in supply and demand schedules and price. In this economic framework, "utility maximization" is not a theoretical assumption that can be dismissed by scanning brains, since "the terms *utility maximization* and *choice* are synonymous" (Gul and Pesendorfer 2008, 7). In a way reminiscent of the behaviorist credo, Gul and Pesendorfer maintain that the only reasonable assumption is that individuals' observed choices are what they want most. This viewpoint precludes any refutation of such theories by neurocognitive data interpreted to disprove the assumption of maximizing behavior.

The second line of defense recalls Milton Friedman's (1953) famous proposal that models ("hypotheses") should be judged according to their fecundity and not according to the empirical validity of their assumptions. Following this line of reasoning, Gul and Pesendorfer argue that neuroeconomists are wrong-headed in their attempt to improve the validity of economic behavioral assumptions by experimental neuroscience data. Theories *are* abstractions, which implies that their merits cannot be judged on the basis of their fit with data which they were not designed to address. As long as economic theories are able to explain the relative welfare generated by different institutional arrangements, it is irrelevant how valid they are from a neurologic perspective.

WHAT ARE THE IMPLICATIONS FOR THE FIELD?

Both proponents and opponents of neuroeconomics foresee fundamental implications for economics. Yet an examination of the field and the literature in neuroeconomics suggests a much more conciliatory conclusion: that neuroeconomics seems to exemplify consilience, the "interlocking of causal explanations across disciplines" (Wilson 1998, 359). One discipline would not supersede others, rather, consilience is a state of interdisciplinarity in which disciplines evolve to become more compatible. The multiplication of neuroeconomics laboratories at major American universities suggests that this is an ongoing development. Economists are learning to collaborate in teams with psychologists and neuroscientists without renouncing their own theoretical frameworks. In these interdisciplinary teams, economists are valued for their understanding of the broad frameworks of expected utility and game theory, which introduce such concepts as Bayesian probability and strategic behavior to neuroscientists who work on models of decision making. Neuroscientists and psychologists, in their turn, provide expertise in experimental design and recording neural data associated with decisions made by subjects, while relating the theoretical variables in economic models to corresponding cognitive functions and their underlying physiological substrate. In this collaboration, a division of labor between economists and neuroscientists still exists, but they strive for theoretical and empirical coherence across disciplinary boundaries. Two examples will illustrate how neuroeconomics produces new empirical data and improves on existing biological and economic theories.

Paul Glimcher of New York University is a psychologist and neuroscientist specializing in the study of sensory perception (the visual pathway) and motor control. In the late 1990s, neuroscientists disagreed about the interpretation of the neural signals recorded in monkeys engaged in a visual task before movement was initiated. Were they signs of the monkey's *attention* to the visual cue, or did those neurons fire because of the monkey's *intention* to initiate a movement? On the basis of these experiments, neuroscientists could not decide between those competing hypotheses. Glimcher's intuition, formulated together with his postdoctoral student Michael Platt in a paper now widely credited for launching neuroeconomics, was that those neurons encoded variables related to the computational goal to be performed by the monkey. Following a Darwinian logic, Platt and Glimcher (1999) reasoned that the monkey's ultimate goal in the experiment was to maximize the juice reward. To achieve this, it is necessary for the monkey to keep track of at least two basic variables: the probability of certain visual cues to yield a reward and the amount of juice associated with a reward. Combined, these variables define the reward which the monkey can expect in the next sequence of the experiment. Manipulating these variables in the experiment confirmed that neurons localized in the region of interest fired in accordance with the reward the monkey could expect.

In this case, the economic theory of expected utility gave a meaning to the data gathered through neuroscientific experiments. More precisely, framing the problem in economic terms allowed the design of new hypotheses to account for a monkey's actions by introducing new variables (intensity and probability of reward) and a new conceptual apparatus (the theory of choice). This implies that the scenario of a clash between data from natural science and social theories might be ill-conceived. Neuroscience is an experimental science producing radically new data, which are in turn molded by theoretical frameworks. This predicts that economics might actually benefit from contact with empirical data about cognition and decision making. Glimcher's lab produced further results in this direction, using game theory to analyze neural activity in strategic decision making by monkeys and humans (Dorris and Glimcher 2004). In these new studies, innovation came less from the use of neural data to study economic choice than from the high yield of the economic theoretical framework used to interpret it: the concepts of mixed strategies and Nash equilibrium showed that random patterns of neuron firing in monkeys facing uncertain choices could be explained as an ordered and optimal response of the monkey's brain attempting to track the best available choice option.[21]

This example is concerned with biologists benefiting from theoretical insights in economics. It might remain true, as Gul and Pesendorfer have argued, that economics can expect no benefit from imaging data provided by neuroscience. A recent paper, however, provides counterarguments to this proposition.

In a paper published in *Science* in 2009, four neuroeconomists at the California Institute of Technology, Ian Krajbich, Colin Camerer, John Ledyard, and Antonio Rangel, chose to attack the free-rider problem, one of the oldest problems in economics, from a new angle. The free-rider problem is the one faced by an individual who can choose to pay or not pay his part of a collective investment, given that the investment will benefit all individuals irrespective of his contributions. (In economic terminology, the investment is a "public good"; a typical example is national defense.) In this situation, models of rational economic decision making and experimental games show that individuals tend to understate their willingness to pay. Each individual prefers to "free ride." The line of reasoning behind this is that if the others pay for the investment, the individual will benefit from it anyway. The aggregation of the individual preferences leads to the suboptimal result that the funds needed to finance the investment are not raised.

This classic negative result in public economics can be much improved by recourse to neurological monitoring of individuals during the phase in which they declare their willingness to pay, Krajbich et al. explain. The individuals' brains are scanned while they choose to contribute to the investment or not, and this data is used to detect any discrepancy between their stated willingness to contribute and their actual desire to see the investment implemented. This is not merely an expensive form of lie detection—fMRI's performance in detecting free riders is just above random. It is the threat of being detected, and the associated monetary punishment, that deters individuals from lying about their real preferences. As it turns out, the social welfare achieved in the experiment corresponds to 93 percent of the optimal outcome. Nearly all of the socially desirable investments are chosen by the participants, versus the 23 percent usually obtained in classic experimental settings. This study demonstrates that economic theorizing and economic policy making are able to capitalize on biological data. In other words, not only can neurological data be used to test a model in social science; such data also can be integrated into the existing frameworks and can yield new results.

Neuroeconomics invalidates the notion that the availability of new types of data will displace theoretical investigations and eventually render them obsolete. Datasets and theorizing do not displace each other, as in a zero-sum game. Rather, what the interdisciplinary relationship between economics and biology demonstrates is that they tend to nurture each other. What are the practical implications for economics?

Traditional education in the framework of rational decision making is in high demand in cognitive neurosciences. Competing neurological hypotheses can be tested against economic theories of utility maximization, and the axiomatic formulation of a choice theory is already used with a comparable purpose: clarifying and selecting between competing neural models in systems neuroscience (Caplin and Dean 2008). The statistical skills of econometricians, where they have a certain comparative advantage, will also probably become valuable in the testing of models of choice. Should economists rejoice, and change none of their old habits? Probably not. The eruption of data of a radically new nature, generated in unfamiliar settings by practitioners outside economics, will demand from economists that they practice their skills in an interdisciplinary way—something they are notoriously poorly trained to do.

Economics, because of its relatively advanced formalism and the united methodological front displayed by its mainstream practitioners, has often demonstrated an overbearing attitude toward other social sciences. Biology has also been described by some economists as a field in which economic "imperialism" could be exerted (Hirshleifer 1985). If the economics profession accepts the possibility that an influential (and not necessarily competing) view of individuals' choices may come from neurobiology, the eruption of new data in neurobiology may discourage the use of confrontational metaphors. The blindness of the economics profession to any data not conforming to its mathematical models has been criticized recently, and calls have been made for more pluralistic methodological teaching within the field (Denis 2009). The emergence of neuroeconomics shows that openness to currents of thought and streams of data coming from outside of economics is certainly needed.

CONCLUSION: DATA CHALLENGES TO SOCIAL THEORY?

In this chapter we have explored the implications of the emergence of radically new data sources for scholarly research. We have compared two social

science disciplines in which empirical research is seen as highly relevant to
theoretical innovation: sociology and economics. We have discussed who
has been making claims for the importance of new data sources, we have
seen how different positions in both sociology and economics have been
pitted against each other, and we have recognized areas of compromise and
blurring of boundaries between different research styles and paradigms. In
this final section, we compare the two case studies in more detail and relate
them to the more general discussion about a "fourth research paradigm,"
which is supposed to underpin the initiatives in building infrastructures for
e-science and e-research.

Perhaps our first conclusion should be that the hypothesis of the fourth
research paradigm, taken literally as proposed in much of the scientific literature, is a simplification of a much more complex reality, and that it risks
losing sight of important dimensions of scientific and scholarly work. This
holds not only for the hyperbolic claims of journalists but also for the claims
that underpin investment schemes for e-science and cloud computing infrastructures by commercial companies such as Microsoft, Amazon, and
Google. To put it bluntly: If we take into account how new data sources
have been implicated in empirical sociology and in economics, a straightforward shift from previous research paradigms to a novel "fourth paradigm"
is improbable.

However, this does not mean that the claim that there is a fourth research
paradigm is nonsensical or lacks veracity. It does represent a valid advocacy
position. Basically, it is a form of standpoint epistemology that tries to shape
the world to its ideal image. Both in sociology and in economics, data-
driven research has taken on new forms that have become highly relevant to
important areas of research. These forms do represent radical innovations in
the field, but not quite in the way envisioned by proponents of the fourth
research paradigm. Detailed study of these patterns of innovation actually
yields more interesting results than the more abstract discussion about the
future of e-research in general.

In both sociology and economics, novel data sources are exploited by
relative outsiders. Commercial counterparts to academic sociology using
powerful micro-level data sources not available to academics have emerged.
In economics, innovation has come from the participation of biologists and
neuroscientists with their neuroimaging instruments in the field of decision
theory. It is a familiar pattern in the history of science that innovation is

fostered by outsiders and by the use of novel instrumentation. Less attention usually is paid to the specific forms of resistance within established scholarly communities. These strategies are quite relevant, though, because they shape the patterns of (inter)disciplinary development that inevitably ensue when new ideas invade a discipline.

In the case of sociology, we have recognized two different forms of resistance: denial of authority and assimilation. The first is evident in the claims that commercial forms of sociology, including market analysis within large companies and freely available social networking tools developed by commercial search engines, lack sophistication and rigor. Seen from the perspective of the methodological standards of the field, this is patently true. However, it remains to be seen whether this criticism will be able to counter the argument that the traditional standards are no longer valid owing to the very large scale of the new types of transactional data. We have also noted that the field of sociology has not yet taken up the challenge of processing geographical data. Since these data have been a staple of geography and some other fields, it will be interesting to see whether new forms of interdisciplinary work on the boundaries of these fields will provide new research methodologies for sociology in general.

Assimilation is a strategy employed by those social scientists who claim that the new data sources are not so new as to require special treatment. From this position, new data should, rather, be treated in the same way as other forms of data with which the field is already familiar. This is a pincer movement: if the data are included in the field's traditional data-processing routines, the methodological standards are also upheld as still highly relevant. An example of this strategy is the claim that having more transactional data does not necessarily mean that we understand more about the role of these transactions. That would require social theory, and theory does not emerge from the data. Although we would not want to claim that theory emerges from data, neither would we want to preclude the possibility that inductive theoretical innovation can happen on the basis of data exploration. Prescriptive methodological notions are usually not very good at capturing the myriad ways in which theories and data interact in daily sociological practice.

In the case of neuroeconomics, we have seen a somewhat different pattern. Though commercial sociology has not really bothered to attack academic sociology, neuroeconomists have staged a frontal assault on the central assumptions of the field of economics in their defense of brain research as a basis for understanding economic decision making in particular and economic behavior in general. In particular, the popular notion of the rationally choosing human has been undermined by the demonstration of emotional factors, supposedly indicated by the activation of particular areas of the brain. In this case, the dominant defense strategy has been one of distancing the two domains from one another. We discussed how this was achieved in the claim that economic theory is indifferent to the neurological basis of decision making. It simply does not have anything to say about the biological basis of behavior, and it cannot be refuted by biological research results. In other words, the neuro-expertise is not disputed but is declared irrelevant. Here another approach in neuroeconomics is relevant, one more subtle than the frontal assault. As we have seen, one of the dominant research streams in neuroeconomics does not limit the validity of economic theory but extends its reach by reinterpreting neurological behavior into economic terms such as the maximizing of utility. Seen from this perspective, neural substrates are actually computing economic puzzles. This is an interesting epistemic move, since it aims to change the field of economics by extending its relevance to experiments and data that formerly were not subject to economic analysis.

To sum up, our analysis shows that traditional theories in social science are not doomed by the new data floods. Economics and sociology have a long tradition of dealing with large amounts of data and are too often portrayed as incapable, as if sociology could be reduced to Talcott Parsons' systems theory and as if economics consisted only of untested mathematical models. Both sciences actually have considerable expertise in dealing with extensive quantitative and qualitative data, as studies based on census data or the field of applied econometrics amply testify.

The history of economics in the postwar period epitomizes how social scientists' exclusive sense of identity led them to erect a strict boundary between their theories of social phenomena and (generic) data generated outside those boundaries. Many professional sociologists seem to appraise "commercially" collected transactional data in a similar way. Because those data were generated and processed outside of academia, without a theoretically guided research schema, they lack the sophistication that traditional sociology deems necessary. Not all social scientists, indeed not all sociologists, adopt such a defensive stance. For instance, management departments in business schools use their organic relationships with companies to get access to transactional data, then use those data for research in finance or marketing.

Technological innovation might be a common factor behind the emergence of extremely large new datasets in different sciences, but the specific type of data produced should also be considered. (See chapter 7 below.) Transactional data are behavioral data of a particular kind: they provide information on the choices made by individuals in relation to other individuals. Whereas traditional sociology (and economics and other social sciences, for that matter) could safely treat each observation as independent from other observations, the point of networks is precisely that modification or suppression of a data point brings changes to the rest of the dataset. Analysis of datasets has already triggered the design of a new theoretical framework of interpretation within the thriving field of social network analysis. A similar conclusion can be drawn with regard to neural data in economics: they foster the development of a behavioral type of economic theorizing in a way that contradicts the picture of a passive landscape of theories overpowered by data.

Finally, the methodological toolkit of the social sciences continues to be transformed and enriched by the eruption of new forms of data. Therefore, we can expect lively theoretical work rather than the demise of social theory. This may go together with an intricate re-drawing of boundaries between approaches within fields and between fields. Moreover, it may result in the splitting of fields (e.g., academic versus commercial sociology) or in the merging of fields (e.g., primatology and economics). Rather than the emergence of a robust fourth paradigm, we are witnessing a myriad of knowledge "patchworks," partly overlapping, and partly contradictory, which are becoming more complicated rather than less so. Having more data may or may not lead to more knowledge, but it certainly leads to a need for more theoretical constructs with which to analyze those data.

NOTES

1. The Sloan Digital Sky Survey (http://www.sdss.org/) laid the foundation for this infrastructure. Examples of publicly available results are Microsoft's World Wide Telescope (at http://www.worldwidetelescope.org) and Google Sky (at http://www.google.com).

2. For responses to Savage and Burrows, see the *European Journal of Social Theory, Sociology, Cultural Sociology*. For responses to Anderson by Kevin Kelly, Daniel Hillis, and others, see http://www.edge.org/discourse/the_end_of_theory.html.

3. Quantitative methods are concerned with attempts to quantify social phenomena and to collect and analyze numerical data. Common tools include surveys,

questionnaires, and secondary analysis of statistical data. Qualitative methods, on the other hand, are more concerned with understanding the meaning of social phenomena. Therefore, they emphasize personal experiences and interpretation over quantification. Commonly used tools include focus groups, participant observation, and the in-depth interview.

4. Particularly in the United States, the positivist tradition remains ubiquitous in sociology. The discipline's two most cited journals, the *American Journal of Sociology* and the *American Sociological Review*, primarily publish research in the positivist tradition. The *British Journal of Sociology*, in contrast, publishes primarily non-positivist articles.

5. Survey research and the collection of micro-economic and transactional data to build government and private statistical databases are the main forms of research in this tradition of empirical sociology.

6. A good example is the development of the Deutsche Universitätsstatistik, which is associated with Herman Conring and Gottfried Achenwall (Schnell et al. 1995).

7. The Chicago School's studies in urban sociology emphasized two other kinds of "empirical" research: fieldwork and ethnographic work, which remained dominant methodologies in American sociology until the 1940s (Park, Burgess, and McKenzie 1925; Thomas and Znaniecki 1920; Coulon 2004).

8. The amount of digital information created, captured, and replicated worldwide in 2007 was 2.25 × 1,021 bits—about 281 exabytes, or 281 billion gigabytes (Gantz et al. 2008). The term *transactional data* covers all sorts of records collected routinely by public and private organizations, such as the duration of a communication between two mobile phone users by their respective companies, or the kind of information collected by cookies installed on the computer of visitors to a website.

9. However, Savage and Burrows don't intend that the sample survey become obsolete. They note that in some areas it will continue to be a central research tool because of the limits of transactional data (2007, 892).

10. This also holds for ethical concerns about anonymity and confidentiality.

11. With this suggestion Savage and Burrows do not mean to sell the sociological soul to the devil of market research. Rather, they emphasize that an involvement with such technical innovations entails reflecting on the methods of such powerful commercial agents and engaging with them in "public sociology."

12. The Internet has become a heavily studied subject on its own, as various sociological conference series testify.

13. See the Social Sciences Week Blog (hosted by the Social Science Information Gateway, and ended in July of 2005), which reflects on changes triggered by technical innovations in sociology.

14. With the advent of computer-assisted survey information collection (CASIC) in the 1980s, and particularly with the expansion of Web-based surveys in the late 1990s, technology revolutionized data collection.

15. In this context, it has also been noted that an engagement with commercial sociology is difficult because market-research agencies are often reluctant to provide detailed insights into their methodological applications (Danielsson 2004).

16. The subtitle of the theme of the American Sociological Association's 100th annual meeting, held in 2005, was "Accounting for the Rising and Declining Significance of Sociology."

17. The term *Complex Systems* (CS) denotes an interdisciplinary research methodology currently in favor in the social sciences and elsewhere. CS research originated from physics and nonlinear systems some decades ago. Its models soon permeated such distant fields as economics, political science, and (more recently) sociology. In social systems, the essence of CS is the characterization of the distributed dynamics of how the interaction of many actors and variables leads to predictable phenomena, which often involve hierarchy, emergence, dynamic structures, and large-scale transitions.

18. Functional magnetic-resonance imaging is the technology often singled out in presentations of neuroeconomics, but a variety of other recording techniques are also used, among them electroencephalograms and magnetoencephalograms, cell recordings, and endocrinological measurements.

19. Daniel Kahneman, the founder of behavioral economics and a co-recipient of the Nobel Prize in Economics in 2002, was recently invited to receive a doctorate *honoris causa* from Erasmus University Rotterdam. When evoking the future of his research program, Kahneman singled out neuroeconomics as a promising venture.

20. Gul and Pesendorfer 2008 circulated as a working paper for three years before appearing in print in a volume presenting a collection of the reactions it generated (Caplin and Schotter 2008).

21. A Nash equilibrium is a state of equilibrium reached when each player knows that each other player will also play his best strategy and thus no player has any incentive left to deviate from his best strategy.

REFERENCES

Acker, Joan. 2005. Comment on Burawoy on public sociology. *Critical Sociology* 31: 327–331.

Adkins, Lisa, and Celia Lury. 2009. Introduction: What is empirical? *European Journal of Social Theory* 12 (1): 5–20.

Alchian, Armen A. 1950. Uncertainty, evolution and economic theory. *Journal of Political Economy* 58 (3): 211–221.

Anderson, Chris. 2008. The end of theory: The data deluge makes the scientific method obsolete. *Wired*, July 16.

Aronowitz, Stanley. 2005. Comments on Michael Burawoy's "The critical turn to public sociology. *Critical Sociology* 31: 333–338.

Beaulieu, Anne. 2000. *The Space inside the Skull: Digital Representations, Brain Mapping and Cognitive Neuroscience in the Decade of the Brain*. PhD diss., University of Amsterdam.

Bell, Gordon, Tony Hey, and Alex Szalay. 2009. Computer science: Beyond the data deluge. *Science* 323 (5919): 1297–1298.

Berger, Peter. 2002. What happened to sociology? *First Things (New York, N.Y.)* 126: 27–29.

Bethlehem, Jelke. 2009. The rise of survey sampling. Discussion Paper 09015, Statistics Netherlands.

Blank, Grant. 2008. Online research methods and social theory. In *The Sage Handbook of Online Research Methods*, ed. N. Fielding, R. Lee, and G. Blank. Sage.

Breiter, Hans C., Itzhak Aharon, Daniel Kahneman, Anders Dale, and Peter Shizgal. 2001. Functional imaging of neural responses to expectancy and experience of monetary gains and losses. *Neuron* 30 (2): 619–639.

Brunt, Liam. 2001. The advent of the sample survey in social sciences. *Statistician* 50 (2): 179–189.

Bulmer, Martin. 1984. *Sociological Research Methods: An Introduction*, second edition Macmillan.

Bulmer, Martin, Kevin Bales, and Kathryn Kish Sklar, eds. 1991. *The Social Survey in Historical Perspective 1880–1940*. Cambridge University Press.

Burawoy, Michael. 2004. Public sociologies: Contradictions, dilemmas and possibilities. *Social Forces* 82: 1603–1618.

Camerer, Colin, George Loewenstein, and Drazen Prelec. 2004. Neuroeconomics: Why economics needs brains. *Scandinavian Journal of Economics* 106: 555–579.

Caplin, Andrew, and Mark Dean. 2008. Dopamine, reward prediction error, and economics. *Quarterly Journal of Economics* 123 (2): 663–701.

Caplin, Andrew, and Andrew Schotter, eds. 2008. *Foundations of Positive and Normative Economics*. Oxford University Press.

Clough, Patricia. 2009. The new empiricism: Affect and social method. *European Journal of Social Theory* 12 (1): 43–61.

Cole, Stephen, ed. 2001. *What's Wrong with Sociology?* Transaction.

Comte, Auguste. 1848. *Discours sur l'ensemble du positivisme*. Mathias. Translated as *General View of Positivism* (Trubner, 1865).

Coulon, Alain. 2004. *L'Ecole de Chicago*. Que Sais-Je?

Couper, Mick. 2000. Web surveys: A review of issues and approaches. *Public Opinion Quarterly* 64: 464–481.

Crompton, Rosemary. 2008. Forty years of sociology: Some comments. *Sociology* 42 (6): 1218–1227.

Danielsson, Stig. 2004. "The propensity score and estimation in nonrandom surveys: An overview." Department of Statistics, University of Linköping; *Report no. 18 from the project Modern statistical survey methods* (available at http://www.statistics.su.se).

Degler, Carl. 1991. *In Search of Human Nature: The Decline and Revival of Darwinism in American Social Thought*. Oxford University Press.

Denis, Andy. 2009. Editorial: Pluralism in economics education. *International Review of Economics Education* 8 (2): 6–22.

Diekmann, Andreas. 2008. *Empirische Sozialforschung: Grundlagen, Methoden, Anwendungen*. Rowohlt.

Dorris, Michael, and Paul Glimcher. 2004. Activity in posterior parietal cortex is correlated with the relative subjective desirability of action. *Neuron* 44: 365–378.

Durkheim, Emile. 1895. *Les règles de la méthode sociologique*. Félix Alcan.

Esping-Anderson, Gøsta. 2000. Two societies, one sociology, and no theory. *British Journal of Sociology* 51 (1): 59–77.

Fischer, Michael, Stephen Lyon, and David Zeitlyn. 2008. The Internet and the future of social science research. In *The Sage Handbook of Online Research Methods*, ed. N. Fielding, R. Lee, and G. Blank. Sage.

Fricker, Ronald, and Matthias Schonlau. 2002. Advantages and disadvantages of Internet research surveys: Evidence from the literature. *Field Methods* 14: 347–367.

Friedman, Milton. 1953. *Essays in Positive Economics*. University of Chicago Press.

Gantz, John, Christopher Chute, Alex Manfrediz, Stephen Minton, David Reinsel, Wolfgang Schlichting, and Anna Toncheva. 2008. The Diverse and Exploding Digital Universe: An Updated Forecast of Worldwide Information Growth through 2011. IDC White Paper (available at http://www.emc.com).

Ghamari-Tabrizi, Berhooz. 2005. Can Burawoy make everyone happy? Comments on public sociology. *Critical Sociology* 31: 361–369.

Glimcher, Paul, Colin Camerer, Ernst Fehr, and Russell Poldrack. 2008. Introduction: A brief history of neuroeconomics. In *Neuroeconomics: Decision Making and the Brain*, ed. P. Glimcher, C. Camerer, E. Fehr, and R. Poldrack. Elsevier.

Gouldner, Alwin. 1970. *The Coming Crisis of Western Sociology.* Avon Books.

Gouldner, Alwin. 1979. *The Future of Intellectuals and the Rise of the New Class.* Macmillan.

Gouldner, Alwin. 1985. *Against Fragmentation: The Origins of Marxism and the Sociology of Intellectuals.* Oxford University Press.

Gray, Jim, and Alex Szalay. 2007. eScience: A transformed scientific method (available at http://www.slideshare.net).

Gul, Faruk, and Wolfgang Pesendorfer. 2008. The case for mindless economics. In *Foundations of Positive and Normative Economics*, ed. A. Caplin and A. Schotter. Oxford University Press.

Hey, Tony, Stewart Tansley, and Kristin Tolle, eds. 2009. *The Fourth Paradigm: Data-Intensive Scientific Discovery.* Microsoft Research.

Hine, Christine. 2006. Computerization movements and scientific disciplines; the reflexive potential of new technologies. In *New Infrastructures for Knowledge Production: Understanding E-Science,* ed. C. Hine. Idea Group.

Hirshleifer, Jack. 1985. The expanding domain of economics. *American Economic Review* 75 (6): 53–68.

Hollands, Robert, and Liz Stanley. 2009. Rethinking "current crisis" arguments: Gouldner and the legacy of critical sociology. *Sociological Research Online* 14 (1) (available at www.socresonline.org.uk).

Horowitz, Irving. 1993. *The Decomposition of Sociology.* Oxford University Press.

Kern, Horst. 1982. *Empirische Sozialforschung: Ursprünge, Ansätze, Entwicklungslinien.* Beck.

Knutson, Brian, G. Elliott Wimmer, Scott Rick, Nick G. Hollon, Drazen Prelec, and George Loewenstein. 2008. Neural antecedents of the endowment effect. *Neuron* 58 (5): 814–822.

Krajbich, Ian, Colin Camerer, John Ledyard, and Antonio Rangel. 2009. Using neural measures of economic value to solve the public goods free-rider problem. *Science* 326: 596–599.

Krugman, Paul. 2009. How did economists get it so wrong? *New York Times*, September 6.

Leonard, Thomas. 2005. Eugenics and economics in the Progressive Era. *Journal of Economic Perspectives* 19 (4): 207–324.

Marx, Karl. 1847. *Misère de la philosophie: Réponse à la philosophie de la misère de M. Proudhon.* A. Frank.

Merton, Robert K. 1975. Structural analysis in sociology. In *Approaches to the Study of Social Structure*, ed. P. Blau. Open Books.

Michels, Robert. 1932. Intellectuals. In *Encyclopedia of the Social Sciences*, ed. E. Seligman. Macmillan.

Mitra-Kahn, Benjamin. 2011. Redefining the Economy: A History of Economics and National Accounting. Ph.D. dissertation, City University London.

Moody, James, and Douglas White. 2003. Structural cohesion and embeddedness: A hierarchical concept of social groups. *American Sociological Review* 68 (1): 103–127.

Mundie, Craig. 2009. The way forward. In *The Fourth Paradigm: Data-Intensive Scientific Discovery*, ed. T. Hey, S. Tansley, and K. Tolle. Microsoft Research.

Osborne, Thomas, and Nikolas Rose. 1999. Do the social sciences create phenomena: The case of public opinion research. *British Journal of Sociology* 50 (3): 367–396.

Osborne, Thomas, and Nikolas Rose. 2004. Spatial phenomenonotechnics: Making space with Charles Booth and Patrick Geddes. *Society and Space* 22: 209–228.

Park, Robert, Ernest Burgess, and Roderick McKenzie, eds. 1925. *The City*. University of Chicago Press.

Platt, Michael L., and Paul W. Glimcher. 1999. Neural correlates of decision variables in parietal cortex. *Nature* 400: 233–238.

Ross, Dorothy. 1991. *The Origins of American Social Science*. Cambridge University Press.

Samuelson, Paul. 1947. *Foundations of Economic Analysis*. Harvard University Press.

Sanfey, Alan. 2003. The neural basis of economic decision making in the Ultimatum Game. *Science* 300 (5626): 1755–1758.

Savage, Mike. 2009. Contemporary sociology and the challenge of descriptive assemblage. *European Journal of Social Theory* 2 (1): 155–174.

Savage, Mike, and Roger Burrows. 2007. The coming crisis of empirical sociology. *Sociology* 41 (5): 885–899.

Savage, Mike, and Roger Burrows. 2009. Some further reflections on the coming crisis of empirical sociology. *Sociology* 43 (4): 762–772.

Schnell, Rainer, Paul Hill, and Elke Esser. 1995. *Methoden der empirischen Sozialforschung*. Oldenbourg.

Schroeder, Ralph, and Jenny Fry. 2007. Social science approaches to e-science: Framing an agenda. *Journal of Computer-Mediated Communication* 12 (2) (available at http://jcmc.indiana.edu).

Stigler, George. 1968. *The Organization of the Industry*. Irwin.

Thomas, William, and Florian Znaniecki. 1920. *The Polish Peasant in Europe and America*. University of Chicago Press.

Thrift, Nigel. 2005. *Knowing Capitalism*. Sage.

Turner, Stephen, and Jonathan Turner. 1990. *The Impossible Science: An Institutional Analysis of American Sociology*. Sage.

Urry, John. 2005. Beyond the science of society. *Sociological Research Online* 10 (2) (available at http://www.socresonline.org.uk).

Vehovar, Vasja, and Katja Manfreda. 1999. "Web surveys: Can the weighting solve the problem?" In *Proceedings of the Survey Research Methods Section, American Statistical Association* (available at http://www.amstat.org).

Westergaard, Harald. 1932. *Contributions to the History of Statistics*. King and Son.

Wilson, Edward. 1975. *Sociobiology: The New Synthesis*. Harvard University Press.

Wilson, Edward. 1998. *Consilience: The Unity of Knowledge*. Knopf.

Zald, Mayer. 1991. Sociology as a discipline: Quasi-science and quasi-humanities. *American Sociologist* 22 (3–4): 165–187.

6 BEYOND OPEN ACCESS: A FRAMEWORK FOR OPENNESS IN SCHOLARLY COMMUNICATION

CLIFFORD TATUM AND NICHOLAS W. JANKOWSKI

There is a growing mountain of research. But there is increased evidence that we are being bogged down today as specialization extends. The investigator is staggered by the findings and conclusions of thousands of other workers—conclusions which he cannot find time to grasp, much less to remember, as they appear. Yet specialization becomes increasingly necessary for progress, and the effort to bridge between disciplines is correspondingly superficial.

—Vannevar Bush (1945/1995)

Formal and informal communication practices have evolved in different ways in response to digital media. Journal publications and books have changed very little beyond creating digital versions nearly identical in structure to their print counterparts. The growing body of research on open access to scholarly publications sheds some light on scholarly communication and digital media, but with a primary focus on formally published work. This is not to suggest a misplaced focus; it does, however, point to gaps in our understanding of evolving modes of informal communication, particularly regarding the use of digital media and the new possibilities of openness that reach beyond open access.

The juxtaposition of widespread adherence to traditional publishing models (access to which typically is not open) and increased openness among informal modes of scholarly communication raises some interesting questions about emerging configurations of open science. On the one hand, academic publishing, also known as formal scholarly communication, is slow to change in response to the vast potential for using digital media to increase openness. Publication of research output is a fundamental component of scientific progress. New knowledge builds on existing knowledge, and publication of new knowledge creates possibilities for future knowledge. Publishing is important in the careers of individual researchers. Open access has been shown to increase the dissemination of new knowledge, but full adoption of it seems to have stalled. On the other hand, there are now a wide variety of openness initiatives within the realm of informal scholarly communication, including enhanced publications, repositories of draft manuscripts, repositories of linked data, open lab notebooks, academic blogs, and structured content ontologies. These projects are demonstrating new possibilities of openness related to increased transparency and improved interoperability of content. This is possible in part because the realm of informal scholarly communication is typically not included in the formal metrics of scientific impact and individual career advancement, and thus the stakes are lower. Informality can facilitate innovation and experimentation; however, it also complicates systematic analysis of whether, and in what ways, these new configurations of openness contribute to open science.

In this chapter we discuss scholarly communication in the context of e-research; thus, we foreground communication practices facilitated by digital media and the Web rather than overtly focusing on the technology itself. The particular attention to openness elevates its importance among other possible ways to examine dissemination of "virtual knowledge." To make this more explicit, the selection of openness as an object of study means that other perspectives not chosen are necessarily excluded. In our view, emerging forms of openness among informal modes of scholarly communication have enormous creative potential. Analyzing the dynamics of these emerging forms holds promise for furthering understanding of "virtual knowledge" in general and scholarly communication in particular.

Against this backdrop, we offer illustrations of both formal and informal communicative forms, focusing on emerging practices in the informal realm and recent digital publishing initiatives by academic publishers. These illustrations serve as a basis for examining the tension and flux in scholarly communication associated with dimensions of openness.

The chapter begins by situating openness and scholarly communication. This is followed by elaboration of the conceptual framework of openness afforded by digital media and the proliferation of user-generated content associated with Web 2.0 (O'Reilly 2005; Vossen and Hagemann 2007). We identify inclusivity and transparency, in addition to access, as dimensions of the *interface of openness* in a communication medium. Correspondingly, the selection of a specific communication technology or platform, and decisions made during its installation, influence the potential for openness. We identify standards, content interoperability, and levels of customization as dimensions of the *infrastructure of openness*. We present examples of innovation in formal scholarly communication for books and journal articles; we also discuss trends in informal scholarly communication. Finally, we reflect on the theoretical and practical import of these developments and suggest areas for additional empirical inquiry related to openness in scholarly communication.

SITUATING OPENNESS AND SCHOLARLY COMMUNICATION

Open-access publishing on the Internet "is demonstrating dramatic and striking gains in the circulation of knowledge" (Willinsky 2005, 29). After a long period of anemic adoption, institutions, funding agencies, and even many publishers are increasingly engaging the possibilities of open access. However, to focus on the free *availability* of academic literature on the Internet—that is, on open access (e.g., BOAI 2002)—is to miss a larger range of open practices emerging in informal venues. The proliferation of Web 2.0 participatory practices associated with the use of blogs, social networks, and wikis has helped to stimulate an appetite for increased open scholarship. In addition, many funding agencies are increasingly expressing high expectations for the development of "new forms of scientific discovery and scholarly research" associated with the affordances of digital media and networked resources (Arms and Larsen 2007, 3). However, this interest is at odds with quality control, academic rewards, and other important activities facilitated by academic publishing (Roberts 1999; Fitzpatrick 2011). In spite of increased transparency and new collaborative possibilities related to openness, formal scholarly communication remains in the decades-old state of crisis. Even as open access seems on the verge of accelerating, with rapid adoption plausible, interesting new practices and innovations in informal scholarly communication remain in relative obscurity.

While informality facilitates opportunities for open exchange, for presentation of new ideas, and for the testing of new claims, the lack of boundaries results in an expansion of what can be considered scholarly discourse, both in terms of content and in terms of contributors. Common to these informal modes of communication is the ethic and practice of openness, which on the surface is consistent with the principles of open science. Openness in science is most visible in the ethos of "communism" that prescribes "open communication of findings," a practice that benefited tremendously from early advances in print technologies (Merton 1979, 474). Such advances facilitated improvements in the accuracy of the knowledge communicated, a more secure system for protecting intellectual property rights, and vastly increased dissemination.

Paradoxically, it appears that use of digital communication media in scholarship has increased openness in such a way as to challenge these long-held principles of open science. For example, the term *radical transparency* refers to the practice of providing access not only to the content produced by contributors but also to information about the organization of the collaboration, and, crucially, to the stakes, or interests, in the collaboration. Moreover, radical transparency makes these resources visible to collaborators and stakeholders alike, as well as to competitors and often the public at large, in contrast with the traditional practice of only providing open access to the final publication. The fact that cooperative publication coexists with competition for intellectual priority points to an inherent tension within the normative structure of science. This tension is attenuated, to some degree, by "disinterestedness," another institutional norm of science, which is the distancing of personal interests or ideologies from scientific inquiry. Disinterestedness, communism of intellectual property, organized skepticism, and universalism "comprise the ethos of modern science" (Merton 1979, 270). This discussion of radical transparency is meant to illustrate an increase in the intensity of tensions created by the possibilities of both openness and closeness. Further, the notion of communal sharing of intellectual resources is often contingent upon academic rewards' having already been extracted from resources to be shared. In other words, only after new knowledge has been formally published (and rewarded), and its novelty diminished, will open access to such work be broadened.

The context within which scholarly communication functions is changing, and this is occurring in parallel to the proliferation of digital versions of materials and Web-based dissemination. Scholarship, in such an environment, goes by different labels (see chapter 1 above), but it is increasingly prevalent in the context of e-research, which is defined as "a form of scholarship conducted in a network environment utilizing Internet-based tools and involving collaboration among scholars separated by distance, often on a global scale" (Jankowski 2009, 7). Delineating the components of e-research in the form of a model is useful here in that it illustrates the relationships of informal and formal modes of communication, which are made visible in a technologically enabled research collaboration environment. Jankowski (2009) has proposed such a model, suggesting three clusters of research activities within a networked environment. (See figure 6.1.)

As with constructions of the notion "science communication" (Garvey et al. 1972), two overlapping activities are identified in figure 6.1, both

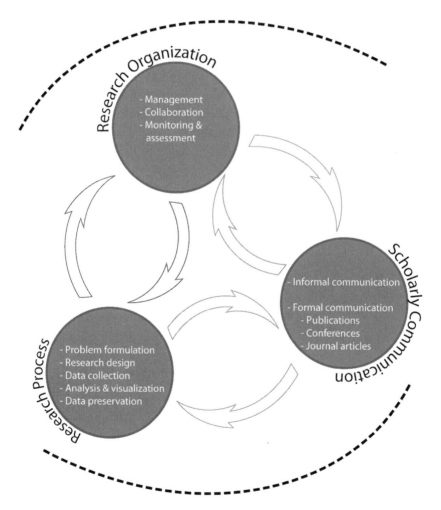

FIGURE 6.1
Components of e-Research (adapted from Jankowski 2009).

oriented toward audiences external to the research project: informal and formal communication. Traditionally, emphasis rested with, and importance was attributed to, formal communication as reflected in ISI-ranked journal articles and monographs released by established scholarly publishers. (The ISI is the Institute for Scientific Information.) These forms of publication are still prominent across the social sciences and the humanities, particularly in North America and Western Europe, and they affect institutional criteria for hiring, tenure, and promotion. This arrangement, however, has come under pressure as institutions struggle to evaluate the proliferation of academic contributions produced in an e-research context (ACLS 2006).

Changes in communication practices vary across disciplinary settings. In his historical account of science and the formation of disciplinary work, Whitley (2000) identifies mutual dependence and task uncertainty as significant for understanding variations in how knowledge is produced. Mutual dependence and task uncertainty are also useful for understanding variations in scholarly use of information and communication technologies (Fry 2006; Fry and Talja 2007). By tracing social and intellectual influences of scientific practice over the past two centuries, Whitley develops an analytical framework that locates scientific work (broadly construed to include the humanities and the social sciences) as primarily a craft that evolved in different ways associated with the particularities of cognitive objects and contextual factors. Practices clustered in relation to mutual dependence (e.g., standardized methods) and in relation to task uncertainty (e.g., the particularity of research objects) have implications for how scientific fields are organized and for how they make use of formal communication venues.

For example, Whitley (2000) claims that scientific fields with high task uncertainty often rely on social networks to interpret research findings once they are published. In a field in which ethnographic methods are used, findings are often descriptive, and data are of little use when not situated in social context. In such fields, empirically based knowledge claims are necessarily localized in a particular social context. Integral to the argument are the research approach and interpretive framework as adapted to particular circumstances. In fields with high task uncertainty, the meaning and the significance of published research results are often ambiguous without an argument to support a particular interpretation. By contrast, in fields with a high degree of standardized research methods—for example, fields with routine laboratory practices and standard raw materials—published research results are understood on the basis of the specific standards used. The validity of new knowledge is contingent upon compliance with a known set of standards.

In other words, a high degree of variability in the way research is conducted limits the potential to standardize research practices, a characteristic that influences the role of scholarly communication. According to Whitley's (2000) account, although the format of journal publication remains very similar across disciplines, the role of publication serves different strategic ends. In a field in which mutual dependence is dominant, published research is often used to establish the priority of common goals and problems, and thus to facilitate coordination of a research agenda within a field or among related fields (ibid., 269). Use of formal communication venues to address issues of strategic importance relies in part on a stable meaning for the results of research.

This is less the case where task uncertainty is dominant, as publication of research would not be readily understood on the basis of standardized practices. Where the object of research is situated in a social context, for example, formulation of problems and goals would be unlikely to find common ground on the basis of published research. Researchers in fields with uncertain and usually unstable research agendas, correspondingly, have more individual autonomy in facilitating a localized research strategy. Addressing issues of strategic importance would involve frequent negotiation and conflict (Whitley 2000, 122–7). Under these circumstances, coordination of goals, problems, and research priorities is typically facilitated through informal social networks rather than through formal publication (ibid., 122–127). These differences in the role of formal communication suggest differences in informal communication. In their explorative case study, Fry and Talja (2007) use Whitley's theory to examine disciplinary uses of digital communication media. In fields with high task uncertainty and low mutual dependence, they find that scholars use informal modes of communication, such as email lists, to coordinate research goals, problems, and priorities (ibid., 123–124).

The fact that the role of scholarly communication varies across different fields has implications for how we understand new communication practices emerging through the possibilities of openness afforded by digital media. It is important here to clarify the distinction between informal and formal modes of scholarly communication. Harley et al. (2010) find very little movement among scholars toward publication of scholarly work in online venues. In spite of the increasing utilization of e-research practices, scholars interviewed across a variety of disciplines overwhelmingly give priority to traditional publication venues when considering career advancement. From the study by Harley et al., it is apparent that the academic reward system, particularly in the United States, shows few signs of deviation from the traditional structure. Although interesting articulations of openness are occurring in the area of informal scholarly communication, most visibly within emerging e-research practices and environments associated with virtual knowledge, there is little research that identifies it as the primary object of inquiry. To address these issues, we propose an analytical framework for openness in scholarly communication. The proposal is followed by examples of openness in both informal and formal venues.

CHANGES IN THE ROLE OF SCHOLARLY COMMUNICATION

Informal scholarly communication manifests itself in a variety of structures, from organized conferences to *ad hoc* discussions. In the traditional sense, few informal modes of scholarly communication are assessed as new knowledge and thus do not substantially contribute to the allocation of academic rewards. At the same time, it is difficult to imagine science and research functioning without informal communication practices. Formal scholarly communication has four distinct functions with respect to academic reward: registering intellectual priority, certifying quality and/or validity of research, disseminating new research, and preserving the scholarly record for future use (Roosendaal and Geurts 1997; Johnson 2004). As will be discussed below, aspects of digital media are being incorporated into formal communication, but these changes are incremental and seldom exploit the social aspects commonly associated with Web 2.0 applications. With notable exceptions (some of which are presented later in this chapter), the formats of academic journals and scholarly books have remained largely unchanged, whereas in modes of informal communication practices are more readily influenced by innovations in popular use. With a limited role in the academic reward system, advances in informal scholarly communication are more closely aligned with advances in popular uses of digital media, and thus provide a site for examination of changes in scholarly communication practices.

Discussions of informal scholarly communication have appeared within studies addressing other aspects of the academic system. This is evident in science communication research (Garvey 1979) and in historical accounts of science and the emergence of academic disciplines (Whitley 2000), both of which have utility in examining the rapid growth and adoption of Web-based informal communication practices. Garvey characterizes formal communication as highly structured, its prime concern being the dissemination of knowledge, which is often "old" by the time it is available in scholarly journals. In contrast, Garvey characterizes informal communication as fluid, adaptive, and often ephemeral, where preliminary research results and new ideas are presented for feedback.

Informal communication operates much in the same way at the beginning of the twenty-first century, although adoption of Web-based communication media renders these practices more visible and, in so doing, provides a basis from which to identify both existing and new practices. For example, Garvey's (1979) original account of expected audiences points to a tension in the utilization of digital media for formal and informal scholarly communication. In academic tradition, new knowledge is first made public when it appears in academic journals. In Garvey's account, scientific communication finds its large potential audience in journal distribution, and informal communication is characterized by a small audience, intentionally limited to public presentations, face-to-face interaction, and distribution of printed-on-paper drafts (154). In comparison, a text published on an academic blog or a video uploaded to YouTube is instantly accessible, with the potential to reach a much larger audience. Whereas academic journals, even when published online, are often restricted through pay-for-access systems, content published openly on the Web is immediately accessible. One widely consulted example of academic use of social media is the YouTube video by Michael Wesch on the meaning of Web 2.0. The video "Web 2.0 . . . The Machine is Us/ing Us" (Wesch 2007) has been viewed more than 11 million times and received more than 23,000 ratings and 8,000 comments as of September 2011. Another example of informal publications by academics having achieved very large audiences is the online version of Fitzpatrick's (2011) scholarly monograph. Made available before the book's publication by the New York University Press, it was consulted more than 20,000 times by nearly 8,000 site visitors, who posted nearly 300 comments.[1]

These examples are not meant to suggest that blogs or videos create a competitive threat to journal publishers, but they do suggest radical change in potential audiences. With the aid of digital media, modes of informal scholarly communication are encountering much larger audiences, even when compared against open access to journal articles and books.

Changes in relative audience size have implications for the respective roles of scholarly communication. As Garvey (1979) notes, new findings and ideas are first presented in informal scholarly communication. Sharing insights and information on an academic blog makes them instantly accessible to the online public, and in so doing provides some degree of intellectual priority, albeit without formal assessment by peer review. However, because informal communication is both central to scholarship and still not very well defined in the literature, it is difficult to isolate. In addition to the overlapping contributions in establishing intellectual priority and to the extent that informal scholarly communication is distributed and maintained on the Web, it can also provide an archival role, thus overlapping another primary function of formal scholarly communication. Content repositories in particular serve an archive function.

Uploading draft articles to the Social Science Research Network[2] and uploading presentation slides to SlideShare[3] are two ways in which scholars are using digital media to distribute informal scholarship. Procter et al. report that a majority of scholars in the United Kingdom occasionally (45 percent) or frequently (13 percent) "use Web 2.0 in novel forms of scholarly communication" (2010a, 4043). These results are based on an expanded definition of scholarly communication that combines the informal and formal modes. Elsewhere, the same authors conclude that a significant minority of scholars "express considerable enthusiasm for change" and an understanding that "benefits may come from relatively unconstrained early dissemination and discussion of their ideas and their findings" (Procter et al. 2010b, 49). However, their enthusiasm is muted by concerns about disrupting the academic reward system and by jeopardizing formal publication opportunities.

This conflict can be understood as a tension between the benefits of establishing intellectual priority through the use of digital media and the risk of losing intellectual priority by waiting for the process of formal publication. At stake in the move to increased openness are the rewards upon which academic careers are based. Academic journals have traditionally provided the "date stamp" that establishes when new knowledge was produced. This establishes when and by whom research results, ideas, theoretical claims, and discoveries are considered new and original. Amid the transformation of scholarly communication and the rush to build new ICT infrastructures,[4] also within the academic publishing sector, the role of formal modes of scholarly communication is being complicated by increasing openness in informal modes. One example is the academic reward system, which is traditionally based on research impact (e.g., publications and citations). Though these ICT infrastructures facilitate new possibilities for open science, there is a tension between the emergence of new forms of open scholarly communication, typically within informal venues, and the academic publishing system, which continues to facilitate the allocation of academic rewards. In other words, scholarly contributions that contribute to increased openness are difficult to measure in terms of research impact in one's field. This points to the need for an increased understanding of openness in scholarly communication, particularly among the many new forms emerging from informal venues.

ANALYTICAL FRAMEWORK OF OPENNESS

Taking this evolution into account, the proposed analytical framework of openness focuses on interfaces and infrastructures of communication media. (See figure 6.2.) Specifically, the interface of openness is defined here as the point of interaction between a user and a communication medium. The interface dimensions include accessibility, inclusivity, and transparency, which collectively provide a basis for examining the practice of openness. Analysis of the interface (and its corresponding dimensions) provides a view of openness in the ways in which digital media are used with respect to their intended functions. In this framework, the infrastructure of openness is embedded in the construction and the operation of the communication venues, each of which utilizes an enabling platform. The infrastructure of openness is defined here as the possibilities enabled or constrained by the interaction among technical standards, modes of interoperability, and levels of adaptability. Although it is not universally the case, we identify scholars as the primary actors at the interface of openness, and technical experts and administrators, as well as scholars, as the primary actors involved in the infrastructure of openness.

To elaborate, the interface of openness is conceived as the place where users act upon digital media to communicate with others. Correspondingly, the possibility for openness is conceived as socio-technological infrastructure, which includes activities such as selecting, configuring, and implementing associated communication resources. By shifting the purview of openness beyond access to published articles (typically the end result of

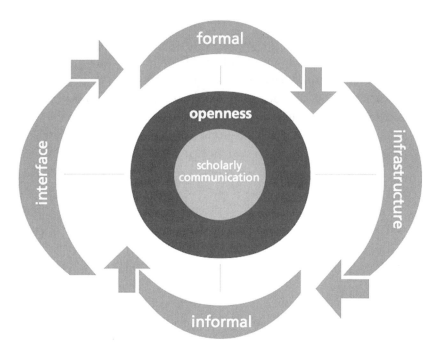

FIGURE 6.2
Diagram of Openness Framework (source: Tatum 2011).

research activity), a larger and more socially complex analytical domain is
revealed. With respect to "virtual knowledge," inclusion of the many and
diverse actors who contribute to new constructions of openness increases
the possibilities for open science embedded in the broader realm of scholarly communication—both formal and informal. As such, analytical focus
is aimed at interaction among human agency, social structure in the form
of situated practices, and material structure in the form of digital media.
Following Orlikowski, we view technology as "both an enabler of, and a
constraint on, human action" (Orlikowski 1992, 25). The conceptual framing of openness as contingent upon interface and infrastructure recognizes
the dual role of technology in facilitating both agency and structure (Virtual
Knowledge Studio 2008).

INFRASTRUCTURES OF OPENNESS
The infrastructure of openness as used here comprises standardization, interoperability, and adaptability. At a system level, the standards employed

have a significant role in shaping the possibilities of openness. We are not so much concerned with which standards are used. Rather, of interest are the ways in which selection and utilization of standards facilitate and/or constrain particular articulations of openness. The next two infrastructure dimensions, interoperability and adaptability, are understood first by establishing relevant technical standards; it is their respective orientations that have a bearing on openness. Issues of interoperability are typically concerned with inter-compatibility of technological components. Here we use the same logic, but applied to content rather than technology *per se*. Apart from whether a communication platform is in compliance with open Web standards, and thus accessible by anyone with Internet access and an active account, we measure content interoperability in terms of intertextuality among internal as well as external resources—specifically the ways in which digital content is compatible with tagging, hyperlinking, and syndication. Concepts of content intertextuality go back to Vannevar Bush's (1945/1995) "mesh of associative trails" and Ted Nelson's (1965) pioneering formulation of hypertext. (See figure 6.3; also see the discussion of Paul Otlet in chapter 3 above.) The capacity for intertextuality is fundamental to the structure of content across the Web, but these capabilities are not always similarly employed.

Technological infrastructure at universities, often vertically constructed, provides an illustrative view of the dynamics of content interoperability. A university installation may utilize proprietary or open-source software, or a combination of both, but the concerns for interoperability are typically prioritized with respect to a complete set of resources (perhaps including access to the Internet, office automation, and the latest installation of e-research infrastructures). The need to keep these resources safe and secure often requires significant and ongoing engagement. Such an effort would necessitate security standards across the campus-wide collection of resources while maintaining interoperability among them, but often at the expense of compatibility with resources outside of the collection. In a university setting, infrastructure is often the dominant consideration in enabling and constraining content interoperability.

In practice, however, the relationship between standards and interoperability can be a bit more convoluted. Standards create a shared technical language that governs how individual software and hardware components communicate with one another (Simcoe 2006, 161). Two international standards bodies, the World Wide Web Consortium and the Internet Engineering

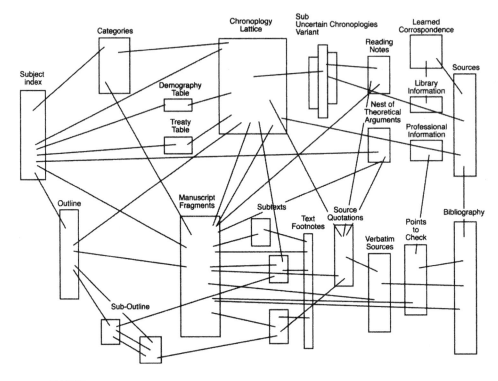

FIGURE 6.3

Nelson's notion of Evolutionary List File (ELF) applied to historiography (source: Nelson 1965, 12).

Task Force (IETF 2010), work closely together, and with others, to create and perpetuate open standards that establish "a formal set of obligations that promote fairness, responsiveness and progress" on the Internet (W3C 2010). Although the Portable Document Format is recognized as an open standard for publishing documents on the Web, its use limits interoperability. First introduced by Adobe in the early 1990s and released as an open standard in 2008,[5] the Portable Document Format provides platform independent sharing of formatted text, graphics, and images within a single document. Developed in an era when sharing documents across different operating systems was problematic, the Portable Document Format employs a rigid internal structure to prevent inadvertent changes to the document content. As a consequence, it also prevents content from being linked to at the content level of word, sentence, or image within the document.

The ways an infrastructure can be adapted for a particular context are shaped by the technical standards employed in a platform and the associated degree of content interoperability. But the potential for user interventions also contributes to how a communication medium can be adapted for particular uses. We define the adaptability dimension as the level at which customization can occur. Adaptability is conceived here as the possibility of change at three levels: that of user customization, that of community-driven process improvements and refinements, and that of institutional customization.

THE INTERFACE OF OPENNESS

Operationally, the interface of openness is defined to include the dimensions of access, inclusion, and transparency. For our analysis, accessibility is a measure of when and to what degree content is made available for distribution and consumption. Inclusivity, on the other hand, depends on the extent to which a communication venue allows others to participate. Indications of inclusivity include when users are able to add comments to published content, to edit published content, to upload new content, and to delete existing content. The transparency dimension involves the visibility of stakeholders associated with the medium, relevant processes, and organizational issues associated with operation of the platform. Most digital resources include information about the site and about its owners, its organizers, and sometimes its participants, often found at the "About" page. Information regarding processes, codes of conduct, limitations, and liabilities is found at a "Terms of Service" or "Rules" page. Indicators of interests are more complicated, and may be impossible to find from information provided in a communication medium. However, examination of the structure and organization of the technology reveals information that, when combined with published information, allows inference regarding the degree of transparency of such platforms (and their administrators). Indicators of this sort include identification of the holder of the domain name and the location of the servers. Specifically, this is the identification of who "owns" the domain name and whether the site is hosted independently, by a related or parent institution, or by a commercial service provider. Things as seemingly innocuous as the registration of the domain name or the site's host point to additional stakeholders in a particular configuration of openness.

The interface for uploading the previously discussed YouTube video (Wesch 2007) offers a range of user-selected parameters that both enable and constrain how the video can be viewed, rated, commented upon, and distributed by both its producer and its viewers. Similarly, the viewing interface enables and constrains how the video can be consumed in conjunction with the content producer's settings. Over time, common usage patterns begin to form the expected use of the medium, at the same time informing developers about future enhancements. In this way, human interaction with the YouTube interface can influence decisions made about future iterations of the infrastructure. In this case, we are interested in changes in the YouTube platform that result in changes to its interface. Orlikowski describes this cycle as an "ongoing interaction of technology with organizations [that] must be understood dialectically, as involving reciprocal causation, where the specific institutional context and the actions of knowledgeable, reflexive humans always mediate the relationship [of the interaction]" (1992, 34). Because the possibility of openness exists among many other features of a particular interface and among many other attributes of a particular technology, it is necessary to operationalize the concepts of interface and infrastructure of openness.

We illustrated the components of our openness framework in figure 6.2. We used this framework to examine openness associated with technological innovations in both formal and informal scholarly communication. We then evaluated the implications of openness with respect to the functions of scholarly communication noted above. Of particular interest are the areas where informal communication practices overlap with the traditional role of formal communication, and the intertextual structures that are co-created through the collaborative use of digital media in informal communication. The results of this analysis enabled us to make explicit the emergence of new academic practices facilitated by digital media, and to provide a framework for examining new features introduced into formal modes of scholarly communication. Identification of the interfacial and infrastructural dimensions of openness provided a comparative basis for what a particular socio-technical installation enables and how it is used.

In the next two sections we review technological advances in both formal and informal modes of scholarly communication. Journal and book publishers continue to experiment with new ways of leveraging the capabilities of digital media, but with careful consideration for their role in facilitating the academic reward system described above. In spite of some rather innovative features, the structure of journal articles and books remains very much unchanged. While access has improved and readership has increased, the benefits provided are limited to specific texts (those deemed publishable). On the other hand, there is significant change taking place among informal modes of communication where there is some overlap in establishing intellectual priority and the archival role of formal publication. More important, the increase of potential audience, the diversity of interconnected communication channels, and the creation of networked content through informal communication practices seem to expand the utility and function of scholarly communication in interesting ways. In the illustrations that follow, we show advanced features added to digital versions of academic journals and books. For informal communication examples, we select typical uses of stable technologies to illustrate the ways in which increased openness facilitates the interconnecting of communication content between and among communication venues.

FORMAL SCHOLARLY COMMUNICATION

As was mentioned earlier, the two main forms of formal scholarly communication are books and journal articles. Here we illustrate how these forms are adapting to the Internet environment. Three book examples are presented: an initiative of the University of Michigan Press, an overview of websites complementing scholarly titles, and a new variant to peer review of book manuscripts.[6] Similarly, three journal examples are presented: illustrations from open-access journals, initiatives by commercial publishers in the social sciences and the humanities, and a new journal format by a major publisher in the natural sciences.

BOOK PUBLISHING

Book publishers have experimented with a range of marketing strategies involving digital media and Web-based distribution, and sometimes in hybrid fashion. The MIT Press, for example, released Mitchell's (1996) *City of Bits* online and in print, with some degree of financial success, according to Thompson (2005, 330–331). Other MIT Press books have since been released in a similar fashion: the revised version of Rheingold's (2000) *Virtual Community*, Willinsky's (2005) *The Access Principle*, and a series of reports on digital media and learning prepared in collaboration with the MacArthur Foundation.[7] In 2007 the University of Michigan Press established "digitalculturebooks," an experimental publishing strategy that makes titles available both as files that can be read online (but not easily printed) and as conventionally bound and printed versions for purchase (Turow and Tsui 2008). Another strategy involves the construction of websites that complement print-based books. Thompson (2005) suggests several reasons publishers consider this approach and constructs a list of "added values" similar to that compiled for other media, such as electronic newspapers (Jankowski and Van Selm 2000).

Thompson (2005) argues that the most substantial change in publishing is occurring in the production and marketing divisions of the enterprise. Readers are generally unable to see such changes, but the changes cover the range of activities in publishing, from receipt of a manuscript through to publication in print or electronic form, including the establishment of a point of sale on the publisher's website. The scope and the intensity of the transformation of the publishing industry suggest that much is in flux. At the same time, the essence of scholarship —its contribution to understanding, to new knowledge, and ultimately to scientific breakthroughs—remains a craft entailing much time and intellectual investment, that is not fundamentally altered by digital innovations.

ACADEMIC JOURNALS

By and large, the role of scholarly journals is based on the publishing traditions developed within specific academic disciplines, and in the social sciences and the humanities these traditions generally place emphasis on text-based argumentation, with attention usually devoted to both theoretical issues and empirical evidence. Journal articles rely on, and are prepared according to, an accepted template, with limited attention to visualization and dynamic presentation of data, little opportunity for reader-author exchange, few internal or external hyperlinks, and almost no accessibility to research instruments and datasets. This sketch, though sweeping, outlines the dominant profile of social science and humanities journal article publishing. It is also prominent among online-only open-access periodicals in many disciplines in the humanities and the social sciences. One example of the application of this template is the *International Journal of Internet Science* (*IJIS*), which is essentially a mirror image of the style and content found in the high-status print-based periodicals in the same area of scholarship. (See figure 6.4.).

The *Journal of Computer Mediated Communication* (*JCMC*), also an online, open-access journal, exemplifies a move in the direction of increased openness though providing full texts in HTML webpages. (See figure 6.5.) Full texts are typically provided only in pdf format, which preserves the format and layout and provides some limited protection from content changes. Originally designed as a solution of cross-platform compatibility, these benefits also limit content interoperability on the Web, insofar as publishing in pdf format is meant for downloading, storing, and reading on a local computer. Content within the pdf wrapper is to some extent isolated from the Web (as was discussed earlier), which diminishes the possibility for search-engine indexing of content elements and which also limits the sort of intertextual constructions possible with HTML. Thus, publishing

Navigate

Home
Mission
Articles
Articles in Press
Book Reviews
Editors
Editorial Board
Editorial Panel
Submit Article
Subscribe
Supporters
Conferences
Contact

Editors

Ulf-Dietrich Reips
(University of Deusto, Spain and IKERBASQUE, Basque Foundation for Science)
Uwe Matzat
(Eindhoven University of Technology, NL)

Editorial Board

Michael Birnbaum
(California State University at Fullerton, USA)
Tom Buchanan
(Westminster University, UK)
Don Dillman

A peer reviewed open access journal for empirical findings, methodology, and theory of social and behavioral science concerning the Internet and its implications for individuals, social groups, organizations, and society.

Volume 4, Issue 1 (2009)

Continuous Measurement of Musically-Induced Emotion: A Web Experiment
Hauke Egermann, Frederik Nagel, Eckart Altenmüller, Reinhard Kopiez
Hanover University of Music and Drama

Abstract: The aim of this study was to determine the validity of the Internet-based ESeRNet software for the measurement of emotional music experiences by comparing the data of this study with those previously collected in a lab experiment. Participants (N = 83) listened to different music pieces online. At the same time they gave a continuous self-report about their emotional state by moving their computer-mouse in a two-dimensional emotion space and indicating chills (strong emotions accompanied by shivers down the spine or goose pimples) by clicking the mouse button. The emotional dimensions assessed were arousal and valence. Participants reported that the music pieces caused different emotional reactions that were not significantly different from the lab study using the same stimuli. Thus, the validity of this Internet-based method could be confirmed. In general, nearly all participants evaluated positively most aspects of the study — with the exception of the participation time. None of the technical parameters investigated at the participants' computers significantly affected the emotional self-report, but an influence of the self-rated concentration on arousal and chill ratings was observed. The results also show that experiments in the Web offer a promising way for emotion research and provide insights on emotions experienced when listening to music in every day life.

Keywords: Emotion, music, Web experiment, continuous rating, Internet

Download full paper

FIGURE 6.4
Screen shot of article in online-only journal (source: http://www.ijis.net).

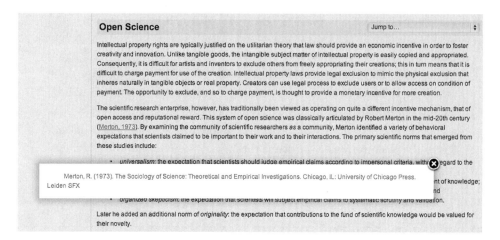

Open Science   Jump to...

Intellectual property rights are typically justified on the utilitarian theory that law should provide an economic incentive in order to foster creativity and innovation. Unlike tangible goods, the intangible subject matter of intellectual property is easily copied and appropriated. Consequently, it is difficult for artists and inventors to exclude others from freely appropriating their creations; this in turn means that it is difficult to charge payment for use of the creation. Intellectual property laws provide legal exclusion to mimic the physical exclusion that inheres naturally in tangible objects or real property. Creators can use legal process to exclude users or to allow access on condition of payment. The opportunity to exclude, and so to charge payment, is thought to provide a monetary incentive for more creation.

The scientific research enterprise, however, has traditionally been viewed as operating on quite a different incentive mechanism, that of open access and reputational reward. This system of open science was classically articulated by Robert Merton in the mid-20th century (Merton, 1973). By examining the community of scientific researchers as a community, Merton identified a variety of behavioral expectations that scientists claimed to be important to their work and to their interactions. The primary scientific norms that emerged from these studies include:

• *universalism:* the expectation that scientists should judge empirical claims according to impersonal criteria, with ⊗ egard to the

Merton, R. (1973). The Sociology of Science: Theoretical and Empirical Investigations. Chicago, IL: University of Chicago Press.   nt of knowledge;
Leiden SFX   nd

• *organized skepticism:* the expectation that scientists will subject empirical claims to systematic scrutiny and validation.

Later he added an additional norm of *originality:* the expectation that contributions to the fund of scientific knowledge would be valued for their novelty.

FIGURE 6.5

Screen shot of HTML formatted journal article (source: http://onlinelibrary.wiley .com).

content in HTML format increases content interoperability within and among journal articles published on the Web. A fundamental open Web standard, HTML facilitates hyperlinking and meta-data attributes within the full text.

In both the *IJIS* and *JCMC* examples, there is open access to articles and open Web standards are employed. However, although *JCMC* articles are available in HTML format, hyperlinking is used primarily for navigation within the text. Instead of linking directly to cited resources, hyperlinks are used to first display the full reference (see figure 6.5) and then to jump to its location in the reference list. This example shows how publishers selectively employ technological affordances in ways that limit the degree of openness. Another example of innovative use of Web features in a closed fashion is the journal *Cell*. Announced in 2009, *Cell*'s initiative was billed at its launch as "tak[ing] full advantage of online capabilities, allowing readers individualized entry points and routes through the content, while using the latest advances in visualization techniques" (Elsevier press release, July 20, 2009).[8] In practice, readers are able to begin with any section and traverse sections through embedded hyperlinks. Literature references are also hyperlinked, often making a direct path to external text locations, but access to external sources is prevented when additional subscriptions are required. (The continued presence of subscription firewalls between journal articles limits the broadening of network potential, particularly with regard to extending intertextuality beyond the individual article. Implications of intertextual hyperlinking are discussed further below.)

Cell published its first issue in the new format in January 2010. (See figures 6.6 and 6.7.) The new format directs reader attention to specific components of an article rather than an all-encompassing presentation or argument. It emphasizes visualizations and multimedia components. Internal and external hyperlinks are included, as are audio interviews with article authors. References with citation rankings are dynamically updated, and an analysis of references indicating frequency of citation is provided. Overall, the "Article of the Future" initiative suggests movement away from the traditional linear structure of the scholarly journal article to an almost postmodern conception of the article emphasizing visual, multiple modes of presentation and online dynamic updating.

There is nothing comparable to Elsevier's "Article of the Future" initiative in the social sciences or in the humanities, although there are some titles exploring incorporation of multimedia. The *International Journal of Learning and Media* (*IJLM*), launched in 2009 by the MIT Press and supported by the MacArthur Foundation, includes a contribution based on YouTube videos (Juhasz 2009), and in January of 2010 *IJLM* organized a Web-based forum discussion involving the journal's editor, two authors, and a respondent. (It is available at http://ijlm.net.) Several periodicals (among them *Journalism Studies, Television & New Media,* and *Information, Communication & Society*) have been experimenting since 2009 with podcasts and videos as supplements to journal issues, but such initiatives are present in only a few of the thousands of periodicals published in the humanities and the social sciences.

Although some observers (Hendler 2007; Whitworth and Friedman 2009) speak of an ongoing "revolution" in academic journal publishing, change of that magnitude is limited to a few scholarly periodicals. Elsewhere, change seems small, incremental, and cautious, at least in the humanities and the social sciences. Change also seems most prominent in those areas that facilitate organizational efficiency (e.g., "back office" manuscript processing) and in marketing and promotion. Though some scholars may incorporate social media into their informal communication practices, this is seldom evident in the journal articles prepared and published by these same academics.

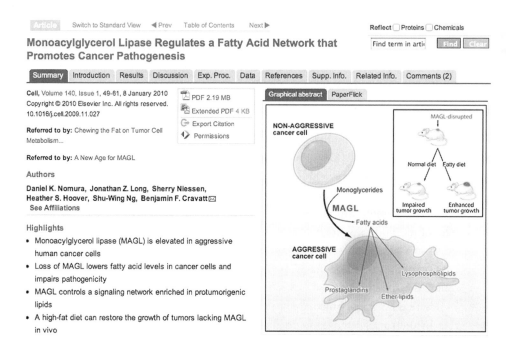

FIGURE 6.6
Screen shot of "Article of the Future," *Cell*, January 2010 (source: http://www.cell.com).

INFORMAL SCHOLARLY COMMUNICATION

Informal modes of scholarly communication are increasingly made visible through the use of digital media. This section presents examples of how informal communication practices are evolving with the use of freely available products and services on the Web. In selecting commonly used applications for illustration purposes, emergent practices that are compatible with open Web standards are foregrounded. Excluded from this selection are the kinds of commercially oriented platforms that limit interoperability either intentionally (e.g., for economic purposes) or unintentionally (e.g., as a result of specific functional needs). As will be discussed below, compliance with open Web standards facilitates the use of explicit intertextual references through hyperlinking (Mitra 1999) from one text to another across different communication platforms.

Illustrative examples include an email list used by the Association of Internet Researchers (AoIR), the incorporation of individual blogs in the

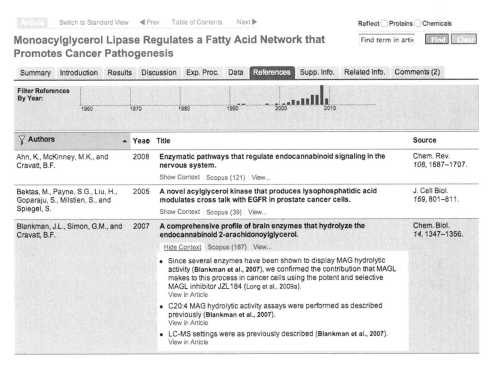

FIGURE 6.7
Screen shot of dynamic references included in "Article of the Future," *Cell*, January 2010 (source: http://www.cell.com).

websites of the Oxford Internet Institute and the Humanities, Arts, Science, and Technology Advanced Collaboratory; syndication of article updates; and the use of a keyword tag cloud by the Science Studies Network. Although contemporary communication platforms can and do include all these functions bundled into a single website, individual examination of these practices sheds light on the role of digital tools and resources in the co-construction of scholarly discourse. A hybrid example, an Enhanced Publications project, illustrates a blending of formal and informal practices.

EMAIL

Scholarly communication using email lists may be the least dynamic contribution to the structuring of scholarly discourse. Nevertheless, simplicity and ubiquity of use and low financial and administrative barriers contribute to the popularity of email lists. In addition, email lists have been shown to encourage inclusivity and equality (Kavada 2010). Common in many fields and disciplines, email lists make use of asynchronous communication in ways that can increase the diversity of topics, scale of participation, and continuity of discourse across time. However, it should be noted that reliance on email lists to ensure an informed group of participants can result in a fragmented community when both email and face-to-face meetings are required to stay informed. Inevitably, not all participants can attend all face-to-face meetings, thus potentially creating inequalities of information access (ibid.).

The Association of Internet Researchers administers an email list known as Air-L. As of 2010, it had more than 2,000 subscribers. Scientists, scholars, researchers, activists, and technologists engage in communication about societal aspects of the Internet. Participation is open but requires registration. Contributions to Air-L discussions cannot be made anonymously, but the list is not moderated. When a registered user sends something to the list, it is instantaneously distributed to all other users.

Most present-day email lists archive contributions. Air-L's archive represents nearly ten years of active engagement, which is open on the Web and can be queried with public search engines. The archive consists of HTML-coded webpages with an ordered list of links, each corresponding to an individual email. Emails are sortable by subject, date, author, or discussion thread. The resulting link structure is internally robust, providing easy navigation throughout the archive with connections to external content through active links embedded in the original email correspondence. Because each email has a unique URL, email content can be linked to as a resource and the archive itself is open to indexing by public search-engine robots. However, the content of the archive is completely static. Other than the internal link structure, its contribution to intertextuality occurs passively, if and when content is linked. Even so, linked content is likely to be findable, and in some cases eminently discoverable, owing to the influence of hyperlinking on search-engine rankings (Tatum 2005).

ACADEMIC BLOGS

Academic blogs are used in a wide range of forms. Some common examples include publication of scientific results, discussion of new ideas, and reflection about scholarly life and culture. Configurations are similarly diverse, ranging from individual blogs to a variety of network structures, such as a loose network of blogs connected through individual contributions to particular topics and a highly selective set of blogs, the content of which is aggregated and presented in a topic-specific stream. In principle, anyone with Internet access and a browser can read and comment on academic blogs. The blog format typically includes published texts presented in reverse chronological order, a place for readers to comment, a display of links to other relevant blogs, and a variety of options for navigating and consuming content. In comparison to email lists, discourse is nonlinear and unbounded, and participation is typically open to the public.

Hyperlinking is a common practice in blogging. Linking documents, collections of documents, and related audio and visual resources creates a content structure that is independent of where (that is, in which servers) the individual pieces are located across the Web (Halavais 2008, 43). This "textured connectivity" of scholarly discourse is created with hyperlinking, by either human or machine (such as databases) actors (Beaulieu and Simakova 2006). In contrast with traditional citations in printed text, the immediacy of hyperlinks facilitates the construction of intertextual discourses, which are dynamic in both production and consumption. A text published on a blog can be commented on by others, updated at a later time, and reacted to in other blogs that link back to the text. The potential for response is both immediate and enduring, something Gray et al. (2008, 114) refer to as the anticipation of "intertextual orders of meaning" that can be created by future "reader/writer contributors." The suggestion is that meaning is more fluid in the co-construction of hyperlinked discourses when the potential for new contributions can develop over time (ibid.). Consumption of hyperlinked discourses is influenced by the opportunities to follow unique paths of hyperlinks in a particular text and by the potential for additions and changes over time.

Syndication protocols, such as RSS or Atom, enable users to subscribe to content from a variety of sources, thereby creating a customized aggregation of content readable in a single location (usually by means of an RSS reader). Through aggregation techniques, a short announcement of the most recent content, often a blog post, is automatically compiled, thus enabling readers to follow the progress of multi-site interactions in a single place. These same aggregation techniques are used to present content from multiple individual voices on, for example, a single institutional website. The website of the Oxford Internet Institute[9] and that of the Humanities, Arts, Science, and Technology Advanced Collaboratory[10] (figure 6.8) are examples of institutional websites that aggregate and publish members' blog posts prominently on their respective home pages.

Being the first person to present findings or to make particular claims on a blog does not formally register intellectual priority, as would be the case in a journal publication, but it does provide a sounding board among peers. In some cases, it signals interest in a particular intellectual territory. These practices seem to serve as groundwork for later submission of manuscripts intended for publication. Ideas and findings communicated on a blog before publication in a journal establish a registration of intellectual priority, insofar as blog content on the Web has a date stamp. One of the main attributes of

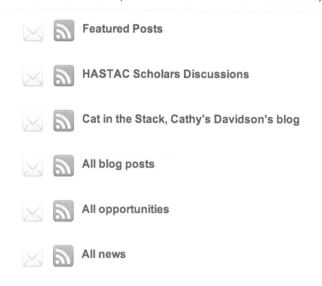

FIGURE 6.8
RSS feeds from HASTAC Humanities Collaboratory (source: http://hastac.org).

blogs (both private, password-protected blogs open only to a select group of individuals and publicly accessible blogs) is the way in which content is contextualized through intertextual hyperlinking, tagging, and aggregation.

SOCIAL TAGGING

Tagging (often referred to as *folksonomy*) is a collaborative form of indexing in which user-generated keywords and associations contribute to a co-produced organization of content. Common sites of tagging include social bookmarking (exemplified by Delicious), photo sharing (exemplified by Flickr), and blog posts. Keyword tags have a dual role: they communicate meaning and they contribute to content structure. Both producers and consumers of digital content can add keyword tags to content. Aggregation of user-generated tagging results in a bottom-up structuring, or taxonomy, of content. Thus, tagging serves to imbue individual content objects with meaning and to establish associations between content—irrespective of formal hierarchy, type, or kind—that would otherwise be imposed by a formal classification system. For example, the tags such as *1950s*, *musician*, and *Jacques Brel* can be simultaneously attributed to a blog post, a video, an image, a music collection, and a top-level website. Implications of social indexing include the abilities to add description to individual content objects, to contextualize content locally and globally, and, in doing so, to categorize these objects among other Web-based content related to each descriptor tag.

Figure 6.9 illustrates the Science Studies Network tag cloud application, which was developed to facilitate contact between researchers with similar interests. The size of individual tags is related to frequency of use. Users enter keywords describing research interests and can click keywords to locate researchers with similar interests.

ENHANCED PUBLICATIONS: A HYBRID APPROACH

The final example brings into focus contemporary tensions between the top-down structure of formal scholarly communication and the bottom-up, emergent structure of informal scholarly communication. For illustrative purposes we will use something we contributed to an enhanced publications project (Jankowski et al. 2011).

Enhancing scholarly publications involves presentation in a Web environment with interlinking of the "objects" of a document, such as data on which the publication is based, supplementary materials, post-publication

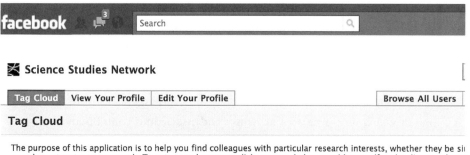

facebook Search

FIGURE 6.9
Tag cloud application developed for use on Facebook by the Science Studies
Network (source: http://apps.facebook.com).

reactions, and secondary analyses. The outcome of our project is the development of enhanced publications for traditionally published books, intended
to introduce book content into the Web environment.

As an important mode of scholarly communication, particularly in the
humanities, the academic book format has seen relatively little enhancement from the affordances of digital media, networked content, and database technologies. Rather than attempting to redefine the book format in a
digital environment, our project[11] focuses on the book in its present form.
The WordPress[12] Content Management System (CMS) is used both for its
relative ubiquity and for its ease of use. Custom plug-ins were developed to
make use of Web 2.0 participatory modes of scholarly communication in
combination with formalized content structures imposed by Semantic Web
formats. (See figure 6.10.)

The hybrid approach reveals tensions between the participatory practices common in Web 2.0 environments (practices associated with informal scholarly communication) and formalized content structures imposed by Semantic Web content ontologies typically envisioned for use with formally published content. A common Web 2.0 practice is to use hyperlinks when citing references and related resources. In this way, books are contextualized within related discourses. This sort of situating of book content actively increases its exposure on the Web through increased access within a network and through increased visibility in search-engine queries. At the same time, book content is also structured through formal object relationships defined in book/website (hybrid) ontology. Exposing book content to the burgeoning Semantic Web also increases its exposure, but in a more passive way and potentially in a more precise way. The benefit of this structure is uncertain,

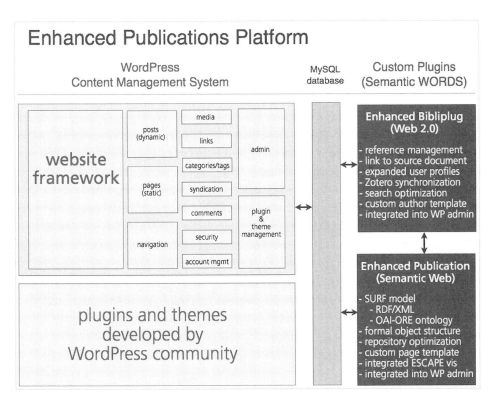

FIGURE 6.10
Semantic WORDS is a suite of plug-ins developed to facilitate Semantic Web formats for the WordPress platform (source: http://ep-books.ehumanities.nl/).

insofar as access to Semantic Web aggregation is still somewhat limited to specialized repositories and machine aggregation that adds additional layers of mediation between humans and the sought-after content. Though Semantic Web projects seem to be increasing in numbers and diversity, which presumably increases interoperability of content on the Web, the expected contribution to scholarly communication is still envisioned as a longer-term investment.

The juxtaposition of formal and informal communication with respect to the emerging practices enabled by Semantic Web and Web 2.0 provides an opportunity to reflect on normative roles within scholarly communication. Both Web 2.0 and Semantic Web provide content structures that facilitate interoperability within and among knowledge domains. Semantic Web structures are often envisioned as a way to create more precise interoperability between concepts and terms within and across knowledge domains while retaining a rigorous hold on the accumulation of new knowledge. Meanwhile, the popularity of Web 2.0 applications in academic use is associated with an evolving form of scholarly communication.

CONCLUSION

Facilitated by the use of digital media, formal and informal modes of scholarly communication have evolved in different ways. In this chapter we have discussed the incorporation of advanced features into digital versions of academic journals and books, and the ways in which increased openness facilitates the interconnecting of communication content between and among informal communication venues. Not surprisingly, formal modes of scholarly communication are slow to adopt aspects of openness beyond open access. Journals that provide a digital version of published articles tend to rely on the pdf format. Though compliant with Web standards, publishing articles in pdf format limits the possibility of intertextual linkages to the document level.

In a Web environment, a pdf document can be linked to as a downloadable document, and links in the text of a pdf document can be made active. In spite of its utility, the logic of document portability employed by the pdf is at odds with the content-interoperability logic of open Web standards. For that reason, the content within a pdf document is excluded from intertextual hyperlinking, a form of networked discourse that creates more precise associations and at the same time contributes to a structuring of domain-specific content. Experiments with online forms of academic book authorship and peer review display a much broader adoption of openness, but at the expense of certification of validity. In the book projects reviewed, open peer review was conducted in the form of comments to the book text published on a blog. The review activity was inclusive, and both the text and the comments were interoperable with linking and tagging techniques. However, it isn't clear what role the open comments may play in the printed text. If the open peer review process is used exclusively in preparation of the final version, it isn't clear what sort of academic certification and recognition the primary author and the publisher can grant.

Informal modes of communication exhibit openness in a variety of configurations. In some cases, informal communication practices also contribute to functions of formal communication. In contrast with traditional accounts of informal communication (communication characterized by smaller audiences and limited distribution), it is now common to register intellectual priority first on a blog or in a video posted online, whereas a journal article would still be locked in a procedure of blind peer review that typically takes months. Numerous Internet venues are being employed to help disseminate new research beyond the formal publication of the article itself. And to some extent, informal communication platforms, content repositories, and networked discourse preserve the scholarly record, both through the automatic date stamping of contributions and through intertextual associations created over time. Something as unsophisticated as the published archive of an email list provides a chronological account of discipline-specific debates, events, and controversies.

We do not interpret the overlap of roles as a competitive threat to the journal publishing industry. Nor do we see the diversity of open practices as somehow disrupting the normative structure of science. Rather, the openness framework stimulates interesting questions about perceptions of open science versus how scholarship is actually practiced. Scholarly communication in a digital context makes these informal practices more visible and, at the same time, gives users and developers the capacity to fine-tune the configuration of openness for each new platform. This seems particularly salient in the humanities and the social sciences, where situated practices preclude some of the more overarching visions of standardized e-science infrastructure (Wouters and Beaulieu 2006). Further empirical research is needed to determine how informal communication media are being adapted in the humanities and the social sciences.

The openness framework developed in this chapter provides an analytical lens for developing a better understanding of informal communication practice. Introduction of this framework is intended to facilitate future development of a theory of openness in scholarly communication, one that will address new questions informed by emerging scholarly practices. For example, can the concept of openness help researchers to generate useful insights about the deployment and utilization of e-science infrastructural resources for humanities and social science research? How is openness configured (or how might it be configured) to facilitate the heightened situatedness and methodological reflexivity of social science and humanities research? What is, or should be, the role of content interoperability standards in relation to e-research? In light of the dynamics discussed in this chapter, how might structure and agency, with regard to technology, be mobilized to explain the role of openness? What theoretical resources can be mobilized to strengthen the knowledge of openness in academic research? If we understand the system of scholarly communication as discursive, there is significant potential in the kinds of intertextual practices identified here as primarily in the purview of informal communication, and as primarily facilitated through the construction of interfaces and infrastructures of openness. These questions, albeit general, provide direction for exploring the potential of Web 2.0 and the Semantic Web in relation to scholarly publishing as conceived through a theory of openness.

The technological capacity envisioned by Vannevar Bush in his 1945 essay "As We May Think" is today quite common and taken for granted. Scholars often "store books, records, and communications" which can be "consulted with exceeding speed and flexibility" (Bush 1945/1995) and can be selected on the basis of association rather than only by indexing. However, the challenge noted by Bush in the passage quoted at the beginning of this chapter is still present. Aided by digital media, the volume of research produced continues to grow, and efforts to structure this content between and among disciplines lack a comprehensive understanding of the potential of openness.

NOTES

1. Detailed in Fitzpatrick's presentation at the University of Michigan in February 2010 and archived at http://deepblue.lib.umich.edu.

2. http://ssrn.com/

3. http://www.slideshare.net/

4. Investment in digital and network technologies intended to enhance research is often referred to as *cyberinfrastructure* in North America and as *e-infrastructure* in Europe. See, for example, Hey and Trefethen 2005 and the introduction to the present volume.

5. International Organization for Standardization (http://www.iso.org).

6. This section of the chapter draws from a presentation made at a research meeting of the Virtual Knowledge Studio for the Humanities and Social Sciences on January 15, 2009. The PowerPoint slides used in that presentation are available at http://www.slideshare.net.

7. As of 2012, the MIT Press has published, in collaboration with and support from the MacArthur Foundation, six book-length titles in the series Digital Media and Learning. These publications are available for sale in printed form or may be downloaded free of charge.

8. Press release (available at http://www.elsevier.com).

9. http://www.oii.ox.ac.uk/

10. http://www.hastac.org/

11. We were primary contributors to this project.

12. Plug-ins developed by WordPress and by the community are available at http://wordpress.org/.

REFERENCES

American Council of Learned Societies (ACLS). 2006. *Our Cultural Commonwealth: The Report of the American Council of Learned Societies Commission on Cyberinfrastructure for the Humanities and Social Sciences* (available at http://www.acls.org).

Arms, William, and Ronald Larsen. 2007. *The Future of Scholarly Communication: Building the Infrastructure for Cyberscholarship*. National Science Foundation & British Joint Information Systems Committee (available at http://www.sis.pitt.edu).

Beaulieu, Anne, and Elena Simakova. 2006. "Textured connectivity: An ethnographic approach to understanding the timescape of hyperlinks." *Cybermetrics, International Journal of Scientometrics, Infometrics and Bibliometrics* 10 (1) (available at http://cybermetrics.cindoc.csic.es).

BOAI. 2002. *Budapest Open Access Initiative* (available at http://www.soros.org).

Bush, Vannevar. 1995. As we may think—*Atlantic Monthly* July 1945. *Journal of Electronic Publishing* 1 (2) (available at http://quod.lib.umich.edu).

Fitzpatrick, Kathleen. 2011. *Planned Obsolescence: Publishing, Technology, and the Future of the Academy*. New York University Press.

Fry, Jenny. 2006. Scholarly research and information practices: A domain analytic approach. *Information Processing & Management* 42 (1): 299–316.

Fry, Jenny, and Sanna Talja. 2007. The intellectual and social organization of academic fields and the shaping of digital resources. *Journal of Information Science* 33 (2): 115–133.

Garvey, William D., Nan Lin, Carnot E. Nelson, and Kazuo Tomita. 1972. Research studies in patterns of scientific communication: II. The role of the national meeting in scientific and technical communication. *Information Storage and Retrieval* 8 (4): 159–169.

Garvey, William D. 1979. *Communication, the Essence of Science: Facilitating Information Exchange Among Librarians, Scientists, Engineers, and Students.* Pergamon.

Gray, Kathleen, Celia Thompson, Rosemary Clerehan, Judithe Sheard, and Margaret Hamilton. 2008. Web 2.0 authorship: Issues of referencing and citation for academic integrity. *Internet and Higher Education* 11 (2): 112–118.

Halavais, Alexander. 2008. The hyperlink as organizing principle. In *The Hyperlinked Society: Questioning Connections in the Digital Age*, ed. J. Turow and L. Tsui. University of Michigan Press.

Harley, Diane, Sophia Acord, Sarah Earl-Novell, Shannon Lawrence, and C. Judson King. 2010. *Assessing the Future Landscape of Scholarly Communication: An Exploration of Faculty Values and Needs in Seven Disciplines.* Center for Studies in Higher Education, University of California, Berkeley (available at http://escholarship.org).

Hendler, James. 2007. Reinventing academic publishing-Part 1. *IEEE Intelligent Systems* 22 (5): 2–3.

Hey, Tony, and Anne E. Trefethen. 2005. Cyberinfrastructure for e-Science. *Science* 308 (5723) (May 6): 817–821.

IETF (Internet Engineering Task Force). 2010. *The Internet Engineering Task Force* (available at http://www.ietf.org).

Jankowski, Nicholas, Clifford Tatum, Zuotian Tatum, and Andrea Scharnhorst. 2011. Enhancing Scholarly Publishing in the Humanities and Social Sciences: Innovation through Hybrid Forms of Publication. In *Public Knowledge Project (PKP) Scholarly Publishing Conference* (available at http://pkp.sfu.ca).

Jankowski, Nicholas, and Martine van Selm. 2000. Traditional news media online: An examination of added values. *Communications: European Journal of Communication Research* 25 (1): 85–102.

Jankowski, Nicholas W. 2009. The contours and challenges of e-research. In *E-Research: Transformation in Scholarly Practice*, ed. N. Jankowski. Routledge.

Johnson, Richard K. 2004. *The Future of Scholarly Communication in the Humanities: Adaptation or Transformation?* (available at http://eprints.rclis.org).

Juhasz, Alexandra. 2009. Learning the 5 lessons of YouTube: After trying to teach there, I don't believe the hype. *International Journal of Learning and Media* 1 (1) (available at http://ijlm.net).

Kavada, Anastasia. 2010. Email lists and participatory democracy in the European Social Forum. *Media Culture & Society* 32 (3): 355–372.

Merton, Robert K. (Ed. Norman W. Storer). 1979. *The Sociology of Science.* University of Chicago Press.

Mitchell, William J. 1996. *City of Bits: Space, Place, and the Infobahn.* MIT Press.

Mitra, Ananda. 1999. Characteristics of the WWW text: Tracing discursive strategies. *Journal of Computer-Mediated Communication* 5 (1) (available at http://jcmc.indiana.edu).

Nelson, Theodor. 1965. A file structure for the complex, the changing and the indeterminate. In Proceedings of 20th National Conference of Association for Computing Machinery.

O'Reilly, Ted. 2005. *What Is Web 2.0—Design Patterns and Business Models for the Next Generation of Software* (available at http://oreilly.com).

Orlikowski, Wanda. 1992. The duality of technology: Rethinking the concept of technology in organizations. *Organization Science* 3 (3): 398–427.

Procter, Rob, Robin Williams, James Stewart, Meik Poschen, Helene Snee, Alex Voss, and Marzieh Asgari-Targhi. 2010a. Adoption and use of Web 2.0 in scholarly communications. *Philosophical Transactions of the Royal Society A: Mathematical. Physical and Engineering Sciences* 368: 4039–4056.

Procter, Rob, Robin Williams, James Stewart, Meik Poschen, Helene Snee, Alex Voss, and Marzieh Asgari-Targhi. 2010b. *If You Build it, Will They Come? How Researchers Perceive and Use Web 2.0.* Research Information Network (available at http://rsta.royalsocietypublishing.org).

Rheingold, Howard. 2000. *The Virtual Community: Homesteading on the Electronic Frontier.* MIT Press.

Roberts, Peter. 1999. Scholarly publishing, peer review and the Internet. *First Monday* 4 (4) (available at http://firstmonday.org).

Roosendaal, Hans E., and Peter A. Th. M. Geurts. 1997. Forces and functions in scientific communication: An analysis of their interplay (available at http://doc.utwente.nl).

Simcoe, Timothy. 2006. Open standards and intellectual property rights. In *Open Innovation: Researching a New Paradigm*, ed. H. Chesbrough, W. Vanhaverbeke, and J. West. Oxford University Press.

Tatum, Clifford. 2005. Deconstructing Google bombs: A breach of symbolic power or just a goofy prank? *First Monday* 10 (10) (available at http://firstmonday.org).

Tatum, Clifford. 2011. Openness and the Formalization of Informal Scholarly Communication. Presented at iCS-OII 2011 symposium on A Decade in Internet Time, Oxford University.

Turow, Joseph, and Lokman Tsui, eds. 2008. *The Hyperlinked Society: Questioning Connections in the Digital Age*. University of Michigan Press.

Thompson, John B. 2005. *Books in the Digital Age: The Transformation of Academic and Higher Education Publishing in Britain and the United States*. Polity.

Virtual Knowledge Studio. 2008. Messy shapes of knowledge—STS explores informatization, new media, and academic work. In *Handbook of Science and Technology Studies*, ed. E. Hackett, O. Amsterdamska, M. Lynch, and J. Wajcman. MIT Press.

Vossen, Gottfried, and Stephan Hagemann. 2007. *Unleashing Web 2.0: From Concepts to Creativity*. Morgan Kaufmann.

W3C (World Wide Web Consortium). 2010. *The World Wide Web Consortium*. Accessed 28 April 2010 at http://www.w3.org/

Wesch, Michael. 2007. *Web 2.0 . . . The machine is us/ing us* (available at http://www.youtube.com).

Willinsky, John. 2005. *The Access Principle: The Case for Open Access to Research and Scholarship*. MIT Press.

Whitley, Richard. 2000. *The Intellectual and Social Organization of the Sciences*, second edition. Oxford University Press.

Whitworth, Brian, and Rob Friedman. 2009. Reinventing academic publishing online. Part I: Rigor, relevance and practice. *First Monday* 14 (8) (available at http://firstmonday.org).

Wouters, Paul, and Anne Beaulieu. 2006. Imagining e-science beyond computation. In *New Infrastructures for Knowledge Production: Understanding E-Science,* ed. C. Hine. Idea Group.

7 VIRTUAL KNOWLEDGE IN FAMILY HISTORY: VISIONARY TECHNOLOGIES, RESEARCH DREAMS, AND RESEARCH AGENDAS

JAN KOK AND PAUL WOUTERS

This chapter analyzes the role of technology in the shaping of research agendas in a field at the interface between the humanities and the social sciences: the history of the family. Family history emerged in the 1970s as a vibrant subfield of social history. It aspired to retrieve the history of "daily life" of the nameless masses, which had always been overlooked in traditional history. Quantification was eagerly adopted as a way to process and reveal meaningful patterns in the snippets of information on ordinary persons found in, for example, tax records, censuses, and parish records of baptisms, marriages, and funerals. The use of the computer as a database engine raised high expectations, not only by analyzing large amount of data, but also by linking across sources and providing new levels of analysis of the data. This was related to a more general move in the early 1970s toward a modernist interpretation of a possible merger of history and the social sciences: the "new history" movement (Burke 2001). In many ways, though with some interesting differences, the current hopes about the role of e-research in the humanities and the social sciences mirror these expectations. An analysis of what actually happened after these research dreams were translated into real research agendas, research projects, and research technologies is therefore relevant to current discussions about the future of e-research in the humanities.

We analyze the specific socio-technical configurations of population databases and advanced data methodologies that are used by both historians and social scientists, including geographic information systems (GIS) technologies. In sketching their histories, we not only look at the technologies; we also look at how particular expectations were inscribed in them. We also analyze how they were expected to be implemented in particular research practices. We do not aim to trace these histories in their full complexities.

Instead, we focus on the extent to which the high hopes have been realized and on what roles these hopes may have played.

In the first section, we consider the role of research dreams and information technology in the development of research programs in the humanities and the social sciences, drawing on the existing literature about promises and expectations in scientific and scholarly research (Brown and Michael 2003), about the development of research agendas as particular forms of research dreams (Shove and Wouters 2006), about research technologies (Joerges and Shinn 2001), and about styles of scientific thought (Crombie 1994; Kwa 2005). We develop a typology of research dreams, and we formulate a number of themes that, on the basis of the literature, can be expected to shape the development of scientific and scholarly fields in relation to new research instruments and programs. We also draw upon our work on research dreams (available at http://www.researchdreams.nl/), research agendas, and the development of modes and styles of research. Research dreams represent the specific form of virtual knowledge that is central to this chapter. Two aspects of virtual knowledge are particularly important: its future-oriented character and its embodiment in research infrastructures and databases. (See the introduction to this volume.)

In the second section, we describe and analyze the history of the field of family history. We describe the research projects and the technologies involved. We delineated the field on the basis of the expert knowledge of one of the authors (Kok). We inspected scholarly journals, monographs, research notes, grant proposals, and websites. In collecting our material, we focused on the introduction and evaluation of ICT-related methods and research projects in the domain of sociological family history. These methods and projects were discussed most extensively in the methodological journals *Historical Methods* and *History and Computing*, and less extensively in "research notes" in family history and social science history journals. In addition, we used the methodological chapters in several monographs in historical demography. We also used grant applications and documentation on the websites providing access to historical censuses or other population data. Finally, we included the regular assessments of the state of their discipline by leading scholars in family history and social science history. From this extensive literature search we extracted 120 documents of different types for further inspection. In selecting these documents, we used the following keywords:

quantitative history/cliometrics[1]
computers
databases
census digitization
record linkage
simulation
GIS
event history
multilevel modeling
(automated) family reconstitution
population projects.

These keywords also mark important trends and landmarks in the development of new research technologies and research dreams in the field of family history.

Apart from charting the interplay between technology and the field of family history, we also present three concrete projects or visions for which we analyzed a related text in more detail. Because of the specialization of one of the authors (Kok), the insights and selection of material was restricted to the more quantitative branches of (academic) family history. This means that qualitative family history, which is also increasingly making use of digital sources, is not covered. We also ignored interesting developments in "amateur" family history, a field in which many people are enthusiastically embracing digital genealogical collections and employing digital tools for the reconstruction of family trees. Such new sites of knowledge production are explored in chapter 1 above.

In the third section, we draw the empirical and theoretical materials together in an analysis of realized research practices in the field of family history in the light of the research dreams as they were formulated at the outset. We also try to present plausible explanations of both success and failure of the research agendas and the dreams, and discuss our conclusions in the context of the current debates about e-research in the humanities.

THE ROLE OF DREAMS IN RESEARCH

DEFINING RESEARCH DREAMS

We define a "research dream" as an elaborate discursive sketch of the future state of the field that is contingent on the presence of particular conditions.

(For example, in the case of a research grant the condition is usually that the grant be funded.) In other words, research dreams are *public dreams*, not private musings. Still, the variety of possible dream formats is considerable. This allows us to be sensitive to the different styles that various authors may tend to use when they try to call up a promising future to convince their peers or funding agencies of the seriousness and relevance of their enterprise. Indeed, this is the defining second aspect of research dreams: they are supposed to be convincing. In other words, research dreams are not merely strings of texts but are *performative*. This is related to a third characteristic of a research dream: it is a *story* in which actors perform particular actions in space and time. This enables us to draw upon narrative analysis to extract the structure of the story and the implied performative effects (Riessman 2008). The fourth aspect of research dreams is that they are *future-oriented*. Research dreams are always stories about the future—they constitute a form of plausible discipline-specific science fiction.

The future-oriented nature of research dreams can be understood with the help of the sociology of expectations as developed by scholars of science and technology (Borup et al. 2006; Brown, Rappert, and Webster 2000a). In the sociology of expectations, the issue is not whether the expectations become true or not. Expectations are not analyzed as predictions, but rather as "bids" in a discursive competition trying to shape the present as much as the future (Berkhout 2006). The analytical distinction between the representation of the future and the actual future is important in this approach. The expectation is discursive, whereas the future that actually emerges is also shaped by material practices and by interactions with other actors and institutions. As Brown and Michael (2003, 7) argue, "representations of the future are both potent resources in constituting the present and the future, but also highly unreliable—the past is littered with failed futures." This means that even failed dreams are analytically interesting because they tell us something about the present. For example, Brown and Michael argue that "breakthrough is probably our most constant and pervasive discursive method for organizing narratives about science, and yet it is also probably our most contested" (2003, 7). In general, futures are analyzed as sites of contestation (Brown, Rappert, and Webster 2000a). An important element of this type of analysis is the inclusion of the act of storytelling itself. In other words, "research dreaming" is a discursive practice which is embedded in a meta-account about past futures (Brown and Michael 2003). For example, historians of the family are usually well aware of past failures which they mobilize to strengthen the case for their particular research dream, either by drawing particular lessons from the failures or by promising to prevent comparable failures to happen. Taking this approach also allows for an analysis of the metaphors, strategies, and (in)consistencies in these stories.

Brown, Rappert, and Webster (2000b) and Wilkie and Michael (2009) distinguish four themes in the sociology of expectations that can help us understand how sociotechnical expectations about the future are constructed and contested. The first concerns how agency is attributed to actors or technological devices. The second relates to the teleological nature of the expectation: to what extent is the future presented as determined by the technology or by its social configuration? The third theme is the role of uncertainties with respect to the future and how these are managed within the future as presented. The fourth theme is called *orchestration*: "What kind of future 'spaces' and 'moments' are opened up or closed down by those actors actively involved in demarcating and furnishing the future?" (Wilkie and Michael 2009, 507). The sociology of expectations pays attention not only to the rhetorical nature of presentations of futures as sites of contestation, but also to the material forms of these presentations.

This last point is particularly relevant to the analysis of research dreams because they come in such a wide variety. A research dream in an article reviewing the current state of affairs in the field of family history has a different form and a different audience than a research grant, and both are different again from a personal memoir written by an editor. In order to be able to draw on the sociology of expectations in science and technology, we need to tease out these different forms. In other words, we need to pay attention to the rhetorical structure, the implicit motifs and metaphors, and the ways in which the relevant dream did or did not circulate within and outside of the field.

HOW TO ANALYZE A RESEARCH DREAM?

The tradition of narrative analysis has developed methods and tools for performing such analyses. *Narrative analysis* refers to a family of methods for interpreting texts that have a story form and pay particular attention to sequences of action:

Narrative analysts interrogate intention and language—*how* and *why* incidents are storied, not simply the content to which language refers. For *whom* was this story constructed, and for what purpose? Why is the succession of events configured that way? What cultural resources does the story draw on, or take for granted? What storehouse of plots does it call up? What does the story accomplish? Are there gaps and inconsistencies that might suggest preferred, alternative, or counter-narratives? (Riessman 2008)

We use two modes of narrative analysis to develop a typology of research dreams in the field of family history: *thematic analysis*, which focuses on the implied meaning of the text, and *structural analysis*, which pays attention to the plot structure and the performative nature of the text.

Our thematic analysis consists of description, comparison, and evaluation of trends in quantitative family history. Thus, we pay attention to the introduction of computers, to the wave of digitization and data processing, to the establishment of databases, to the specific form of census digitization, to the problem of record linkage and automated family reconstitution, to the use of modeling and simulation, to the use of visual tools such as GIS, to the orientation toward event history and multilevel modeling, and to population projects. Partly, these topics rely on each other and form part of one trajectory; partly, they also form parallel trajectories only occasionally related to each other. We will use the concept of a cycle of innovation to describe this non-linear and loop-rich development.

For the structural analysis, we apply the characterization of prospecting the future proposed by Michael (2000). Michael is concerned with characterizing the ways in which the future is represented in accounts which are performed in the present. He has developed a schema of dichotomies: distal/proximal distance from the present, individual/collective subjectivity, substantive/instrumental rationality, positive/negative valency, and slow/fast speed. Michael also characterizes the plot structure of future representations that may be relevant to the analysis of research dreams:

To enunciate a research question, to formulate a research programme, to outline a prospective technological system, to posit the coordination of industry, government and university sectors in the pursuit of "sound technoscience"—all these entail statements made (or rather performed) in the present that draw (on) the past and the future. That is to say, there is a "fabrication" of past and future that make these enunciations, formulations, outlines and positings seem eminently sensible and doable. Thus, the past is represented as entailing some problem (e.g. the chaotic state of science policy), some absence (e.g. the lack of transplantable human organs), some wrong (e.g. environmental degradation), and the future is represented as the "place" where solutions are realized, presences manifested, and wrongs righted. (2000, 22)

Another approach to characterizing the plot structure of historical accounts was developed by the American historian Hayden White, who, borrowing from linguistic theory, proposed that writing history is itself based on a particular plot structure (White 1973). White distinguishes four different kind of emplotments, each based on a different poetic structure or trope: tragedy, romance, comedy, and satire. In tragedy, fate unfolds irrespective of the activities of the actors and often against their best intentions. Comedy is based on happy endings in which contradictions are resolved harmoniously. Romance depicts the development of the hero's character and his or her victory over evil forces after numerous trials and tribulations. Satire emphasizes the meaninglessness of change and undermines itself by refusing to resolve its contradictions (contrary to tragedy and romance). White's central idea is that history writing inevitably falls into one of these four forms of emplotment (which we inherited from the nineteenth century), and that in this sense "progress" in history writing does not exist. No matter how many data are collected, in the end history is shaped by the historian's choice of a particular plot.

RESEARCH DREAMS AND RESEARCH PRACTICES

We are not only interested in the "fine structure" of individual research dreams; we also wish to tease out the dynamics of the interaction between research dreams and research practices, which may give rise to new research dreams and (partly) changed practices. In other words, we are also interested in the relationship between the fine structure of research dreams and their roles in research practices. Rather than studying one particular representation of the future in detail, we are interested in the characteristics of the process of "research dreaming" as both a discursive and a material practice. We expect this to give us a better understanding of the interplay between promise and practice in the creation of new forms of (digital) human sciences. Van Lente (2000) has traced the transformation from promise to requirement in a case study of the history of High Definition Television. He draws the conclusion that the ideograph of technological progress functions as a yardstick for the present and a signpost for the future: "Thus, what starts as an *option* can be labeled as a technical *promise*, and may subsequently function as a *requirement* to be achieved, and a *necessity* for technologists to work on, and for others to support." (60) Van Lente and Rip (1998) propose that the historical development of research dreams can be analyzed as the entwinement of successive loops of a "promise-requirement cycle." (See figure 7.1.)

The promise-requirement cycle can also be used to explain failures of expectations, for example those that turn out to have been too optimistic:

From this perspective, the reason for these too optimistic initial promises and expectations is *not* that forecasters or futurists are ignorant or short-sighted. Instead, promises are strategic resources in promise-requirement cycles. Initial promises are set high in order to attract attention from (financial) sponsors, to stimulate agenda-setting processes (both technical and political) and to build "protected spaces." Promises thus

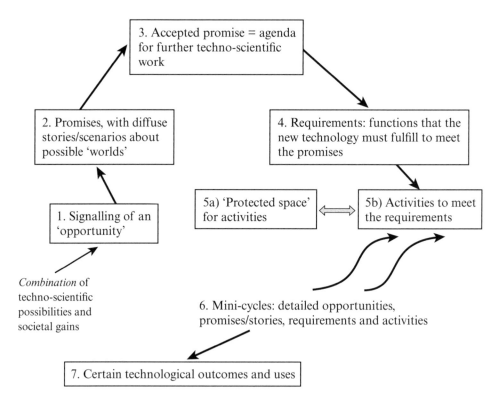

FIGURE 7.1
The cycle of promise. Adapted from van Lente and Rip 1998.

play a role in the social processes that are part of technological development. (van Lente and Rip 1998, 150)

This goes together with a "revisionist attitude"—past expectations are often rationalized in the light of the new present:

More usually, these revisionist histories tend to forget or silence complexity and contingency, transforming a resultant technology into a hero of its own making. Similarly, past disappointments tend to be rationalized such that they present a reduced threat to new and successive expectations. That is, past failures are often isolated as special or peculiar cases with little technically or organizationally in common with the newly proposed promissory solution. (Borup et al. 2006)

The public nature of expectations about the future also means that they are cultural resources for communities that influence one another. Past research dreams affect present and future dreams.

In this chapter, we adopt the sociology of expectations approach to analyze technology-inspired research dreaming in a particular field of history. We examine how promises about the research possibilities offered by computing were received in the field and what kind of dynamics they set in motion. We make use of the notion of the promise-requirement cycle. However, we are equally interested in the narrative style in which these promises were presented. For three representative cases we selected typical texts, which we discuss in boxes. In analyzing their narrative content, we make use of both Michael's typology and White's typology.

DREAMS AND PRACTICES OF COMPUTATIONAL FAMILY HISTORY

FAMILY HISTORY, POPULATION HISTORY, SOCIAL SCIENCE HISTORY

A relative latecomer to the "new history" movement of the early 1970s, family history soon became a lively sub-discipline, with many practitioners publishing in the *Journal of Family History* and (beginning in 1996) in *The History of the Family: An International Quarterly* and also in journals dedicated to (historical) demography, social history, and women's history. From the outset, family history was characterized by two very different approaches (Tilly and Cohen 1982). One used methods and sources characteristic of traditional historiography to disclose "sentiments" and expectations regarding roles and relationships within the family. The other focused on using quantitative methods to gain insight into structures and processes related to the family. Details found in old census manuscripts were categorized and aggregated for the purpose of studying variations and long-term changes in household size and composition. Parish records of marriages, baptisms, and funerals were used to reconstitute families and to aggregate their histories into marriage, fertility, and mortality rates.

In this section, we focus on the research agendas, the data needs, and the results of the latter approach, quantitative family history, which we treat as essentially coterminous with historical demography and population history. Population history focuses generally on larger aggregates than family history, which is dedicated to understanding how the micro level of individuals and families responded to and shaped—through their reactions and strategies—larger social structures and processes (Hareven 1987). Historical demography/quantitative family history can be considered as part of "social science history." Although not found in academic curricula, social science history can be considered an "interdiscipline" with a journal (*Social Science History*), an association (Social Science History Association), and international conferences (annually in the United States, biannually in Europe). Members of the association come mainly from history, sociology, economy, political studies, and anthropology. Practitioners of social science history are dedicated to applying theories from the social sciences to historical topics and to using formal methods of hypothesis testing (Kousser 1977; Baker 1999). These methods generally include quantitative ones; in that sense, social science history is one of the last strongholds of "cliometrics," or quantitative history,[2] which lost its popularity among historians at large in the early 1980s (Reynolds 1998; Wetherell 1999).

Family historians and social science historians were early and avid users of information and communication technologies. "The computer" promised to assist with calculating, with the storing of research material, with automatic record linkage, and with visualization of data. How were these expectations translated into agendas for infrastructures and research? How did ICT-inspired projects affect the field of family history and social science history at large, and what kind of research dynamics did they engender? Did they lead to new research questions, and did these new questions lead to technical innovation? How was this "new knowledge" received in the field of history at large? To what extent was the decline of "cliometrics" associated with disappointed expectations regarding ICT innovations? Although we focus on family and population history, we put our analysis within the broader context of the development and reception of social science history.

CREATING LARGE MICRO-DATASETS FOR RESEARCH

Quantitative family history and historical demography came into being in the 1950s when a Frenchman named Louis Henry devised the method of using parish records to reconstitute families. The method was extremely time-consuming. (See Rosental 2003.) Soon, however, computers began to be used to store and process the large amounts of data involved in population history projects. In one of the first projects to use computers for these purposes, in 1966, the Department of Demography at the Université de Montréal attempted to link all the data on the entire French population of the St. Lawrence Valley in the seventeenth and eighteenth centuries taken from the nominal censuses. In 1975 it was reported that "the manna gathered in the presbyteries is still feeding our computers." The researchers were aiming to publish a monograph on the parish of Quebec from 1621 to 1716 and were quite vague about their future research ideas: "other investigations . . . will always be possible; for example, a study of first names, places of residence, the importance of signatures, or a study of the household at various censuses" (Légaré et al. 1975, 7). However, in the final section of the project's report we find two arguments that recur in similar introductions to large historical demography projects. First, the reconstituted historical population is portrayed as a "laboratory" in which demographers can study universal social processes. Second, it is envisaged that historians and demographers will learn from one another's techniques and research strategies, and that the database exemplifies "mutually beneficially interdisciplinary collaboration" (ibid., 7). A second noteworthy forerunner was the Demographic Database at Umea University in Sweden, which reconstituted the populations of several northern Swedish regions from the seventeenth century on. The database (http://www.ddb.umu.se) is still being expanded and is widely used. In contrast with the two first examples, the project of Jacques Dupâquier and Denis Kessler at the Ecole des Hautes Etudes en Sciences Sociales in Paris used a sample method, seeking to collect all data pertaining to 3,000 French families whose surnames started with the letters Tra from nineteenth- and twentieth-century parish and tax records (Dupâquier and Kessler 1992). The aim was to study structural transformation in French society (e.g., by studying changed occupations) and the effects of economic and political crises on family life. The database has not been completed, but its material has been used for a number of studies.[3]

These large databases, and the numerous others that were constructed in the late 1980s and the 1990s (for overviews, see Thorvaldsen 1998; Hall et al. 2000; Dillon and Roberts 2006), can be seen as a second round in a cycle of database creation. Their initiators responded to criticism leveled at the way the early cliometricians had handled historical information. According to the critics, the cliometricians, in "transforming data into categories that computers can analyze" (Fitch 1984, 240), had squandered the original information in the historical sources: they had, when working in teams, induced arbitrary categorization (e.g., of occupations), and they had stored the data in such a way that the analyses could not be repeated (Stone 1979). Thus, the new databases tried to process the data in such a way that as much of the original information as possible was retained, adding the codes that would ease statistical handling as extra variables. Furthermore, the appearance of arbitrariness in categorization was reduced through extensive documentation of what classification had been used, e.g., on household typology or historical occupations. With respect to the latter, more and more databases now offer the standardized code for historical occupations HISCO (Van Leeuwen, Maas, and Miles 2002).

Creating a large historical database with microdata is time-consuming and thus costly in nearly all cases. In the research agendas that accompanied the grant proposals, the project leaders sought to justify the costs by suggesting diverse fields of research that could be pursued only through their project. In most of these agendas we find common themes reiterated, with some variation depending on the disciplinary affiliation of the team's principal members and the sources available for digitization. In various projects, the discourse of the population "laboratory" was pursued, but obviously newly emerging projects had to indicate why their design offered a better or at least a new angle on the universal human processes to be uncovered. This implies that in creating a project's research dream it was necessary to take the agendas of other projects into account. These other projects' claims of universality needed to be contested in order to create a niche for the new project without disqualifying the competitors' scientific credibility. Thus, the Historical Sample of the Netherlands (begun in 1989), which endeavors to reconstruct the life histories of 80,000 randomly sampled individuals born between 1811 and 1922, emphasizes its uniqueness by stating that it alone has complete information on migratory moves in the Netherlands, and thus does not suffer from the loss of observation which often severely limits the use of data assembled in villages or small regions. (See the box on *Dreaming of new techniques for migration history* below.) Moreover, the database designers promise perfect conditions for studying the effects of religious diversity as well as the interplay of geographic mobility with social mobility, fertility. and mortality (Mandemakers 2001, 2006). Likewise, a large database with reconstructed life histories in Flanders found a niche through a different data design from the Dutch one. Here, entire families comprising several generations were traced in their geographic moves, their careers, and their family formation. This design offers the possibility of adding a kinship perspective to behavioral patterns (Matthijs and Moreels 2010). A final example of a special niche is a database constructed from the detailed records of Tasmanian convicts. The "paper Panopticon" created by the penal authorities makes it possible to "follow the convicts in sickness and health, and even into the outer reaches of madness. We can reconstruct the families and the life experiences they left behind" (Bradley et al. 2010).

A common theme in project proposals for large databases is the "data gap." Although historical databases often cover extended periods, adding earlier or later periods is considered necessary to chart the fundamental historical processes of the country in question. For instance, the current extension to the present of the Scanian Database at Lund University, which has complete information on the inhabitants of nine parishes in the Swedish province of Scania in the period 1646–1895, claims to remedy the "true lacuna of knowledge about the most fundamental processes in the making of the modern family, and society" (Bengtsson et al. 2005). Because microdata pertaining to the twentieth century are hard to come by, this project promises to study the backgrounds of the long-term fertility decline, and to disclose early-life-course experiences related to the often ill-understood demographic choices made by contemporary individuals. Because people from the same villages are studied, it is possible to develop an intergenerational perspective in the research. In a similar vein, the Canadian Century Research Infrastructure (see box) aims to create microdata files with samples from censuses conducted between 1911 and 1951 for the purpose of finding out how Canada had so quickly turned into a highly urbanized and industrialized country in that period:

What are the social, economic, demographic, cultural, and political changes that explain Canada's profound transformations during the twentieth century? To what extent have these changes varied across the land and among different individuals and groups? And how do these changes in Canada compare with, and relate to, developments in other countries around the world? (Gaffield 2007, 55)

Typically, the research vision does not rely on just one research topic, however broadly conceived. It is expected that the project will encourage interdisciplinary projects, and that it will attract new kinds of users (e.g., "media scholars will be able to contribute to our understanding of the history of communications by focusing on the question posed in the 1931 census that asked if each household had a radio"). Finally, and quite typically, Gaffield suggests that the new infrastructure will engender entirely new research questions: "even more important, the CCRI will raise questions about the making of twentieth-century Canada that we have not yet even imagined" (63).

CENSUS MANUSCRIPTS

Census manuscripts form the basis of some very large and successful projects, of which the most noteworthy is IPUMS (which stands for Integrated Public Use Microdata Series). This project of the Minnesota Population Center standardized the so-called public use 1 percent samples of the US censuses, enriched them with standardized codes, and created an interface that enabled researchers to download entire datasets or selected variables, and to use mapping facilities (Ruggles and Menard 1990; Sobek and Ruggles 1999; Ruggles et al. 2003). And in a project called IPUMS International, the Minnesota Population Center harmonized the available census samples from many countries from the second half of the twentieth century, retaining their original content. The latter project has a bold vision:

We can look forward to a harmonized database with hundreds of millions of records representing the majority of the world's population. It will not only open new opportunities for comparative cross-national research, but it will also provide researchers in many countries with research tools more powerful than they have ever had before. (Ruggles et al. 2003, 65)

Thus, IPUMS offers standardized and easily accessible census samples from all over the world. What can new census projects offer? The North Atlantic Population Project (another project of the Minnesota Population Center) aims at complete digitization of the late-nineteenth-century census

Dreaming the Canadian Century Research Infrastructure (Gaffield 2007)

In this project the past is represented as entailing the problem of a conflict in the field: the struggle between researchers using the census data as a solid base for making statements about historical reality and more "postmodern" researchers critiquing these census surveys as power moves by the elites. These two approaches had been interpreted as mutually exclusive in the discipline. Yet the project claims it can combine both and thereby bring a new consensus to the field. This is done by seeing both the questioner and the respondent as "authors" of the historical documents produced by the Canadian censuses. The future is represented as the "place" where solutions are realized by the potential of the new research infrastructure to bring these opposing perspectives together in a productive union. Questioning the question therefore no longer invalidates the data produced by the census. It has now become an additional source of data, potentially even strengthening the interpretation of the census data themselves. Technically, this leads to a method of analyzing "multi-authored" documents, a very feasible project indeed. This will only make the project more attractive: "The fact that a continuing debate is often framed in the dichotomous terms of quantitative/qualitative or realist/constructivist helps explain why the CCRI aims to attract those researchers who are paying increasing attention to the importance of situating documents (e.g. census enumerations) in larger social, economic, cultural, and political contexts." (Gaffield 2007, 62) In terms of Michael's (2000) schema, the future is posited as close to the present in time, as carried by collective subjectivities (bringing groups together), and as an unambiguous positive valency (the conflict is posited as a negative situation for the field). There are no specific referents to speed, but this may point to an expectation that the resolution brought about by the new infrastructure works instantaneously. To sum up, this project description has a plot structure of "comedy" in White's typology (1973), because it brings salvation and dissolves antagonisms.

---

manuscripts of several countries in the North Atlantic region. Its design allows study of minority groups, such as the indigenous populations of Norway and Canada. Also, communities can now be studied in their integrity. Since data on entire populations are available, extensive linkages across census can be undertaken, entire life histories can be reconstructed, and contextual variables (e.g., occupational structure of the localities) can be used to further enrich the analysis of behavioral patterns. In short, the project promises a data-rich and comparative approach to topics such as industrialization, fertility transition, and migration (Roberts et al. 2003).

Either in the form of a sample or in the form of data on entire populations, every historical database and all intended users were faced with the
unusual specter of a "data flood" and confronted by the challenge to find
meaningful patterns in the mass of data. All of them were facing the problem
of reworking those patterns into convincing historical narratives.

A CYCLE OF DATA-HANDLING TECHNIQUES

In addition to unprecedented facilities for storing data on historical populations, the computer offered powerful support to those seeking to quantitatively unearth and understand the patterns in the behavior of those populations.
There was an expectation that family history could now move away from
the necessarily impressionistic study of historical texts, which were, almost
by definition, reflections of the lives and worldviews of the elite. Looking
back on more than thirty years of ICT-enabled methodology, we can dis-
cern the promise-requirement cycle we introduced in the previous section.
Methods were, obviously, geared to data, and evolved as the quality, scope,
and accessibility of data improved. This was not a linear process; often data-
collection strategies changed in response to disappointing results and/or budget constraints. In trying to make sense of the often very scant information on
individuals available, historians tried out different techniques that, however,
repeatedly brought them derision from qualitative historians and from social
scientists. The efforts of "cliometrics" were disqualified as "ugly" history by
historians, and their use of statistics was seen as amateuristic by social scientists.
Over the course of years the statistical methods improved considerably, but
social science history became more and more entrenched in the camp of social
scientists and more and more distanced from the humanities.

The early users of computers in family history were particularly enthusiastic about automatic record linkage. By using algorithms that compared
(variations of) names, people could be linked across parish and tax or criminal
records, across sources in different localities, and across the decennial censuses.
There was intense discussion of the appropriate methods, especially in the
1970s (e.g., Skolnick 1971; Katz and Tiller 1972; Kelly 1974; Guth 1976).
However, the technique soon reached its limits, and it became clear that
expectations had been raised too high. Myron Gutmann berated the "sentiment" that "record linkage will solve all historical problems" as "a sentiment
that led to a large number of ill-planned and improperly completed disserta-
tions, and even to badly-put together work by senior scholars who should

have known better" (1977, 155). Improving automated record linkage was no solution; the technique was too expensive, and new projects in this direction were not likely to be funded. We see here a second cycle starting, turning away from "wide speculations to more practically oriented assessments" (Geels and Smit 2000, 881). Thus, Gutmann admonished his peers to turn away from record linkage and to think of alternative research strategies. The solution could lie in better sources with already linked data, such as published genealogies or population registers (see below). Or one could minimize linkage problems by using a surname letter sample (a solution adopted by the Tra project in France) or a sample in a base population to be traced in other sources (a solution adopted by the Historical Sample of the Netherlands).

A number of family historians worked with original census documents containing rich information on the occupations, ages, and family relations of people within households. However, when it came to interpreting the meaning of the co-residence patterns the researchers ran into difficulties because it was not known how large the potential pool of relatives was. For instance, did one find so few co-residences of adults with their elderly parents because those parents were already deceased, or because the parents could choose among many surviving children, or because the cultural preference was to live in a small, "nuclear" family? Thus, to understand the actual findings one had to know the range of potential outcomes given rates of fertility and mortality. If actual findings deviated from that range, one might claim to have found norms prescribing avoidance of co-residence with kin. For this reason, household historians from the Cambridge Group for the History of Population and Social Structure began to experiment with computer simulations. The reminiscences of the project's participants offer interesting insight into a "mini" promise-requirement cycle and the vague but "grandiose" plans that set it in motion. In June of 1971, Eugene Hammel, Kenneth Wachter, and Peter Laslett embarked on a limited project (expected to take a few months at most) to design a Monte Carlo simulation that could predict household composition: "What could be simpler. . . . Simulations always look straightforward on paper." Once the computer work was done, "the chief labour would . . . be the reconceptualization of hypotheses" (Wachter and Hammel 1986, 392). However, it proved extremely difficult to come up with realistic demographic rates. The process of fine-tuning took years. "What was the computer simulation project? A mix of grandiose plans and endlessly petty details." (ibid., 400) In the meantime, the participants faced computer problems as well as the skepticism of established historians. ("It's all bunk," the historian George Homans exclaimed during a seminar.) Moreover, the simulations required a new round of empirical data gathering. In the end, the project resulted in an influential, but not undisputed, reinterpretation of English household history (Wachter et al. 1978; see also Ruggles 1986; Ruggles 1987; Smith 1989; King 1990). Eventually, the experts themselves began to doubt the usability of the method. Simulation designers had ignored migration and overlooked the fact that demographic behavior is transmitted across generations and clustered within families, making it nearly impossible to predict the range of demographic outcomes (Schofield 1985; Ruggles 1993). However, the majority of family historians had always mistrusted simulations. "Historians," Nancy Fitch commented, "find it difficult to believe that something almost wholly made up, like the fictitious population generated by a set of microsimulation computer runs, could yield better information about a historical process than a 'real' historical document." (1980, 128)

Around 1980, criticism of historians' use of quantitative methods intensified. Quantitative history was attacked for its lack of compelling research questions (Judt 1979), and influential historians pleaded for a return to cultural studies and to the narrative (Stone 1979). Conversely, social scientists pointed out that the results of quantitative history were meager at best. The reconstituted local populations were often small, not allowing for significance tests. Moreover, historians tended to compare means (e.g., average age at marriage, average age at last birth) aggregated at the level of villages or even whole provinces. By comparing the demographic means of regions with different characteristics (e.g., religious composition), they often fell into the trap of "ecological inference fallacy" by assuming that group means applied to all individuals. Moreover, their emphasis on the mathematical mean as indicator of the average was attacked harshly: "Statistics is about probabilities; only by misunderstanding laws of probability can historians believe that their statistical results suggest that the world might be governed by regular laws." (Fitch 1984; 250)

The promises of technological innovation in history are made in highly contested, competitive areas. Those promises are evaluated not only in terms of whether they provide more reliable data and better research results, but also in terms of whether the results fit the type of history writing that holds most appeal to the scholarly community, the funding agencies, and the general

Dreaming of New Techniques for Migration History (Hogan and Kertzer 1985)

Hogan and Kertzer aim to introduce a new methodology for migration history by adopting analytical techniques from demography. The argument is that many ways of analyzing migration histories are based on net migration data. This leads to a serious underestimation of migration flows and does not allow for an understanding of the factors that shape migration behavior, which may differ at different stages of an individual's life course. The authors therefore argue for the use of complete migration data by the assembly and analysis of residential histories at the individual level from population registers. Moreover, they argue for the use of more advanced, probabilistic, and multivariate statistical techniques within the framework of a longitudinal research design borrowed from the field of demography. The authors hint at the lack of statistical training in the field of history as an obstacle for the realization of their research dream, but they expect that the unambiguous advantages of their analytical techniques will be "of immediate relevance" (29). They aim to lower the barrier by pointing to a host of computer programs that enable this type of more advanced statistical analysis, but they clearly expect that the results themselves will be convincing. "As more data become available from population registers, and analysts become more comfortable with the idea of focusing on the hazard rate of migration, we anticipate that multivariate methods . . . will become more important in historical migration study." (29) This is in line with Michael's model of the plot structure of future representations. The future is seen as the place where the "wrongs" of the past are solved. Michael's scheme of dichotomies seems less relevant, however, with the exception of the positive/negative valence dichotomy. In terms of the audience of this research dream ("for whom was the story constructed?"), Hogan and Kertzer seem to orient themselves to a relatively specialized expert audience, less to historians in general. Overall, we can characterize this research dream as proposing new tools for answering old questions. In terms of White's typology of historical narrative, perhaps "tragedy" would be the best characterization, since the uptake of longitudinal research designs is presented as more or less inevitable, although it would be a drama with a unequivocally positive valence.

public. Thus, in the 1980s social science historians saw themselves challenged to come up with better sources, better techniques to convince statisticians, and better concepts to convince other historians. A new cycle started with more realistic and scaled down expectations. Historical demographers began to focus on projects to collect longitudinal data on individuals. By creating micro-datasets with life histories, they could avoid the problems of record

linkage, simulation, and ecological fallacy. The historical population registers
of several countries, which kept daily records of people, were seen as an ideal
source for this approach (Gutmann and Van de Walle 1978; Mandemakers
2006). Moreover, individuals were not to be pressed into categories for which
meaningless means were calculated. Instead, new techniques allowed them
to be studied in their individual variability. "Event history" techniques based
on survival analysis offered demographic behavior in the form of probabilities (or "hazards") at the individual level. Historians were particularly pleased
that the method (based on observed person-years) solved the old problem
of loss from observation (Alter 1988). An integrating approach was found in
the concept of the *life-course*. The life course can be defined as the sequence
of positions in specific life domains (such as residence, work, and family) of a
particular person in the course of time. Life-course analysis studies sequences
and the timing of transitions to new positions. The timing reveals the demographic choices of individuals, but also the normative pressure emanating
from society at large and the interdependencies between related individuals
(Hareven 2000). Moreover, by studying the relation between transitions in
different domains, social history could once again bring together such facets
of life as work, family, and migration. And because the models could include
time-dependent covariates as well as "competing" independent variables, the
approach promised that demography would at last be able to study processes
(e.g., parenthood) instead of isolated events (e.g., childbirths) (Hobcraft 2006;
for an overview, see Kok 2007). By now, the technique has been applied
frequently in demographic research—for example, in the influential comparative Eurasia project (Bengtsson et al. 2004; Tsuya et al. 2010). The cycle of
elaborating techniques of working with micro-level data has not yet ended.
Event history modeling based on longitudinal microdata has been accused of
"atomistic fallacy" (Courgeau 2002) since it focuses on individuals and tends
to underplay the role of their communities and extended (kin) networks.
Thus, social science historians have been advised to include network analysis in their toolbox (Wetherell 1999) and to apply multi-level modeling to
understand the effects of shared environments, be they families or localities
(Clubine-Ito 2004).

VISUALIZATION

When it comes to *visualizing* the mass of data collection in historical population databases, we see once again an intricate cycle of high expectations,

Dreaming the Great American History Machine (Miller and Modell 1988)

This is a case of developing software in the context of early-1980s university Unix computing for historical research. It complements the other two cases in that it is a visualizing device developed mainly for teaching more advanced historical methods. The authors indicate that they deliberately refrained from including a lot of "new social history" in their course, but wanted to focus on classical questions. The software is basically a map of the United States on which data from a variety of sources can be projected and statistically analyzed in a rudimentary descriptive way. In contrast to the other two cases, the authors do not claim to solve a problem or correct a wrong from the past. Rather, they claim that the novelty of their application is the possibility for interaction with large amounts of data that opens up new ways of doing analytically sophisticated empirical historical research. They started their work by reflecting on earlier experiences with teaching the use of computers in history courses. An important motif is the wish to put the kind of questions historians are interested in more centrally in courses using computerized data. The article is written as a report on the experiences in using the Great American History Machine, looking back rather than forward. The course substantiated that interaction lead to more active involvement and engagement by the students. Only in the appendix do the authors explicitly discuss future developments. Here, the modesty of the authors is striking. They argue that the GAHM is already a useful "reference tool to specialists in a number of areas of American history" but that its use as a research tool would require enhancement in a number of directions (133). The specification of these enhancements remains at the technical level, however, and is clearly strongly tied to the Andrew/Unix system developed by Carnegie Mellon University (a Unix release still in use). This research dream is strongly focused on the technology. The technology is central in shaping the future. The text is mainly written for colleagues in the field who are also interested in teaching new methods to students of American history. In Michael's terms, this dream is instrumental, is close to the past, is directed to the collective, has an unambiguous positive valence, and has a fast speed.

disappointments, and a new round of technical innovations accompanied by more realistic research agendas, which in their turn try to be compelling by sketching appealing futures for research. Initially, computer cartography was hailed as a relatively simple and powerful tool for historians (e.g., Holland 1972). GIS, which combined mapping with the manipulation of an underlying database with spatial information, raised expectations even higher, particularly after microcomputers became widely available (Foote 1992). Interestingly, GIS was often promoted as a concession to those historians who were dissatisfied with cliometrics and with the formal hypothesis testing of social science historians. Thus, the Great American History Machine, one of the first online GIS applications (see box), was described as a way to help historians in "the essence of their methodology [which] seems to be the inductive and iterative search for patterns" (Miller and Modell 1988). By and large, however, historians eschewed GIS. Knowles (2008) distinguishes two reasons for this: first, the "fuzzy" data characteristic for historical information cannot be fitted properly to the spatial databases; second, the "logocentric" historians are not used to studying images (Knowles 2008, 2; see also Knowles 2000). Although the proponents of GIS recognize that the current use of GIS is limited and "application-driven," they seem more convinced than ever before that historians will turn *en masse* to GIS, either because the disciplines of history and geography are seen as converging (Bailey and Schick 2009) or because GIS fits perfectly with the "spatial turn" in the humanities at large (Bodenhamer 2007).

CONCLUSIONS

Large databases with standardized, well-documented data and refined techniques of analyzing them have changed the fields of family and population history almost beyond recognition. Social science historians have demolished much of the conventional wisdom about the family and society. For example, the notion that modernization (industrialization, urbanization) would be accompanied by a shift to small families was destroyed when historical family reconstitutions disclosed that small families had been widespread in Western European in the past (Hareven 1987). The more household information was processed, the more complicated the local and temporal variation in household forms appeared. Similarly, modern historical demography has put into perspective the idea of a common European fertility transition characterized by family limitation beginning in the second half of the nineteenth century. New techniques disclosed deliberate birth control in several "pre-transitional "populations. The question was raised: "Should [we] speak of multiple fertility declines occurring in distinct contexts and for different reasons?" (Szołtysek 2007)

The knowledge produced by constantly refined techniques has become better in the sense of rigorously tested, but it fits less and less comfortably in historical syntheses and narratives. The lingering dissatisfaction with the "ugly" history produced by the cliometricians increased in the 1980s. Swierenga (1999) recalls that the president of the American Historical Association "warned against elevating to a predominant place a 'technical problem-solving' approach that is 'severely vision-limiting.'" Social science history could not escape the paradox of having to refine its technology while avoiding functional thinking, which reduced its visionary capacities. As we have seen, social science historians have abandoned the search for "regular laws" and now focus on "probabilities," which hold even less meaning for most historians. Historians, in their turn, were inspired by postmodernism and the "literary turn" and have come to find "meaning" in the many, equally "true" worldviews of the historical actors themselves.

How do quantitative family historians and database builders respond to the fact that they have "fallen out of favor" and seem unable to provide meaning (Milanich 2007)? Some seem to abandon the hope that they ever will win back mainstream historians and predict that the facilities will be used only by social scientists. (See, e.g., Sobek and Ruggles 1999, 106.) As often happens with promises about technological innovations, the process of "societal embedding" (Geels and Smit 2000, 876) had been neglected. In this case, this embedding might have implied securing lasting commitments for projects from universities and making sure that new generations of scholars are prepared to work within the projects. Various authors comment on the neglect of statistical training in historical curricula and point at ways of redressing it. (See, e.g., Reynolds 1998; Wetherell 1999; Steckel 2007.) In fact, several large database projects now run summer schools to provide new generations of researchers with up-to-date technical skills. Others authors state that historians should pool resources and work more collaboratively in order to benefit from applications such as GIS. (See, e.g., White 2008.) Some argue for multidisciplinary teams on the ground that the combination of skills demanded by state-of-the-art historical demography transcends the capacities of individual scholars and even of individual disciplines (Kok 2007). By expanding the scope of regional micro-datasets (e.g., through encouraging direct comparisons between them—see Alter, Mandemakers, and Gutmann 2009), new questions can be raised and new users attracted.

Another problem is that social science historians were confined too long to the "protected space" they had created in the form of social science history journals and specialized meetings. Obviously this space gave social science historians opportunities to fine-tune their techniques. But it also made it easier for mainstream historians to ignore them. Apparently, it is really difficult to adopt the "strategic game" of moving research dreaming away from the protected space and to realign with other historians. An interesting move in this direction is the redesign of the database interfaces to accommodate different kinds of usage. For example, the interface of the Canadian Century Research Infrastructure (CCRI) provides access to many kinds of texts about the background of census-taking, the different meanings that census variables could have for the governments, the local census-takers, and the people who were counted. Thus, according to Gaffield,

the CCRI is intentionally designed to build on the strengths of both social history and cultural history by enabling an integrated sociocultural epistemology. Our approach is based on the concept of multiauthored sources: Defined as "contextual data," the CCRI provides users with historical evidence related to the substantive content of the census microdata under examination. (2007, 58)

The history of the adoption of computing in historical research is a history of high hopes and great disappointments. This is already evident in the metaphors that historians themselves choose to use in their articles on computing—some muse on "a love affair gone sour" (Swierenga 1984) and others pine for "a marriage made in heaven" (Keats-Rohan 2000). Indeed, many database, visualization, and research projects seem to have been launched with high expectations but not to have produced many convincing results. However, it would be wrong to see those dreams only as misjudgments. In fact, "new historians" were highly successful in attracting funds and attention. In time, social science historians learned to readjust their dreams and conceived more realistic research strategies by creating more useful datasets and by improving their analytic skills and techniques, and social scientists found their more nuanced research results increasingly convincing. However, their findings failed to capture the imagination of historians who could not use them as building blocks for syntheses or who merely found them trivial. It remains to be seen whether or not a new round in the cycle of improved research infrastructures will attract a new generation of practitioners or even win back mainstream historians.

All this seems to point to a combination of success and failure, if we take the actors' goals as the criteria for success. The various research dreams have indeed fed into the promise-requirement cycle cited earlier in this chapter.

This has created a specific research stream in the field of family history. At the same time, the greater dream of a modernist footing for larger swaths of the historical field has not been realized. On the contrary, many historians have turned away from statistical and probabilistic analysis. It remains to be seen whether the particular Canadian dream of combining modernist and post-modernist history writing will be realized.

Research dreams and their implementation in historical databases as research infrastructure are a form of what was called "virtual knowledge" in the introduction to this volume. Virtual knowledge points to the potential that is not yet realized in research plans and proposals. Taken at face value, this seems obvious since it is true for every novel research plan. However, in most of the research dreams discussed in this chapter, virtuality plays an additional role. It is not entirely defined for exactly what research questions the proposed databases as research infrastructures will be the solution. Often the expectation that they will generate new research of a higher quality is set forth in rather generic terms. The justification of the dream is a specified deficit in current knowledge. But the research dream itself is actually a new research infrastructure (in the form of a huge data set combined with tools for analysis) that can become the source of unspecified new lines of research and knowledge. These new research lines are virtual in a double sense: they do not yet exist and they are not yet well defined. The research dreams we analyzed are actually proposals for new research structures that are imbued with the ambition to generate novel forms of knowledge of which only the contours are clear. It should therefore come as no surprise that failures to meet the specifications will not hinder the cycle of promise. The generative potential of the virtual remains real, even if a particular expectation is not met. Virtual knowledge is in this sense a very hard type of knowledge indeed.

What struck us while analyzing the various research dreams is their uniform narrative structure. Nearly all of them seem to be based on a particular deficit model. Lack of knowledge about the history of the family is a wrong that has to be corrected, and it will be corrected when more data-research facilities collect more data (some of them new in kind) and when those data are subjected to more advanced statistical analysis. The dream subsequently is fulfilled only partially, after which the cycle starts again. The partial failure does not deter the historians from chasing a new version of the same dream. In a way, it is perhaps not surprising that this type of dream is so dominant. We hypothesize that a particular plot structure holds a paradigmatic position in a particular discipline: one simply has to phrase one's promises in the structure of the dreams and promises of the past. A "new," original plot structure would probably be too risky in the competitive setting in which these dreams have to function. It would be interesting to test this hypothesis in comparison with other disciplines. Do we indeed find homogeneous plot structures within disciplines, but not across disciplines? An alternative hypothesis that is compatible with our research is that it is not the discipline but the particular epistemic style (Crombie 1994) that is the determinant of the type of research dream. According to this explanation, data-oriented fields like family history would share a deficit model in which the quest for data is dominant, while fields with another research style can be expected to have another dominant narrative structure in their research dreaming. A third alternative explanation, still compatible with our findings, is that it is not so much the field or the research style but the position of the "research dreamer" that shapes the narrative structure. Researchers in a particular field would be expected to dream on the basis of a type of deficit model, since they are required to create novelty in their specialty. Technology developers such as e-science infrastructure builders, on the other hand, may tend to dream the "tragedy" type of dream, in which science is steamrolled by the inevitable push of the latest technologies. Research funders may take yet another perspective. A systematic cross-comparative research setup focusing on the interaction of narrative structure, field, research style, and types of research dreaming actors is needed to address these different hypotheses.

Such a comparative research design may also throw new light on the interaction between the promise-requirement cycle and the narrative structure of research dreams. Apparently, the promise-requirement cycle we have illustrated here with the case of family history entails recurrent narrative structures for the promises involved. Thus, we can conclude that the real creativity involved in research dreaming lies in putting new and competitive "content" within a more or less traditional plot structure. The dream "plot" is not original, but the activity of research dreaming nevertheless is a highly creative activity, creating new venues for research, educating new generations of researchers, and building up new research infrastructures. The challenge for e-humanities or digital humanities may be to build up a reflexive tradition of research dreaming that is aware of the limitations of the research dreams and of the high probability of failure but, at the same time, values the creativity of the process of dreaming.

NOTES

1. Cliometrics gained popularity from the late 1950s on, particularly in economic history. Its leading advocates are Robert Fogel and Douglass North.

2. Another noteworthy stronghold is econometric history, with journals such as *Journal of Economic History* and *Explorations in Economic History*.

3. See http://www.ehess.fr/ldh/theme_TRA/Theme_TRA-Intro.htm.

REFERENCES

Alter, George. 1988. *Family Life and the Female Life Course: The Women of Verviers, Belgium, 1849–1880*. University of Wisconsin Press.

Alter, George, Kees Mandemakers, and Myron Gutmann. 2009. Defining and distributing longitudinal historical data in a general way through an intermediate structure. *Historical Social Research (Köln)* 34 (3): 78–114.

Bailey, Timothy J., and James B. M. Schick. 2009. Historical GIS: Enabling the collision of history and geography. *Social Science Computer Review* 27 (3): 291–296.

Baker, Paula C. 1999. What is social science history, anyway? *Social Science History* 23 (4): 475–480.

Bengtsson, Tommy, Cameron Campbell, and James Z. Lee, eds. 2004. *Life under Pressure: Mortality and Living Standards in Europe and Asia, 1700–1900*. MIT Press.

Bengtsson, Tommy, Martin Dribe, and Christer Lundh. 2005. Linking the past to the present: 20th century Sweden from a long-term micro perspective. Presented at annual meeting of Social Science History Association, Portland, Oregon.

Berkhout, Frans. 2006. Normative expectations in systems innovation. *Technology Analysis and Strategic Management* 18 (3): 299–311.

Bodenhamer, David J. 2007. Creating a landscape of memory: The potential of humanities GIS. *International Journal of Humanities and Arts Computing* 1 (2): 97–110.

Borup, Mads, Nik Brown, Kornelia Konrad, and Harro van Lente. 2006. The sociology of expectations in science and technology. *Technology Analysis and Strategic Management* 18 (3): 285–298.

Bradley, James, Rebecca Kippen, Hamish Maxwell-Stuart, Janet McCalman, and Sandra Silcot. 2010. Research note: The founders and survivors project. *History of the Family* 15 (4): 467–477.

Brown, Nik, and Mike Michael. 2003. A sociology of expectations: Retrospecting prospects and prospecting retrospects. *Technology Analysis and Strategic Management* 15 (1): 3–18.

Brown, Nik, Brian Rappert, and Andrew Webster, eds. 2000a. *Contested Futures: A Sociology of Prospective Techno-Science.* Ashgate.

Brown, Nik, Brian Rappert, and Andrew Webster. 2000b. Introducing contested futures: From looking into the future to looking at the future. In *Contested Futures: A Sociology of Prospective Techno-Science*, ed. N. Brown, B. Rappert, and A. Webster. Ashgate.

Burke, Peter. 2001. *New Perspectives on Historical Writing.* Pennsylvania State University Press.

Clubine-Ito, Christopher. 2004. Multilevel modeling for historical data: An example from the 1901 Canadian census. *Historical Methods* 37 (1): 5–22.

Courgeau, Daniel. 2002. New approaches and methodological innovations in the study of partnership and fertility behaviour. In *Dynamics of Fertility and Partnership in Europe: Insights and Lessons from Comparative Research*, volume 1, ed. M. Macura and G. Beets. United Nations.

Crombie, Alistair C. 1994. *Styles of Scientific Thinking in the European Tradition.* Duckworth.

Dillon, Lisa, and Evan Roberts. 2006. Longitudinal and cross-sectional historical data: Intersections and opportunities. *History & Computing* 14 (1/2): 1–7.

Dupâquier, Jacques, and Denis Kessler, eds. 1992. *La société française au XIXe siècle: Tradition, transition, transformations.* Fayard.

Fitch, Nancy. 1980. The household and the computer: A review. *Historical Methods* 13 (2): 127–137.

Fitch, Nancy. 1984. Statistical fantasies and historical facts: History in crisis and its methodological implications. *Historical Methods* 17 (4): 239–254.

Foote, Kenneth E. 1992. Mapping the past. A survey of microcomputer cartography. *Historical Methods* 25 (3): 121–131.

Gaffield, Chad. 2007. Conceptualizing and constructing the Canadian Century Research Infrastructure. *Historical Methods* 40 (2): 54–64.

Geels, Frank W., and Wim A. Smit. 2000. Failed technology futures: Pitfalls and lessons from a historical survey. *Futures* 32 (9–10): 867–885.

Guth, Gloria J. A. 1976. Surname spellings and computerized record linkage. *Historical Methods Newsletter* 10 (1): 10–19.

Gutmann, Myron P. 1977. The future of record linkage in history (review essay). *Journal of Family History* 2 (2): 151–158.

Gutmann, Myron P., and Etienne Vandewalle. 1978. New sources for social and demographic history: the Belgian population registers. *Social Science History* 2 (2): 121–143.

Hall, Patricia K., Robert McCaa, and Gunnar Thorvaldsen, eds. 2000. *Handbook of International Historical Microdata for Population Research.* Minnesota Population Center.

Hareven, Tamara K. 1987. Family history at the crossroads. *Journal of Family History* 12 (1): ix–xxiii.

Hareven, Tamara K. 2000. *Families, History and Social Change: Life Course and Cross-Cultural Perspectives.* Westview.

Hobcraft, John. N. 2006. The ABC of demographic behaviour: How the interplays of alleles, brains and contexts over the life course should shape research aimed at understanding population processes. *Population Studies* 60 (2): 153–187.

Hogan, Dennis P., and David I. Kertzer. 1985. Longitudinal approaches to migration in social history. *Historical Methods* 18 (1): 20–30.

Holland, Reid A. 1972. Urban history and computer mapping. *Historical Methods Newsletter* 6 (1): 5–9.

Joerges, Bernward, and Terry Shinn, eds. 2001. *Instrumentation Between Science, State, and Industry: Sociology of the Sciences Yearbook 22.* Kluwer.

Judt, Tony. 1979. A clown in regal purple: Social history and the historians. *History Workshop Journal* 7 (1): 66–94.

Katz, Michael, and John Tiller. 1972. Record-linkage for everyman: A semi-automated process. *Historical Methods Newsletter* 5 (4): 144–150.

Keats-Rohan, K. S. B. 2000. Prosopography and computing: A marriage made in heaven? *History & Computing* 12 (1): 1–11.

Kelly, Dennis. 1974. Linking nineteenth-century manuscript census records: A computer strategy. *Historical Methods Newsletter* 7 (2): 72–82.

King, Miriam L. 1990. All in the family? The incompatibility and reconciliation of family demography and family history. *Historical Methods* 23 (1): 32–40.

Knowles, Anne K. 2000. Introduction. Special issue: Historical GIS: The spatial turn in social science history. *Social Science History* 24 (3): 451–470.

Knowles, Anne K. 2008. GIS and history. In *Placing History: How Maps, Spatial Data, and GIS Are Changing Historical Scholarship*, ed. A. Knowles and A. Hillier. ESRI.

Kok, Jan. 2007. Principles and prospects of the life course paradigm. *Annales de Demographie Historique* 1: 203–230.

Kousser, J. Morgan. 1977. The agenda for social science history. *Social Science History* 1 (3): 383–391.

Kwa, Chunglin. 2005. *De Ontdekking van het Weten*. Boom.

Légaré, Jacquies, André LaRose, and Raymond Roy. 1975. Reconstitution of the seventeenth century Canadian population: An overview of a research program. *Historical Methods Newsletter* 9 (1): 1–8.

Mandemakers, Kees. 2001. The historical sample of the Netherlands (HSN). *Historical Social Research (Köln)* 26 (4): 179–190.

Mandemakers, Kees. 2006. Building life course datasets from population registers by the Historical Sample of the Netherlands (HSN). *History & Computing* 14 (1): 87–108.

Matthijs, Koen, and Sarah Moreels. 2010. The Antwerp COR*-database: A unique Flemish source for historical-demographic research. *The History of the Family. An International Quarterly* 15 (1): 109–115.

Michael, Mike. 2000. Futures of the present: From performativity to prehension. In *Contested Futures: A Sociology of Prospective Techno-Science*, ed. N. Brown, B. Rappert, and A. Webster. Ashgate.

Milanich, Nara. 2007. Whither Family History? A Road Map from Latin America. *American Historical Review* 112 (2): 439–458.

Miller, David W., and John Modell. 1988. Teaching United States history with the Great American History Machine. *Historical Methods* 21 (3): 121–134.

Reynolds, John R. 1998. Do historians count anymore? The status of quantitative methods in history, 1975-1995. *Historical Methods* 31 (4): 141–148.

Riessman, Catherine K. 2008. *Narrative Methods for the Human Sciences*. Sage.

Roberts, Evan, Steven Ruggles, Lisa Y. Dillon, Ólöf Gardarsdottir, Jan Oldervoll, Gunnar Thorvaldsen, and Matthew Woollard. 2003. The North Atlantic Population Project. *Historical Methods* 26 (2): 80–88.

Rosental, Paul-André. 2003. The novelty of an old genre: Louis Henry and the founding of historical demography. *Population-E* 58 (3): 97–130.

Ruggles, Steven. 1986. Availability of kin and the demography of historical family structure. *Historical Methods* 19 (3): 93–102.

Ruggles, Steven. 1987. *Prolonged Connections: The Rise of the Extended Family in Nineteenth-Century England and America*. University of Wisconsin Press.

Ruggles, Steven. 1993. Confessions of a microsimulator: Problems in modeling the demography of kinship. *Historical Methods* 26 (4): 161–169.

Ruggles, Steven, Miriam L. King, Deborah Levinson, Robert McCaa, and Matthew Sobek. 2003. Ipums-International. *Historical Methods* 36 (2): 60–65.

Ruggles, Steven, and Russell R. Menard. 1990. A public use sample of the 1880 U.S. census of population. *Historical Methods* 23 (3): 104–115.

Schofield, Roger. 1985. Historical demography in the 1980s: A review essay. *Historical Methods* 18 (2): 71–75.

Shove, Elizabeth, and Paul Wouters. 2006. The bases of interactive agenda setting. Background paper for Economic and Social Science Research Council (ESRC) Interactive Agenda Setting workshop, Abingdon (available at http://www.lancs. ac.uk).

Skolnick, M. H. 1971. A computer program for linking records. *Historical Methods Newsletter* 4 (4): 114–125.

Smith, James E. 1989. Method and confusion in the study of the household. *Historical Methods* 22 (1): 57–69.

Sobek, Matthew, and Steven Ruggles. 1999. The IPUMS project. An update. *Historical Methods* 32 (3): 102–110.

Steckel, Richard H. 2007. Big social science history. *Social Science History* 31 (1): 1–34.

Swierenga, Robert P. 1984. Historians & computers: Has the love affair gone sour? *Organization of American Historians Newsletter*, November: S2–S4.

Swierenga, Robert P. 1999. Computers and historical research: personal reflections. Presented at Regional History Meeting, Spring Arbor College (available at http:// www.swierenga.com).

Szołtysek, Mikolaj. 2007. Science without laws? Model building, micro histories and the fate of the theory of fertility decline. *Historical Social Research (Köln)* 32 (2): 10–41.

Stone, Lawrence. 1979. The revival of narrative: Reflections on a new old history. *Past & Present* 85 (1): 3–24.

Thorvaldsen, Gunnar. 1998. Historical databases in Scandinavia. *History of the Family. An International Quarterly* 3 (3): 371–383.

Tilly, Louise E., and Miriam Cohen. 1982. Does the family have a history? A review of theory and practice in family history. *Social Science History* 6 (2): 131–179.

Tsuya, Noriko O., Wang Feng, George Alter, and James Z. Lee. 2010. *Prudence and Pressure: Reproduction and Human Agency in Europe and Asia, 1700–1900*. MIT Press.

Van Leeuwen, Marco H. D., Ineke Maas, and Andrew Miles. 2002. *Historical International Standard Classification of Occupations* (Dutch, English, French, German, Norwegian, and Swedish edition). Leuven University Press.

van Lente, Harro, and Arie Rip. 1998. Expectations in technological developments: An example of prospective structures to be filled in by agency. In *Getting New Technologies Together: Studies in Making Sociotechnical Order*, ed. C. Disco and B. van der Meulen. Walter de Gruyter.

van Lente, Harro. 2000. Forceful futures: From promise to requirement. In *Contested Futures: A Sociology of Prospective Techno-Science*, ed. N. Brown, B. Rappert, and A. Webster. Ashgate.

Wachter, Kenneth W., Eugene A. Hammel, and Peter Laslett. 1978. *Statistical Studies of Historical Social Structure*. Academic Press.

Wachter, Kenneth W., and Eugene A. Hammel. 1986. The genesis of experimental history. In *The World We Have Gained: Histories of Population and Social Structure,* ed. L. Bonfield, R. Smith, and K. Wrightson. Blackwell.

Wetherell, Charles. 1999. Theory, method and social reproduction in social science history: A short jeremiad. *Social Science History* 23 (4): 491–499.

White, Richard. 2008. Foreword. In *Placing History: How Maps, Spatial Data, and GIS Are Changing Historical Scholarship*, ed. A. Knowles and A. Hillier. ESRI.

White, Hayden. 1973. *Metahistory: The Historical Imagination in Nineteenth Century Europe*. Johns Hopkins University Press.

Wilkie, Alex, and Mike Michael. 2009. Expectation and mobilisation: Enacting future users. *Science, Technology & Human Values* 34 (4): 502–522.

ABOUT THE AUTHORS

SMILJANA ANTONIJEVIĆ is an Assistant Professor of Culture and Technology at Roskilde University. Her research intersects the areas of communication, culture, and technology, focusing on scholarly collaboration in virtual environments, digital humanities, digital nonverbal communication and affective computing, trust in online interaction, psychological aspects of blogging, digital rhetoric, and the use of new media during crises.

ANNE BEAULIEU is a Project Manager in the Groningen Energy and Sustainability Programme. She joined the University of Groningen after several years as a senior research fellow at the Koninklijke Nederlandse Akademie van Wetenschappen (KNAW), where she also served as Deputy Programme Leader of the Virtual Knowledge Studio for the Humanities and Social Sciences between 2005 and 2010. A dominant theme in Beaulieu's work is the importance of interfaces for the creation and circulation of knowledge. Her past research projects at the KNAW focused on data sharing, knowledge networks, and visualization and visual knowledge. She has also done extensive work in the field of digital humanities, on new (ethnographic) research methods, and on ethics in e-research. (In English, the KNAW is known as the Royal Netherlands Academy of Arts and Sciences.)

VICTOR BEKKERS is a Professor of Public Administration and Public Policy in the Department of Public Administration at Erasmus University Rotterdam. He is also dean of the Erasmus Graduate School for the Humanities, Social and Behavioural Sciences. His research focuses on how the course, the contents, and the organizations of policy processes in public administration change as a result of the penetration of information and communication technologies (including new media) into these processes and as a result of the innovation potential of these technologies. He has published numerous articles, books, and book chapters on these topics.

SARAH DE RIJCKE is an Assistant Professor in the Centre for Science and Technology Studies at Leiden University. Her current research focuses on the impact of research evaluation on the primary process of knowledge production. She previously held a postdoctoral position at the Virtual Knowledge Studio in Amsterdam, where she participated in the research project "Network Realism. Making knowledge from images in digital infrastructure."

STEFAN DORMANS is an Assistant Professor in the Department of Geography, Planning and Environment at Radboud University Nijmegen. His current research focuses on social movements, webometrics, and ethnographic and discursive methods. He holds a PhD in urban and narrative geographies. From 2008 until 2010 he worked on academic collaboration as a postdoctoral researcher at the Virtual Knowledge Studio of the KNAW.

NICHOLAS W. JANKOWSKI is a Visiting Fellow in the KNAW's e-Humanities Group. He is the initiator and a co-editor of the journal *New Media & Society,* a founding board member of the European Institute of Communication and Culture (Euricom), and the editor of the Hampton Press book series Euricom Monographs: New Media and Democracy. He edited *E-Research: Transformation in Scholarly Practice* (Routledge, 2009) and co-edited *The Long History of New Media* (Peter Lang, 2011).

JAN KOK is a Professor of Comparative History of the Life Course at Radboud University Nijmegen. A member of the e-Humanities Group of the KNAW, he is also co-editor-in-chief of *The History of the Family*.

MATTHIJS KOUW recently completed his PhD work at the Virtual Knowledge Studio within the Faculty of Arts and Social Sciences at Maastricht University. Based on an ethnographic study of the use of simulations and models in hydrology and hydrodynamics, geotechnical engineering, and ecology, his dissertation discusses how simulations and models make knowledge of risks more or less visible and to what extent their use makes technological cultures susceptible to risks. He holds an MA in philosophy and an MSc in Science and Technology Studies from the Universiteit van Amsterdam. He also has experience in software development.

CLEMENT LEVALLOIS is a Research Associate at Erasmus University Rotterdam with a background in economics and management and the history and sociology of science. He currently studies the emergence and significance of neuro-social sciences, using methodologies from the e-humanities (text mining, network analysis, and data visualization).

REBECCA MOODY studied political science and obtained a PhD in public administration in 2010 from the Department of Public Administration at Erasmus University Rotterdam. It was based on a study of the influence of Geographic Information Systems on policy design and agenda setting. She is currently examining how visual images and technologies influence public policy making.

ANDREA SCHARNHORST is Head of e-Research at the Data Archiving and Networked Services (DANS) institute. She is also a member of the e-Humanities group at the KNAW. She has a background in physics and in philosophy of science. Her current work on modeling the science system and visualizing the evolution of knowledge orders can best be characterized as being part of the information sciences.

STEPHANIE STEINMETZ is an Assistant Professor of Sociology at the University of Amsterdam and a senior researcher at the Erasmus Virtual Knowledge Studio in Rotterdam. She is involved in the project "Improving Web survey methodology for social and cultural research," focusing on methodological issues of Web surveys and the acceptance of new Web-based data collection methods within sociology. Her main research interests are quantitative research methods, social stratification, gender and educational inequalities, and the history of sociology.

CLIFFORD TATUM is a PhD candidate at Leiden University's Centre for Science and Technology Studies. His research examines the role of openness in scholarly communication. He is project manager of Academic Careers Understood through Measurement and Norms (ACUMEN) and an associate researcher at the KNAW e-Humanities Group in Amsterdam.

CHARLES VAN DEN HEUVEL is Head of Research of History of Science at the KNAW's Huygens Institute for the History of the Netherlands. His research interests include the history of architecture, fortification, and town planning, the history of cartography, the history of science of the Early Modern period, and the history of information science. His e-humanities research focuses on the use of visualizations and annotations in historical disciplines.

BAS VAN HEUR is an Assistant Professor of Social Geography in the Department of Geography at Vrije Universiteit Brussel. His research is concerned with the politics of urban development and the role of research in engaging with and analyzing urban development strategies and their effects. He has published empirical research on creative industries, digital heritage, small cities, and the built environment of universities and more theoretical work on cultural political economy in various international journals and edited volumes.

PAUL WOUTERS is a Professor of Scientometrics and the Director of the Centre for Science and Technology Studies at Leiden University. He was Programme Leader of the Virtual Knowledge Studio for the Humanities and Social Sciences from 2005 to 2010. He is interested in information practices in relation to scientific and scholarly research. He has published on citation theories, the history of the Science Citation Index, virtual research environments, data sharing, e-research and the computational bias in e-science, and the paradoxes of science communication.

SALLY WYATT is Programme Leader of the KNAW's e-Humanities Group and a Professor of Digital Cultures in Development at Maastricht University. With Andrew Webster, she edits the Health, Technology and Society book series, published by Palgrave Macmillan. Her research focuses on digital inequalities and on the everyday uses of Web-based technologies by people looking for health information and by scholars engaged in research.

INDEX